Current Issues in Expert Systems

International Lecture Series in Computer Science

These volumes are based on the lectures given during a series of specially funded chairs. The International Chair in Computer Science was created by IBM Belgium in co-operation with the Belgium National Foundation for Scientific Research. The holders of each chair cover a subject area considered to be of particular relevance to current developments in computer science.

The Correctness Problem in Computer Science (1981)
R. S. BOYER and J. STROTHER MOORE

Computer-aided Modelling and Simulation (1982)
J. A. SPRIET and G. C. VANSTEENKISTE

Probability Theory and Computer Science (1983)
G. LOUCHARD and G. LATOUCHE

New Computer Architectures (1984)
J. TIBERGHIEN

Algorithmics for VLSI (1986)
C. TRULLEMANS

Databases (1987)
J. PAREDAENS

Current Issues in Expert Systems (1987)
A. van LAMSWEERDE and P. DUFOUR

Current Issues in Expert Systems

Edited by

A. van Lamsweerde

Institut d'Informatique
Facultés Universitaires de Namur, Belgium

P. Dufour

Faculté des Sciences
Université de l'État à Mons, Belgium

1987

ACADEMIC PRESS
Harcourt Brace Jovanovich, Publishers
London   San Diego   New York   Berkeley
Boston   Sydney   Tokyo   Toronto

ACADEMIC PRESS LIMITED
24–28 Oval Road
London NW1 7DX

U.S. Edition published by
ACADEMIC PRESS INC.
San Diego, CA 92101

British Library Cataloguing in Publication Data

Current issues in expert systems.—
   (International lecture series in computer science).
   1. Expert systems (Computer science)
   I. Van Lamsweerde, A.   II. Dufour, P.
III. Series 006.3′3   QA76.76.E95
   ISBN 0-12-714030-1

Photoset by Paston Press, Loddon, Norfolk and printed by
St. Edmundsbury Press Ltd., Bury St. Edmunds, Suffolk

Contributors

Kaihu Chen Intelligent Systems Group, Department of Computer Science, University of Illinois at Urbana-Champaign, 1304 West Springfield Avenue, Urbana, Illinois 61801, USA

William J. Clancey Knowledge Systems Laboratory, Stanford University, 701 Welch Road, Palo Alto, California 94304, USA

Peter Jackson Department of Artificial Intelligence, University of Edinburgh, 80 South Bridge, Edinburgh EH1 1HN, Scotland

Peter Hammond Logic Programming Group, Department of Computing, Imperial College of Science and Technology, University of London, 180 Queen's Gate, London SW7 2BZ, England

Heedong Ko Intelligent Systems Group, Department of Computer Science, University of Illinois at Urbana-Champaign, 1304 West Springfield Avenue, Urbana, Illinois 61801, USA

Frank Kriwaczek Logic Programming Group, Department of Computing, Imperial College of Science and Technology, University of London, 180 Queen's Gate, London SW7 2BZ, England

Ryszard S. Michalski Intelligent Systems Group, Department of Computer Science, University of Illinois at Urbana-Champaign, 1304 West Springfield Avenue, Urbana, Illinois 61801, USA

Norihisa Suzuki IBM Tokyo Research Laboratory, 5–19 Sanbancho, Chiyoda-ku, Tokyo 102, Japan

Preface

Computers so far have been used mostly to process *data*. Typically, the same sequences of actions are performed repeatedly to compute new values from old ones; they work on well-structured universes with complete information.

For more than twenty years, Artificial Intelligence has been concerned with the "old dream" of letting computers mimic the ways human experts solve difficult problems. In such a case, computers have to process *knowledge representations*. Typically, sequences of inferences have to be performed in a quite versatile way to derive new useful knowledge from old one; the surrounding universe is usually ill-structured, uncertain and incomplete.

Early work in AI was concerned with general problem-solving procedures. Attempts to apply such techniques to large real-world problems were mostly unsuccessful, usually because of the enormous size of the search space of alternatives to be considered. Major progress was made in the mid-1970s by allowing the problem-solving process to make use of separate sources of explicit knowledge about highly specific problem domains. This gave rise to a first generation of expert knowledge-based systems. It then appeared that some of the techniques used for representing, organizing, inferring, communicating and acquiring knowledge were transposable or generalizable to many application domains. The next step now is to make such techniques more powerful and flexible and to find effective software and hardware architectures to implement them efficiently. This yet unbeaten challenge is at the core of various fifth generation computer projects.

Expert Systems formed the theme of the 1985 International Professorship in Computer Science, hosted jointly by two Belgian universities: the Facultés Universitaires de Namur and the Université de l'Etat à Mons. This annual professorship is organized by the Belgian National Science Foundation (FNRS) with the financial support of IBM Belgium. Its aim is to invite guest lecturers to speak on a selected topic in Computing Science and to contribute papers to be collected and published in book form. We tried to organize the course contents so as to cover the major issues in Expert Systems, namely the following:

- What are the various sources of knowledge to be identified, and how should they be formalized, organized and allowed to cooperate?
- What are the appropriate inference processes on these sources, and how should they be automated?
- What kind of techniques are needed to make an expert system able to teach and/or explain its reasoning?

- What kind of techniques are needed to enable an expert system to learn?
- What kind of machine architectures are needed to improve drastically the performances of an expert system?

As a result, the actual course programme was as follows.

P. Jackson (University of Edinburgh), *Logic for Expert Systems?*

P. Hammond, F. Kriwaczek and M. Sergot (Imperial College), *Logic Programming for Expert Systems.*

R. S. Michalski (University of Illinois), *Machine Learning and Automation of Knowledge Acquisition.*

W. Clancey (Stanford University), *Building Expert Systems for Explanation and Tutoring.*

N. Suzuki (University of Tokyo), *Knowledge Engineering Workstations.*

Each of these topics deserved approximately 30 hours of lectures. Quite naturally, all courses presented two kinds of material: an introductory tutorial to the subject being covered and research contributions. It seemed sensible not to include in this book the first kind of material if it was found in other books for which the lecturers had contributed (Jackson, 1986; Clark and McCabe, 1984; Michalski *et al.*, 1984, 1986; Sleeman and Brown, 1982). This book is therefore organized as follows.

In a first introductory chapter, Jackson briefly discusses some confusions that frequently arise regarding the various roles that logic can play in the design and implementation of an expert system. Various limits of predicate calculus as the main knowledge representation language and of deductive inference as the main mode of reasoning are analysed and illustrated. The author advocates a framework in which multiple representation formalisms and reasoning mechanisms can be integrated. This view is actually taken and illustrated in several chapters of this book.

Chapter 2 concentrates on a specific class of expert systems that might be of widespread use in the future. Advice-giving systems are intended to provide assistance in formulating and solving everyday problems. Partial solutions have to be built incrementally and interactively by the user and the system until a point is reached where both parties agree. The user here has rights of rejection, second opinion or negotiation. The system must reason about knowledge as well as about beliefs. Thus intentional systems are needed that are capable of simulating attitudes people adopt towards propositions. Beside the syntactic and semantic components of a statement expressing some piece of knowledge or belief, one must also define a pragmatics component in which rules for interpreting the statement in some context of use are specified. After presenting the specific features of advice-giving and discussing specific representational and control issues related to it, Jackson details a novel architecture for such systems based on a game-theoretic approach for interpreting first-order logic and for dealing with pragmatics. Knowledge and belief fragments are represented internally by frame-based structures made of syntax, semantics and pragmatics slots, which are activated by demons associated with them; entities from syntactic slots are evaluated by semantic rules according to a game-theoretic interpretation of logic, while pragmatic rules tell the semantic rules which strategy to choose for controlling the game. The proposed architecture is evaluated on the basis of the current implementation of these ideas.

There is an obvious connection between advice-giving systems and intelligent tutoring systems (ITS), as both have to reason about knowledge and belief states of the partner. In Chapter 3 Clancey presents a tutorial survey on ITS. First, a general architecture for such systems is described briefly, and various possible teaching scenarios are discussed together with their relation to theories of instruction. Various examples of existing ITS are then described and compared. The discussion progressively reveals some of the basic abilities "clever" ITS should have, for example the ability to solve the problems submitted to the student, the ability to analyse the differences between the student and the system plans, a generative behaviour in discovering student misconceptions, the separation of teaching knowledge from domain knowledge, and the suitability of system initiatives. This presentation sets the framework for Clancey's own work, which is reviewed in the next chapter.

Chapter 4 presents the key ideas behind the evolution of a major expert-system project, from which many lessons can be drawn. Clancey explains the main design decisions leading from the GUIDON rule-based tutoring system, including the reconfiguration of MYCIN into NEOMYCIN and NEOMYCIN's generalization in the heuristic classification shell HERACLES. It is shown how the evolution process follows two orthogonal paths: getting richer knowledge representations by making meta-knowledge more and more explicit, and getting more abstract and general problem-solving procedures (from infectious-disease problem solving to diagnosis problem solving and teaching diagnosis problem solving). Following these paths, one gets system shells and instructional systems that can be used for any expert system developed from the corresponding shells. The need for separating various kinds of knowledge (e.g. domain knowledge, problem solving knowledge and meta-knowledge) and for distinguishing among various roles of knowledge (e.g. strategic, structural and support knowledge) and among various models (e.g. problem-solving, student and dialogue models) is illustrated and substantiated in great depth throughout this chapter.

Machine learning is being recognized as a more and more important issue. The topic addressed in Chapter 5 is somewhat related to the previous one. The borderline between a teacher and a learner is not always very clear as the teacher has to learn about the student behaviour. Inductive inference is among the most powerful learning strategies. It consists of generating plausible and useful hypotheses that explain observed events or facts and predict unobserved ones. In this chapter Michalski, Ko and Chen develop a general learning methodology involving a special kind of inductive infer- ence; they call it part-to-whole generalization because the description of a structured object is inferred from descriptions of parts of it, as opposed to instance-to-class generalization, where the description of a class of objects is inferred from a description of selected instances of this class. Given a partial sequence of objects or events characterized by a list of attribute–value-range pairs, the technique described produces a specification of plausible proper- ties of any object or event in the complete sequence. The methodology thus amounts to a simple form of domain-independent qualitative prediction. In order to reduce substantially the search space of possible descriptions, various typical description models are used to constrain the syntactic patterns of the derivable properties. The system background knowledge includes generation rules associated with each model and heuristics for selecting most promising descriptions. The power and generality of the method presented is illustrated through a variety of interesting examples.

The rest of the book is concerned with specific software and/or hardware support for implementing expert systems. Chapters 6 and 7 might be seen as variations on the theme "All you can do with PROLOG". A short and general overview of some of the issues raised in using PROLOG as implementation vehicle for decision support systems (DSS) is presented in Chapter 6. After recalling the general architecture underlying such systems, Kriwaczek advocates the appropriateness of if–then rules and their coding in PROLOG as the unique medium for the piecewise development of the data, model and dialogue components of a DSS. This view should of course be contrasted with that substantiated in Chapter 1.

In Chapter 7 Hammond describes an approach for implementing a command-driven front-end to an interactive logic programming environ- ment. The key idea is to introduce an explicit Horn clause definition of the grammar of the command language that is kept separate from the declarative description of the interaction with the user and from the implementation of the commands. As in generic syntax-directed editors, the grammar defini- tion is used for example for detecting and explaining incorrect command forms, prompting the user for command components or supporting alterna- tive concrete syntactic forms for commands.

Several expert systems mentioned in this book use frame-based structures for representing one source of knowledge or another. There is a growing interest for the object-oriented approach both in the AI and Software Engineering communities. Chapter 8 is concerned with machine architectures for supporting real-world expert systems developed according to this approach. Suzuki first gives a brief account of the history, trends and characteristics of workstations for expert-system development. A short overview on object-oriented language concepts is presented next, mainly through some language features of SMALLTALK-80, which are used in the next section. The author then discusses the design philosophy and the main architectural decisions that he took in the design of a general-purpose, bytecode emulating microprocessor for SMALLTALK-80. A wise constraint on this design was to avoid substantial rewriting of any part of the source program of the standard SMALLTALK-80 Virtual Image. Comparative data are given to show how the resulting product behaves better than other existing systems. On another hand, the design of bug-free hardware is a very important concern. To support this, Suzuki in a final section develops a methodology for functional specification and verification of hardware using Concurrent PROLOG. The principle is to write the input and output assertions, the functional specification and the hardware specifications all in Concurrent PROLOG and then to check consistency between them by running the code against test data. Bugs can then be discovered at the early stages of the design. These ideas are illustrated through the construction of such a specification for a complex memory system of a high-performance personal computer.

We hope that this collection of papers will provide a representative account of some of the fascinating issues that deserve further investigation for future expert systems to exhibit some form of "intelligent" behaviour. We wish to express our deep gratitude to all the lecturers who have accepted to share their time and knowledge with us. It was a unique opportunity for the Belgian scientific community to learn and exchange ideas with them. The permanent effort of the Belgian National Science Foundation to promote education and research at the highest level is also gratefully acknowledged. We are much indebted to IBM Belgium, who created the professorship and provided the necessary funds; Mr t'Kint de Roodenbeke helped us a great deal in solving some organizational problems. Finally, we are grateful to all the people in Namur and in Mons who provided everyday help and support during the course; among them, Christiane Decoux and Yves Deville deserve special thanks.

AXEL VAN LAMSWEERDE
PIERRE DUFOUR

Jackson, P. (1986). *Introduction to Expert Systems*. Reading, Mass.: Addison-Wesley.

Clark, K. L. and F. G. McCabe (1984). *Micro-PROLOG: Programming in Logic*. Englewood Cliffs, N.J.: Prentice-Hall.

Michalski, R. S., Carbonell, J. G. and Mitchell, T. M. (eds.) (1984). *Machine Learning—An Artificial Intelligence Approach*. New York: Springer Verlag.

Michalski, R. S., Carbonell, J. G. and Mitchell, T. M. (eds.) (1986). *Machine Learning—An Artificial Intelligence Approach*, Vol. 2. Morgan Kaufmann.

Sleeman, D. and Brown, J. S. (eds.) (1982). *Intelligent Tutoring Systems*. New York: Academic Press.

Contents

3. Intelligent tutoring systems: A tutorial survey

William J. Clancey

4. From GUIDON to NEOMYCIN and HERACLES
in twenty short lessons

William J. Clancey

5.   **Qualitative prediction: the SPARC/G methodology for inductively
     describing and predicting discrete processes**

Ryszard Michalski, Heedong Ko and Kaihu Chen

8. Knowledge-engineering workstations

Norihisa Suzuki

1. Logic for expert systems?

PETER JACKSON

Abstract. The advent of logic programming languages has led to calls for an approach to expert-systems design and implementation that involves using predicate calculus as the main knowledge representation language and deductive inference as the main reasoning mechanism. This chapter attempts a critical review of the assumptions upon which such calls are based, and tries to anticipate some of the problems that might attach to a strong version of the logicist's programme. It is argued that logic may have a central role to play, both in the formulation of knowledge and the specification of system behaviour, but that this role will not obviate the need for other knowledge-representation languages and expert-system architectures.

1 INTRODUCTION

In recent years, a number of writers have argued for the application of logic programming techniques to knowledge-based systems (e.g. Kowalski, 1980; Clarke and McCabe, 1982; Furukawa *et al.*, 1984). The main arguments that have been put forward can be summarized as follows:

(1) logic, as a knowledge-representation language, has a clearer seman- ·tics than many other systems, such as frames, and should therefore be used in preference to them;

(2) deductive inference is the correct mode of reasoning for computers to employ, because it is the only one that is well understood;

(3) logic programming languages, such as PROLOG, are good implementation vehicles for expert-systems applications, given pattern-matching primitives and a keyed database;

(4) logic could act as a unifying medium, integrating program specification and expert-systems technology.

This chapter examines some of the assumptions behind these arguments, and mentions some recent work relevant to their assessment.

CURRENT ISSUES IN EXPERT SYSTEMS
ISBN 0-12-714030-1

2 LOGIC AS A KNOWLEDGE REPRESENTATION LANGUAGE

As noted in Smith and Brachman (1980), the term "representation of knowledge" contains a fundamental ambiguity. One construal is the *subjective genetive* reading, which implies that knowing is an activity that requires the manipulation of representations. The other is the *objective genetive* reading, which is more concerned with knowing as a state consisting in the possession of representations.

This section argues that the use of pure logic as a knowledge-representation language neglects knowledge representation as activity in favour of knowledge representation as accomplished fact. It is therefore consonant with the objective genetive reading, but not the subjective genetive one.

To begin with, take the question of order, i.e. the order in which propositions are listed in a declarative logic database. In logic, one can draw exactly the same inferences from the set of propositions $\{P_1, P_2, P_3\}$ as one can from the set $\{P_3, P_2, P_1\}$, or any of the other four permutations. In the majority of propositional knowledge bases, this simply isn't the case; clauses are carefully hand-ordered to control the way in which search spaces develop during procedural interpretation. This is evidence of a category mistake. It doesn't make sense to order propositions in the way that it does to order utterances or inscriptions.

This often combines with a second source of confusion, that involving the semantics of connectives. Propositional representations of the form $P_1 \mathbin{\&} P_2 \mathbin{\&} \ldots \mathbin{\&} P_n$ are frequently interpreted to mean "first try to prove P_1, then $P_2, \ldots$, then P_n", where the order of the P_i is highly significant for the procedural interpretation. Yet, in logic, $P_1 \mathbin{\&} P_2$ is entirely equivalent to $P_2 \mathbin{\&} P_1$. We are making a pun on & which contaminates its logical meaning as a propositional connective with some of the connotations of the corresponding sentence connective in natural language, concerning temporal sequence, causality, enablement, and so on.

Thirdly, there is the danger of a category mistake involving mood. The same proposition is sometimes given a different informal reading in different contexts. Thus

$$P_1 \mathbin{\&} P_2 \mathbin{\&} \ldots \mathbin{\&} P_n \to Q$$

can receive any of the following readings:

"to make Q true, make P_1 and $\ldots$ and P_n true"
"whenever P_1 and $\ldots$ and P_n are true, make Q true"
"to show that Q is true, show that P_1 and $\ldots$ and P_n are true"

These readings are subtly different; some have an imperative feel to them, while others don't. Consider the difference between "if x is a missile, then x

is ready" and "if x is a missile then make x ready!". The former implies that, at the time of utterance, the missiles are ready, while the latter implies that they aren't.

Such difficulties arise because of a failure to distinguish between different kinds of entity: namely propositions, which have only truth values, and sentence tokens, which can have other properties, such as serial order and illocutionary force. This is evidence for a confusion between semantics and pragmatics in the way in which the formalism is used for knowledge representation in the subjective genetive sense. These properties are typically smuggled into the formalism, and, as such, they are not formally represented anywhere.

3   DEDUCTION AS THE MAIN MODE OF REASONING

When experts are attempting to solve ill-structured problems, such as performing medical diagnoses, their reasoning does not seem to be fundamentally deductive in character. Pople (1973, 1982) has argued that a crucial aspect of diagnostic reasoning is the ability to formulate problems in a structured way that makes them more amenable to solution, and the principal mode of inference employed appears to be abductive. Abductive inference is concerned with the generation of hypotheses that would explain observed facts, rather than generating the logical consequences of a collection of facts and rules.

Many data-interpretation tasks that human beings routinely perform, such as speech understanding and plan recognition, are difficult, if not impossible to formulate as deductive tasks. Rather, they involve inference to the best explanation. It is arguable that many expert-system tasks, such as medical diagnosis, are also of this character, in that the deductive inferences that can be drawn are trivial compared with the non-deductive inferences required in the formation, scheduling and confirmation of hypotheses.

Problem-solving strategies such as "try and turn ill-structured problems into well-structured ones by partitioning the hypothesis space" require for their realization associative mechanisms rather than deductive ones. One can implement associative mechanisms in a logic programming language, of course, but this should not be confused with deductive inference. Similarly, appeals to meta-theory miss the point, since the arbitrary use of meta-level axioms to enhance or edit object-level deduction is generally unconstrained by such niceties as soundness and completeness, as McDermott (1986) has recently pointed out.

Lest these remarks be considered as unsubstantiated criticisms, the difficulties raised will be illustrated in the context of MECHO, a program for solving problems in high-school Newtonian mechanics (Bundy, 1978; Bundy et al., 1979). MECHO is chosen not because it is a flagrant example of such problems, but rather because it is one of the few logic-based systems in the literature that has made a systematic attempt to apply propositional representations of knowledge to complex problem solving. The number and nature of the perturbations to the syntax and semantics of the first-order calculus that were required to harness a logical language to the ends of artificial intelligence are extremely instructive.

MECHO was not implemented in PROLOG directly, but rather in MBASE, an interpreter written in PROLOG. A MECHO knowledge base is a list of clauses of the general form $P \leftarrow Q_1, \ldots, Q_n$, where P is the conclusion and the Q_i are conditions. As in PROLOG, a query that unifies with P is construed as a procedure invocation, and the unifier can be considered as a mechanism for passing parameters to the Q_i.

The associative mechanisms employed by MECHO are called "schemata", and they are mainly used to encode general knowledge about such things as pulley systems, for example

sysinfo(pullsys, [Pull, Str, P1, P2], [pulley, string, solid, solid]
[supports(Pull, Str), attached(Str, P1), attached(Str, P2)]).

sysinfo is a meta-predicate that takes four arguments. **pullsys** says that this schema is meant to represent a typical pulley system. The second argument is simply a list of the components of a pulley system, while the third argument contains type information about these components. The fourth argument contains a list of relationships that hold between these components.

This is obviously a perfectly valid way of doing programming, and under certain circumstances it can even be efficient. The point is that there is nothing very propositional about such representations, for example the way in which type information is represented by an implicit mapping between two lists. Neither is accessing and applying such information deduction, in any interesting sense.

Similar things can be said about meta-rules that control object-level deductions. Consider the following example:

method(strategy(dbinf), function(Arguments = > Values), Newgoal)
← all-bound(Arguments), use-function-properties(Newgoal).

This states that the default inference method, **dbinf**, will prove **Newgoal**, a function relation of **Arguments** that returns **Values**, if all the arguments given to the function in **Newgoal** are bound, and if the inferences are performed using "function property pruning" (Bundy, 1977). This is a way of using control information to evaluate a predicate–argument composition of the form $f(a_1, \ldots, a_n)$ in which one of the a_i is uniquely determined once all the other a_i are known. In terms of conformity to the syntax and semantics of the first-order calculus, it is difficult to see what this has to offer over and above the average LISP function. The form and content of such axioms appears to be more or less unconstrained. The most that can be said about such rules is that they are a more explicit way of exercising program control and structuring information than the hand-ordering of clauses and conditions. (In fairness, they are also ingenious, and they do the job.)

The MECHO work is *not* an example of the kind of double-think that confuses deduction with logic programming. It *is* an example of the kinds of extralogical mechanisms that are necessary if one wishes to recast non-deductive reasoning processes in a deductive mould. For further examples, the reader is referred to Jackson (1986, Chap. 11); those given above should be sufficient for present purposes.

4 LOGIC PROGRAMMING LANGUAGES AS IMPLEMENTATION VEHICLES

There is not much to say here, except that PROLOG is in many ways an excellent programming language that may rival LISP as soon as the programming environments of the respective languages are comparable. A good book on how to do knowledge-based programming (as opposed to conventional programming or database query) in PROLOG would also be beneficial in this regard. Everything else is a matter of taste and upbringing.

5 LOGIC AS A SPECIFICATION LANGUAGE AND ANALYTIC TOOL

It is difficult, though probably not impossible, to disagree with Newell (1982) when he suggests that logic is *the* primary tool for the analysis of human knowledge. This is because the principle of rationality must be allowed to stand as a regulative ideal, even if it has neither descriptive nor prescriptive force where human reasoning is concerned. One could argue that expert systems should be entirely rational, even if human beings aren't—but then everything depends on one's definition of rationality. Construals that require that all conclusions reached be sound in the deductive sense are probably too narrow, since they rule out inference to the best explanation. Once one liberates rationality from the chains of deduction (sorry about the pun), "logic for expert systems" again appears to neglect the subjective genetive aspects of knowledge representation, i.e. the way in which representations are typically used to solve problems.

However, the adoption of logic as a specification language need not be hampered by such epistemological and psychological considerations, so long as one's claims are not too strong. Kowalski's (1984) suggestions concerning the creation of "runnable specifications" using logic programming techniques are interesting, although very short on detail. The following questions immediately arise:

(1) How should the specification be derived during the design process?
(2) How can one integrate the syntax and semantics of extended logics for dealing with such things as time and uncertainty?
(3) How can one reason about meta-logical properties of one's system, such as soundness, completeness and consistency?
(4) How does one get from a runnable specification to a performance system?

Such matters cannot be dealt with in any depth here, although they are central to work in progress on logic-based expert systems tools (Jackson *et al.*, 1985; Reichgelt and van Harmelen, 1986).

Thus the process of deriving a specification ought to depend upon some classification of expert-systems tasks, and some criteria for mapping tasks onto representation schemes and control regimes (Reichgelt and van Harmelen, 1985). Typical expert-system tasks, such as diagnosis and design, appear to be related to particular problem solving paradigms, such as heuristic classification and constraint satisfaction (Chandrasekaran, 1985; Clancey, 1985). A formal description of the control regime that realizes the appropriate inference structure should form part of the specification of any expert system.

The fact that one may need to integrate logics of different expressive power within the same specification calls for more than one level of representation and novel compilation techniques (Reichgelt, 1986). Although modal treatments of time are typically superior to first-order treatments in terms of ease of expression and extensibility, they tend to be inferior from a computational point of view. Therefore there appear to be benefits attached to the strategy of allowing the knowledge engineer to express himself in one notation while the interpreter deals with another, equivalent one.

Reasoning about meta-logical properties of knowledge bases requires close attention to issues in man–machine interaction, the construction of environments that extend the procedural power of logic-based formalisms, and the provision of special purpose logic interpreters (Jackson, in press). One approach involves regarding the interaction between a knowledge engineer and a developing knowledge base as a language game, and using a game-theoretic interpretation of logic to help the knowledge engineer explore the consequences of additions and retractions. Embedding a logic-based system in an object-oriented environment can help structure propositional representations of knowledge in a way that benefits both the exercise of flexible control and the intelligibility of the knowledge base.

The problem of compiling runnable specifications of expert-systems architectures into high-performance systems that are not limited to deductive inference, is one that has to be solved by any proponent of the logic-based approach. One technique involves using a meta-level specification of a particular control regime to generate a special-purpose interpreter; thus there is no reason why the language used to specify a control regime need be the language that runs it at execution time. The reader is invited to consult van Harmelen (1986) for a review of the issues and a number of proposals.

6 SUMMARY AND CONCLUSIONS

"Logic for expert systems" means different things to different people. Such slogans tend to confuse the rather different roles that logic can play in the design, evaluation and implementation of an expert system. The present chapter has attempted to do no more than clarify some of the issues and suggest that some of the arguments for logic in various roles are more convincing than others.

The case for logic as the sole representation language and deductive inference as the sole reasoning method appears to be very weak. Pure logics expressive enough for expert-systems applications are typically hard to write interpreters for, and don't have many nice meta-logical properties. Logics that have been adulterated in various ways can easily degenerate into data and programming structures.

Logic programming languages appear to be suitable implementation vehicles for many expert-systems applications, although where serious analysis has been attempted equally serious problems have emerged (e.g. Sharpe, 1984). It will be some time before PROLOG programming environments match those described by Sheil (1983) for exploratory programming in LISP. The case for multiple paradigm programming put forward by Bobrow (1984) also has something to recommend it.

Logic as an analytic tool and runnable specification language appears to have something to offer, although no-one seems to have asked the knowledge engineers if that is indeed what they want! The assumption always appears to be that enough syntactic sugar will make predicate calculus acceptable to all classes of user. Some kind of integration of object-oriented programming and logic programming seems to hold out the most hope in this respect.

Ultimately, nothing is as convincing as an existence proof. When it can be demonstrated that logic, in one or more of the four roles outlined in this paper, has something significant to offer over and above more heterogenous methods for representation and reasoning, we will all become logicists (even if we go on behaving irrationally). People will then wonder, with the benefit of 20–20 hindsight, why papers like this were ever written.

REFERENCES

Bobrow, D. G. (1984). If Prolog is the answer, what is the question? *Proc. Int. Conf. on Fifth Generation Computer Systems ICOT*, pp. 138–145.

Bundy, A. (1977). Exploiting the properties of functions to control search. DAI Research Rep. 45, Dept of Artificial Intelligence, Univ. Edinburgh.

Bundy, A. (1978). Will it reach the top? Prediction in the mechanics world . *Artificial Intelligence* **10**, 129–146.

Bundy, A., Byrd, L., Luger, G., Mellish, C. and Palmer, M. (1979). Solving mechanics problems using metalevel inference. *Expert Systems in the Micro Electronic Age* (ed. D. J. Michie), pp. 50–64. Edinburgh: Edinburgh University Press.

Chandrasekaran, B. (1985). Generic tasks in expert system design and their role in the explanation of problem solving. Paper presented at NAS/ONR Workshop on *Artificial Intelligence and Distributed Problem Solving.*

Clancey, W. J. (1985). Heuristic classification. Rep. KSL 85-5, Knowledge Systems Lab., Stanford Univ.

Clarke, K. L. and McCabe, F. (1982). PROLOG: A language for implementing expert systems. *Machine Intelligence 10* (ed. J. Hayes and D. J. Michie), pp. 455–470. Chichester: Ellis Horwood.

Furukawa, K., Takeuchi, A., Kunifuji, S., Yasukawa, H., Ohki, M. and Ueda, K. (1984). MANDALA: A logic based knowledge programming system. *Proc. Int. Conf. on Fifth Generation Computer Systems ICOT*, pp. 613–622.

Jackson, P. (1986). *Introduction to Expert Systems*. Reading, Mass.: Addison-Wesley.

Jackson, P. (in press). On game-theoretic interactions with first-order knowledge bases. *Non-Standard Logics for Automated Reasoning* (ed. P. Smets). London: Academic Press.

Jackson, P., Reichgelt, H. and van Harmelen, F. (1985). A flexible toolkit for building expert systems. Tech. Rep. EdU-2, Expert Systems Toolkit Project, Dept of Artificial Intelligence, Edinburgh Univ.

Kowalski, R. (1980). *SIGART Newsletter* No. 70 (Special Issue on Knowledge Representation, ed. D. E. Smith and R. J. Brackman), p. 44. New York: Association for Computing Machinery.

Kowalski, R. (1984). Logic programming in the fifth generation. *Knowledge Engng Rev.* **1**, 26–38.

McDermott, D. (1986). A critique of pure reason. Unpublished paper.

Newell, A. (1982). The knowledge level. *Artificial Intelligence* **18**, 87–127.

Pople, H. E. (1973). The formation of composite hypotheses in diagnostic problem solving: An exercise in synthetic reasoning. *Proc. 3rd Int. Joint Conf. on Artificial Intelligence*, pp. 1030–1037. Los Altos, California: Morgan Kaufmann.

Pople, H. E. (1982). Heuristic methods for imposing structure on ill-structured problems: The structuring of medical diagnostics. *Artificial Intelligence in Medicine* (ed. P. Szolovitz), pp. 119–185. Boulder, Colorado: Westview Press.

Reichgelt, H. (1986). A comparison of first-order and modal treatments of time. Unpublished paper.

Reichgelt, H. and van Harmelen, F. (1985). Criteria for choosing representation languages and control regimes for expert systems. *Expert Systems 85: Proc. 5th Technical Conf. of the British Computer Society Specialist Group on Expert Systems* (ed. M. Merry), pp. 21–30. Cambridge: Cambridge University Press.

Reichgelt, H. and van Harmelen, F. (1986). A prototype for a logic-based toolkit for expert system construction. Tech. Rep. EdU-11, Expert Systems Toolkit Project, Dept of Artificial Intelligence, Edinburgh Univ.

Sharpe, W. P. (1984). Logic programming for the law. *Research and Development in Expert Systems* (ed. M. A. Bramer), pp. 217–228. Cambridge: Cambridge University Press.

Sheil, B. (1983). Power tools for programmers. *Datamation*.

Smith, D. E. and Brachman, R. J. (eds.) (1980). *SIGART Newsletter* No. 70 (Special Issue on Knowledge Representation). New York: Association for Computing Machinery.

van Harmelen, F. (1986). A categorization of meta-level architecture. Tech. Rep. EdU-14, Expert Systems Toolkit Project, Dept of Artificial Intelligence, Edinburgh Univ.

2. Towards an architecture for advice-giving systems

PETER JACKSON

Abstract. Current applications of logic to expert systems leave a good deal to be desired in terms of both expressive adequacy and the specification of control. These problems are discussed in the context of advice-giving systems driven by goal-directed dialogue. It is suggested that viewing the interaction as a language game may allow some difficulties with reasoning about belief and the control of inference to be addressed in a more intuitive manner.

1   INTRODUCTION

Applications of logic to expert systems are often unsatisfactory with regard to both the expressiveness of the representation language and the facilities provided for controlling deduction. This is because the epistemological assumptions underlying the equation of human problem-solving with theorem-proving are typically too strong, while the control regimes under which inference is performed are often too weak. These problems are discussed in the context of advice-giving systems, and an architecture based on language games is outlined that may have certain advantages over more conventional approaches. A prototype advisor on personal finance is described, and difficulties inherent in the design are noted. Finally, an attempt is made to assess the approach and relate it to recent work on epistemic and doxastic logic.

1.1   What Are Advice-Giving Systems?

The majority of current expert-system applications appear to perform tasks like fault-finding and medical diagnosis, which are essentially analytic in that they involve identifying the description of some particular case with a specific node in some predetermined classification network (Chandrasekaran, 1983). A growing number of systems also perform tasks that are mostly synthetic, in that they have a strong planning or design component: R1

CURRENT ISSUES IN EXPERT SYSTEMS
ISBN 0-12-714030-1

(McDermott, 1982) might be considered as falling into this class. Of course, few programs fit neatly and exclusively into one or the other of these categories; thus MYCIN's (Shortliffe, 1976) diagnostic capability could be regarded as an analytic skill, while its ability to recommend therapies could be regarded as synthetic.

One can also conceive of systems that perform slightly more open-ended tasks, having both an analytic and a synthetic component, for example systems able to advise on everyday topics, such as financial and legal matters to do with housing and insurance. There is a large potential demand for such systems, although the number of available programs is small at the present time. There are many reasons for this, but I should like to focus upon the following considerations.

(1) The facts and goals of advice-giving are less well defined than fault-finding or medical diagnosis, so it is harder to know what constitutes success, how hard to try and when to stop. It is also more difficult to draw the line between knowledge and belief, or to distinguish fact from opinion.

(2) The structure of the problem addressed in the course of an advisory dialogue may not map onto a discrimination net or some other convenient organizer, so it is harder to know where to begin and how to develop the session. Many expert systems rely on a global control regime, which deprives the user of any initiative in the problem-solving process.

(3) It is not enough for an automatic advisor to solve a problem to its own satisfaction; a solution is no good if the client does not understand and accept it. The system therefore needs to be capable of providing explanations that are clearer and more concise than traces of rule application, and it should also be prepared to look for another solution if the user has reasonable grounds for rejection.

One might call such programs *interactive incremental problem solvers*. Their function is to formulate, refine and attempt to solve a stated problem via a goal-directed conversation with a user (hence interactive), in which possible and partial solutions are proposed as a function of the current formulation of the problem (hence incremental). In other words, the dialogue is an integral part of the problem-solving process, and not an "intelligent front end" that has been added on afterwards. Thus the inferential capacity of the problem-solver and the inferential demands of the dialogue need to be rather more carefully matched than is usually the case. I want to argue that one way of doing this involves reasoning about belief, yet doxastic reasoning must itself be tightly controlled if it is to be both computationally effective and intelligible to the user. This raises a number of issues concerning the way in which beliefs are represented in a knowledge-based system.

1.2   Knowledge Representation For Advice-Giving

Experts employ many different kinds of knowledge in the execution of their duties. In addition to possessing particular facts and general rules relevant to their domain, they also have strategies for applying domain knowledge and dealing with clients. Thus an expert needs to be able to reason about both his own beliefs and those of his client.

Naive applications of logic to expert systems generally concern themselves exclusively with the truth or falsity of propositions. That is to say, knowledge is represented as a set of propositions, Δ, which constitutes a knowledge base. If a proposition P is in Δ then P is deemed to be true, and the expert e is said to know that P. If P is not in Δ, but is logically implied by Δ, then P is true and e knows that P. It is often assumed that if P is not a tautological consequence of Δ, then P is false and e knows that $\sim P$.

There are several epistemological problems associated with this. Some of them derive from the fact that the axioms of epistemic logic that appear to justify the approach are too strong. Let us write $K_e P$ for "e knows that P", while $\Delta \vdash P$ will denote that P is a tautological consequence of Δ.

(1) Experts have been known to be wrong. Hence Δ may not be veridical, in which case the usual epistemic axiom $K_x P \supset P$ will not hold.

(2) Expert knowledge may not be complete. Thus it may not be the case that $\Delta \vdash P$, although P is in fact true. Negation as failure tends to confound $\sim K_e P$ with $K_e \sim P$, by replacing $K_x P \supset P$ with $(K_x P \supset P)$ & $(P \supset K_x P)$.

(3) Experts may not be conscious of all the logical consequences of what they know. Thus, the fact that $\Delta \vdash P$ may not be sufficient for us to say that $K_e P$. The epistemic axiom $K_x(P \supset Q) \supset (K_x P \supset K_x Q)$ is too strong when chains of reasoning may exceed resources.

(4) How do we know that Δ is consistent? If $\Delta \vdash P$ and $\Delta \vdash \sim P$, is it the case that $K_e P$ or $K_e \sim P$ or $\sim K_e P$?

The assumptions implicit in (1)–(4) arc not justified in all expert-systems applications, particularly those that involve advice-giving. Giving advice often means offering suggestions on the basis of partial information, much of which is taken on trust. Knowledge-based programs need to be able to *entertain* propositions, i.e. represent them to themselves without having to make up their minds about whether or not they are true.

Most applications of logic to expert systems are interested in gaining both the expressive power of the predicate calculus under a complete interpretation and syntactic rules deduction that can be shown to have desirable meta-logical properties in the limit case of infinite resources. In applying logic to advice-giving, one is really concerned with argument, in that a system's ultimate goal is to convince the user (and itself) that the advice offered is worth following, using only such resources as are at its disposal. I want to suggest that *it is profitable to view argument as a kind of language game in which valid forms of inference constitute no more than ideal strategies that an actual system may or may not have the resources to follow*.

The question then arises as to which interpretation of which calculus might provide a basis for a representation language whose underlying assumptions were more acceptable.

2   A GAME-THEORETIC INTERPRETATION OF LOGIC

The game-theoretic interpretation of logic selected as a starting point for the formalization of these ideas is due to Hintikka (1973, 1983). In this approach, any attempt to establish the truth or falsity of an expression Φ in an interpreted language **L** is correlated with a two-person, zero-sum, perfect information game $\mathbf{G}\Phi$, played according to the rules of **L**. These games can be thought of as constituting "idealized processes of verification" (Hintikka, 1976, p. 216).

Informally, one can think of the two players as oneself and "Nature", and the game consists of one seeking support for Φ, while Nature looks for a refutation. In seeking to establish the truth of a statement, the players may adopt either a minimizing or a maximizing role with respect to it . The encumbent of the minimizing role (MIN) will attempt to gather evidence against the statement, while the encumbent of the maximizing role (MAX) will try to find evidence for it. It is best to think of oneself starting a game in the MAX role, and Nature starting in the MIN role. Arguments involving negation will result in role reversal, as we shall see below.

2.1   Game Rules for Connectives and Quantifiers

In what follows, let the Greek letters Φ, Γ, Ψ, Π, possibly with numeric subscripts, be meta-variables standing for propositional constants, and let Φ_x, Γ_x, etc. stand for propositional functions of x.

Let the syntax of **L** be that of the propositional calculus, and let $\mathbf{G}\Phi$ denote a game played on Φ, a well-formed formula of **L**, according to the following semantic rules.

(G.&) If Φ is (Γ_1 & . . . & Γ_n) the MIN chooses some Γ_i such that $1 \le i \le n$, and the players play GΓ_i.

(G.~) If Φ is ~Γ then MAX and MIN swap roles, and the players play GΓ.

Courtesy of **(G.&)**, MIN is free to choose the conjunct least favourable to the proof, thereby minimizing MAX's chances of winning. The role reversal in **(G.~)** ensures that I win if the negated expression turns out to be false and that Nature wins if it turns out true. Games for disjunction and the material condition can be derived via the usual equivalences, for example

(G.v) If Φ is ($\Gamma_1 v$ . . . $v \Gamma_n$) then MAX chooses some Γ_i such that $1 \le i \le n$, and the game goes on with respect to it.

Hintikka assumes a complete interpretation **k** for the atomic propositions and the game rules provide for the recursive evaluation of complex expressions relative to **k**. The basic idea is that, if a sentence Φ of a language **L** is true in **k**, i.e. if **k** is a model of Φ, then this can be shown using only the game rules of **L**. Hence

(G.T) Φ is true iff I have a winning strategy in GΦ.

The proof of **(G.T)** is on the construction of Φ, and the truth tables for the connectives. However, the fact that I have a winning strategy in GΦ does not guarantee that I will win. For example, if I choose P during **G**(~(P & Q)), where P is true in **k** but Q is false, then I lose unnecessarily. Similarly, the converse of **(G.T)**,

(G.F) Φ is false iff there is a winning strategy for Nature,

requires that Nature make the right choices, since if she chooses P during **G**(P & Q), where P is true in **k** but Q is false, then she loses unnecessarily. Thus game-theoretic semantics is only sound in practice if optimal choices are made by both sides. On the other hand, if good choices *are* made, then such proofs clearly involve less search than more conventional methods.

Hintikka also suggests quantification games, which assume a non-empty domain **D** of individuals.

(G.U) If Φ is ($\forall x$)Γ_x, where Γ_x is a one-place propositional function, then MIN chooses some d from **D**, and the game goes on with respect to $\Gamma_{d/x}$. where $\Gamma_{d/x}$ denotes the result of substituting d for x in Γ_x uniformly.

This rule is intuitively comprehensible in terms of the implicit conjunction of the universal. One may derive a similar rule for the existential via the usual equivalences, which is comprehensible in terms of its implicit disjunction:

(G.E) If Φ is $(\exists x)\Gamma_x$ then as above, except that MAX chooses.

Thus game choices made during **(G.U)** and **(G.E)** reduce quantification games to propositional games in a finite number of steps, while the latter reduce to the atomic case in a finite number of applications of **(G.&)** and **(G.~)**.

2.2   High Games and Low Games

If one uses logic for the purposes of expert problem solving then one may have only a partial interpretation for the atomic propositions. In such circumstances, it is helpful to think of such an interpretation as a set of models, i.e. an incomplete description of some world. This can be represented by a knowledge base, Δ: a set of sentences describing the beliefs of an expert e as before. The difference is that we do not make any of the assumptions noted earlier. Thus Δ may be inaccurate, incomplete, not closed under logical deduction, and even inconsistent.

This complication necessitates that one specify a further set of games to be associated with logical operators. Those provided above I have called *high games*, and these cope with the presence of operators in Φ. Those provided below I have called *low games*, since these cope with the presence of operators in the elements of Δ. For example, with $(P \& Q) \in \Delta$, MAX ought to win **G**P, but the game rules given so far do not provide for this.

Let the set of all expressions in Δ containing occurrences of the predicate governing an atomic proposition Φ be Δ^Φ. Then for each $\Psi \in \Delta^\Phi$ there is a subgame $\mathbf{F}(\Phi, \Psi)$, with the following rules:

(F.T) If $\Psi = \Phi$ then MAX wins;

(F.~) If $\Psi = \sim\Pi$ then MAX and MIN swap roles and play $\mathbf{F}(\Phi, \Pi)$.

The rationale for **(F.T)** and **(F.~)** is similar to **(G.T)** and **(G.~)**. As a preamble to **(F.&)**, let an occurrence of an atomic formula Φ be *oddly negated* in a formula Π if it stands in the scope of an odd number of negation symbols, and *evenly negated* otherwise. In other words, if Φ is oddly negated then it would appear as a negative literal in a normal form (such as conjunctive normal form) that drives negation in. If Φ is evenly negated then it would appear as a positive literal.

(F.&) If $\Psi = (\Pi_1 \& \ldots \& \Pi_n)$ then the players play $\mathbf{F}(\Phi, \Pi_i)$ for some i such that $1 \le i \le n$, at MAX's choice if Φ occurs in Π_i evenly negated, or at MIN's choice if Φ occurs in Π_i oddly negated. If $\mathbf{F}(\Phi, \Pi_i)$ is drawn then $\mathbf{F}(\Phi,$

Ψ) is drawn. Otherwise, the winner of $\mathbf{F}(\Phi, \Pi_i)$ must also win $\mathbf{G}(\Pi_j)$ for all j such that $j \neq i$ and $1 \leq j \leq n$ to win $\mathbf{F}(\Phi, \Psi)$, else $\mathbf{F}(\Phi, \Psi)$ is drawn.

The rationale behind (**F.&**) is that $\Pi_1 \,\&\, \ldots \,\&\, \Pi_n \vdash \Pi_i$, but this requires two qualifications for the game rules to be sound.

One is that the player who gets choice of conjunct should depend upon whether $\Pi_1 \,\&\, \ldots \,\&\, \Pi_n$ may be used to confirm Φ or refute it (even though the choice appears superficially to be a MAX one). For example, if Ψ were $(\sim\Phi \,\&\, \Pi)$ then, given the choice, MAX would always choose to play $\mathbf{F}(\Phi, \Pi)$ for a draw, rather than lose $\mathbf{F}(\Phi, \sim\Phi)$. Similarly, if Ψ were $(\Phi \,\&\, \Pi)$ then MIN would always choose $\mathbf{F}(\Phi, \Pi)$ over $\mathbf{F}(\Phi, \Phi)$.

The second qualification takes into account the fact that $(\Pi_1 \,\&\, \ldots \,\&\, \Pi_n)$ may not be in Δ at all, but may be a subexpression of an element of Δ, such as $\Psi = \sim(P \,\&\, Q)$. Thus MIN should win $\mathbf{F}(P, \sim(P \,\&\, Q))$ if and only if he can show that Q, for obvious reasons. In the case where $\Psi = (\Pi_1 \,\&\, \ldots \,\&\, \Pi_n)$ *is* in Δ, we may allow that the Π_j are trivially true.

There is a simple analogue to (**F.&**) for disjunction:

(**F.v**) If $\Psi = (\Pi_1 \,v \ldots v\, \Pi_n)$ then the players play $\mathbf{F}(\Phi, \Pi_i)$ for some i such that $1 \leq i \leq n$, at MAX's choice if Φ occurs in Π_i evenly negated, or at MIN's choice if Φ occurs in Π_i oddly negated. If $\mathbf{F}(\Phi, \Pi_i)$ is drawn then $\mathbf{F}(\Phi, \Psi)$ is drawn. Otherwise, the winner of $\mathbf{F}(\Phi, \Pi_i)$ must win $\mathbf{G}(\sim\Pi_j)$ for all j such that $j \neq i$ and $1 \leq j \leq n$ to win $\mathbf{F}(\Phi, \Psi)$, else $\mathbf{F}(\Phi, \Psi)$ is drawn.

The quantifier rules are also analogous, except that they assume that no quantifier ever occurs in the scope of negation, for reasons that will become clear.

(**F.U**) If $\Psi = (\forall x)\Pi_x$ then the players play $\mathbf{F}(\Phi, \Pi_{d/x})$, where $\Pi_{d/x}$ denotes the result of substituting uniformly a constant d of MIN's choice for x in Π_x if Φ is a substitution instance of an oddly negated formula occurring in Π_x, and a constant of MAX's choice otherwise. The winner of $\mathbf{F}(\Phi, \Pi_{d/x})$ is the winner of $\mathbf{F}(\Phi, \Psi)$.

The rationale behind (**F.U**) is that $(\forall x)\Pi_x \vdash \Pi_{d/x}$ for all $d \in \mathbf{D}$, the domain of individuals. The qualification concerning who chooses the constant is to prevent MAX always drawing $\mathbf{F}(Fa, (\forall x) \sim Fx)$ by playing $\mathbf{F}(Fa, \sim Fb)$, where b is any constant not equal to a, and MIN from always drawing $\mathbf{F}(Fa, (\forall x)Fx)$ by choosing to play $\mathbf{F}(Fa, Fb)$.

The analogue for the existential quantifier is straightforward:

(**F.E**) If $\Psi = (\exists x)\Pi_x$ then the players play $\mathbf{F}(\Phi, \Pi_{d/x})$, where $\Pi_{d/x}$ denotes the result of substituting uniformly a constant d of MAX's choice for x in Π_x if Φ is a substitution instance of an oddly negated formula occurring in Π_x, and a constant of MIN's choice otherwise. The winner of $\mathbf{F}(\Phi, \Pi_{d/x})$ is the winner of $\mathbf{F}(\Phi, \Psi)$.

Jackson (1987, Chap. 3) shows that these rules are sound, given optimal choices, but not complete. Briefly, **(F.&)** can be seen to be sound by analogy with the rule of &-elimination, but **(F.v)** is weaker than v-elimination, since it is *not* the case that $\Delta = \{P \vee Q\} \vdash P \vee Q$. MAX does not have a winning strategy in $G(P \vee Q)$, given Δ and the extra game rules given above, although given $\Delta = \{P\}$ or $\Delta = \{Q\}$, MAX *does* have a winning strategy. Thus, to win an argument on $P \vee Q$, MAX must say *which* of P and Q is true.

Similarly **(F.U)** is sound by analogy with $\forall$-elimination, but **(F.E)** is weaker than $\exists$-elimination, since it is not the case that $\Delta = \{(\exists x)Fx\} \vdash (\exists y)Fy$. This is because, once MAX has chosen a/x in $G((\exists x)Fx)$, MIN is free to choose b/y such that $b \neq a$. Giving MIN the option of choosing exemplars for existential variables turns out to be more confining than the usual restrictions on $\exists$-elimination, such as those described by Lemmon (1965, Chap. 3) and Quine (1974, Chap. 37). Thus it is *not* the case that $(\exists x)Fx$ is equivalent to $\sim(\forall x) \sim Fx$, and the rules given above are only sound if no quantifier occurs in the scope of negation.

We assume, in playing $\mathbf{G}\Phi$, that the game halts if a player wins a subgame $\mathbf{F}(\Phi, \Psi)$ in Δ^Φ, while if Δ^Φ is exhausted without a winner being found then $\mathbf{G}\Phi$ is drawn. This is a three-valued logic, since it is possible that Δ logically implies neither Φ nor $\sim\Phi$. The propositional subset of the logic is equivalent to that defined by Kleene's strong connectives under a complete interpretation, since it does not preserve the law of identity.

As an example, assume that I assert that $(\forall x)(\exists y)Rxy$, and $\Delta = \{(\exists y)(\forall x)Rxy\}$.

1. $(\forall x)(\exists y)Rxy$	MAX = Peter
2. $(\exists y)Ray$	MIN = Nature chooses a/x
3. Rab	MAX chooses b/x

4. $(\exists y)(\forall x)Rxy$	Δ
5. $(\forall x)Rxc$	MIN chooses c/y
6. Rac	MAX chooses a/x

I can only draw, because $Rac \neq Rab$. There are several things to notice here.

First, a natural-deduction proof method in the low game would have gone on to derive $(\forall x)(\exists y)Rxy$ from $(\exists y)(\forall x)Rxy$ along the lines of:

| 7. $(\exists y)Ray$ | $\exists$-introduction |
| 8. $(\forall x)(\exists y)Rxy$ | $\forall$-introduction |

with the latter step being valid because a does not occur in the assumption at line 5. The game-theoretic proof cannot go forward, because MAX and MIN disagree about who y is.

Secondly, having played such a language game, it is possible that one or both players may be said to explicitly believe propositions that they did not believe before. This may be so for several reasons. For example, the truth of a proposition Φ may have been only implicit in Δ, prior to the playing of $G\Phi$, not consciously believed by anyone. Also, after the game described above, I now know that Nature believes that $(\forall x)Rxc$. This might furnish me with a winning strategy in any replay of $G((\forall x)(\exists y)Rxy)$, given certain additional conventions that required players to make consistent choices between games. Finally, one can imagine situations in which I come to believe $(\forall x)Rxc$ myself, instead of just believing that Nature believes it. This would depend upon further conventions concerning who should accept whose word for what at the end of a language game, depending upon its outcome.

Therefore it is interesting to consider the development of *doxastic theories* over a series of games, i.e. theories of the players' explicit beliefs based on the outcomes of games played so far. However, the additional conventions required to do this are not really a part of the semantics of the language, but rather its pragmatics. This is because the properties in which we are interested are no longer semantic properties of propositions, such as truth and falsity, but pragmatic properties of sentence tokens in some context of use, such as sincerity and appropriateness.

3 REASONING ABOUT BELIEF AND ABOUT CONTROL

In the terminology of speech act theory (Austin, 1962; Searle, 1965) the typing of a sentence token to a knowledge based system can be considered as a *locutionary* act which the interpreter processes in some *illocutionary* context, for example as a voluntary assertion by some agent. Computational side effects that result, such as outputs to the user and modifications to the system's data structues, can be regarded as the token's *perlocutionary* effect. This section outlines game rules for the speech acts of asserting and asking, which allow the incremental construction of doxastic theories and seek to enforce felicity conditions. Game-playing strategies for the connectives can then be defined that perform limited inference with respect to the doxastic theories so derived. These strategies are deployed as a function of certain indices associated with a proposition at interpretation time, which represent the illocutionary force of the associated speech act.

3.1 Some Pragmatic Games

Let $\mathbf{A}$ and $\mathbf{B}$ be players. Let $\mathbf{A}$'s belief system be $\Delta_\mathbf{A}$ and let $\mathbf{B}$'s be $\Delta_\mathbf{B}$. If $\mathbf{A}$ asserts that Φ to $\mathbf{B}$, written $\Phi_{(>,\mathbf{A},\mathbf{B})}$, then

(1) if $\mathbf{A}$ is sincere then Φ is true in $\Delta_\mathbf{A}$;

(2) $\mathbf{A}$ should not believe that $\mathbf{B}$ already believes that Φ;

(3) $\mathbf{B}$ will accept that Φ, unless it is false in $\Delta_\mathbf{B}$.

These can be regarded as simple *felicity conditions* that might reasonably govern the behaviour of participants in a man–machine interaction. (1) states that if $\mathbf{A}$ asserts that Φ and $\mathbf{A}$ is sincere, then $\mathbf{A}$ believes that Φ. (2) states that $\mathbf{A}$'s assertion of Φ should not be redundant, if it is to be appropriate. (3) states that $\mathbf{B}$ should accept $\mathbf{A}$'s assertion at face value, so long as he does not believe it to be false. More complex conditions can be imagined, but these may serve for now.

Hereinafter, let "α believes that Φ", written $L_\alpha\Phi$, denote explicit belief, defined as $\{\Phi : \Phi \in \Delta_\alpha\}$, and $\Delta_\alpha \vdash_\mathbf{G} \Phi$ denote game-theoretic derivability using the $\mathbf{F}$ and $\mathbf{G}$ rules. We do not assume that $L_\alpha\Phi$ if $\Delta_\alpha \vdash_\mathbf{G} \Phi$, because it is possible that $L_\alpha\Phi$, and $L_\alpha \sim(\Phi \,\&\, \sim\Pi)$, but $\sim L_\alpha\Pi$. Thus $\Delta_\alpha \vdash_\mathbf{G} \Phi$ is consistent with $\sim L_\alpha\Phi$, but inconsistent with $L_\alpha \sim\Phi$ if Δ_α itself is consistent.

Let us assume that the players play a series of games, and that the results of previous games (win, lose, or draw) are stored and accessible to both players. $\mathbf{A}$ and $\mathbf{B}$ are only aware of each other's beliefs as a function of this record of who asked, asserted, accepted and rejected what. Let our knowledge of $\Delta_\mathbf{A}$ courtesy of previous games be $\delta_\mathbf{A}$ and our knowledge of $\Delta_\mathbf{B}$ be $\delta_\mathbf{B}$. Thus δ_α is simply the set of propositions $\{\Phi : L_\beta L_\alpha \Phi\}$ that any observer β would believe that α believed, solely as a function of game outcomes.

In the general case it is unlikely that δ_α, Δ_α, and $\{\Phi : \Delta_\alpha \vdash_\mathbf{G} \Phi\}$ will be identical. In other words, we cannot assume that all of α's beliefs are evident, or that α believes all the game-theoretic consequences of his beliefs. However $\delta_\alpha \subset \Delta_\alpha$ if α is sincere, while $\Delta_\alpha \subset \{\Phi : \Delta_\alpha \vdash_\mathbf{G} \Phi\}$ if α is rational.

Negative introspection is defined as $\{\sim L_\alpha\Phi : \text{it is not the case that } \Phi \in \Delta_\alpha\}$. Nested beliefs can be defined as $\{L_\alpha L_\beta\Phi : \Phi \in \delta_\beta\}$, since the record of previous games is common knowledge. The special case of $L_\alpha L_\alpha\Phi$ denotes positive introspection about α's beliefs; note that $L_\alpha\Phi \supset L_\alpha L_\alpha\Phi$ will not hold as long as $\delta_\alpha \not\subset \Delta_\alpha$.

The felicity conditions for $\Phi_{(>,\mathbf{A},\mathbf{B})}$ can now be sharpened up:

(1) the sincerity condition requires that $L_\mathbf{A}\Phi$, and not merely that $\Delta_\mathbf{A} \vdash_\mathbf{G} \Phi$;

(2) the appropriateness condition requires that neither $L_A L_B \Phi$ nor $L_A L_B \sim \Phi$;

(3) the acceptance condition now requires that **B** accept Φ unless he can maintain that $\Delta_B \vdash_G \sim \Phi$.

Let us extend the game-theoretic approach from the semantics of the representation language to its pragmatics. He who makes an assertion is clearly in the MAX role, while the listener plays the MIN role of critic. If **A** asserts that Φ then

(1) **B** wins if he can show that $L_A \sim \Phi$ or $\sim L_A \Phi$ or $L_A L_B \Phi$ or $L_A L_B \sim \Phi$;

(2) **A** wins if Φ is felicitous and **B** accepts that Φ;

(3) the game is drawn if **B** can maintain that $\Delta_B \vdash_G \sim \Phi$.

However, we need to consider under what conditions **B** can succeed in rejecting Φ. The assertion $\sim \Phi_{(>,B,A)}$ cannot be judged infelicitous of itself, since neither $L_A L_B \Phi$ nor $L_A L_B \sim \Phi$. We must therefore require that **B** give reasons $\{\Pi_1, \ldots, \Pi_n\}$ for rejecting Φ such that the assertion of each Π_i is felicitous. Thus **B**, who was in the MIN role in the game $\mathbf{G}(\Phi_{(>,A,B)})$, must swap roles with **A** when defending his rejection of Φ. Even if the game is ultimately drawn, **B**'s justification will have enlarged δ_B, giving him less room for manoeuvre next time. As shown at the end of Section 2, play reveals strategies that your opponent may subsequently be able to use against you—for example, conceding the Π_i may give **A** a winning strategy in a later game.

A similar analysis can be applied to questions. If **A** asks **B** if Φ, then

(1) if **A** is being sincere then it is not the case that either $L_A \Phi$ or $L_A \sim \Phi$, regardless of whether or not $\Delta_A \vdash_G \Phi$;

(2) The same appropriateness conditions apply here as applied to assertions, together with $\sim L_A \sim L_B \Phi$;

(3) **A** accepts **B**'s answer Π so long as he cannot maintain that $\Delta_A \vdash_G \sim \Pi$.

The analogous game-theoretic account is straightforward. **A** is in the MIN role in $\mathbf{G}(\Phi_{(?,A,B)})$, since **A** is the critic of the reply that **B** will give in his role of MAX. If **A** asks **B** if Φ, then

(1) **B** wins if he can show that $L_A \Phi$ or $L_A \sim \Phi$ or $L_A L_B \Phi$ or $L_A L_B \sim \Phi$ or $L_A \sim L_B \Phi$;

(2) **A** wins if **B** cannot answer;

(3) if **B** answers Π then the winner of $\Phi_{(?,A,B)}$ is the winner of $\Pi_{(>,B,A)}$.

Having asked $\Phi_{(?,\mathbf{A},\mathbf{B})}$, and received a positive reply, **A** is hardly in a position to reject Π simply by asserting $\sim\Phi$, since this would undermine the sincerity of the original question. Rather, **A** must impugn a premise upon which **B**'s answer rests, for example if $\Pi = P$ has reasons $\{Q \& \sim (Q \& \sim P)\}$ then **A** may counter with $\sim Q$, so long as $\sim L_\mathbf{A} L_\mathbf{A} Q$, but not with $Q \& \sim P$.

Given just two speech acts, one can have embedded games, for example MIN asking questions designed to cast doubt on MAX's assertions, MAX asking questions of MIN while attempting to find an answer, and so on. Regardless of how primitive these rules are, the potential of the game-theoretic approach may at least be apparent. In addition to providing an interpretation scheme for classical logic, it also provides us with a framework for drawing non-classical inferences, such as conversational implicatures.

3.2   A First Attempt at Game-Playing Strategies

The valuation of the Φ in the assertion "Φ is true" and the question "is Φ true?" *could* proceed along identical lines. The difference between the two speech acts would be the use to which the semantic valuation of Φ is subsequently put, i.e. their perlocutionary effects in terms of program actions. The idea explored here is that, just as one can associate semantic rules of evaluation with syntactic rules of construction, so one can define pragmatic rules that associate evaluation strategies with semantic rules.

The explanation and examples given below are confined to two-person conversation games and the speech acts of asserting and asking. Let the set of mood indices be $\{>, ?\}$ as before, and the set of agent indices be $\{\mathbf{S}, \mathbf{U}\}$, standing for the system and the user respectively. Let $\Phi_{(>,\mathbf{U},\mathbf{S})}$ denote the assertion of Φ by the user, $\Phi_{(?,\mathbf{U},\mathbf{S})}$ denote the user asking if Φ, and so on. Let $\Delta_\mathbf{S}$ denote the system's non-doxastic theory, i.e. its knowledge base, and $\delta_\mathbf{U}$ the system's beliefs about the user's beliefs, i.e. its user model. The intention is that the semantic evaluation strategy associated with Φ should be some function of the indices that constitute its context.

To clarify the issues, let us attempt to derive a strategy for **S** in **(G.&)** as a function of the mood associated with the conjunction. Together with the role reversal of **(G.~)**, this will suffice to give strategies for all the other connectives. Strategies for quantification games are much harder to specify, and beyond the scope of this chapter.

If **U** asserts that Φ then any language game played on Φ should have **U** as MAX and **S** as MIN, since $\Phi_{(>,\mathbf{U},\mathbf{S})}$ implies that $L_\mathbf{U}\Phi$, if **U** is sincere. **S**'s role, as consumer and critic of the information supplied, is to check that Φ is consistent with what both parties already believe.

Suppose that $\Phi = \Pi_1 \& \ldots \& \Pi_n$. The *slow game* for & is to play **(G.&)** on each of the conjuncts until a winning move is found, backtracking over losing decisions, but this will be expensive in terms of both CPU and storage. The decision problem for the propositional calculus is NP-complete, while in the case of the predicate calculus it is undecidable, so this game may be slow indeed!

Three *quick games* are possible that attempt to trade completeness against computational cost.

(1) The *felicity game*. Before accepting $\Phi_{(>,U,S)}$, **S** would like to satisfy itself that Φ does not conflict with information already supplied by **U**. If $L_S L_U \sim \Phi$ then **U** is not sincere, while if $L_S L_U \Phi$ then **U** is repeating himself. **S** could also check that neither $L_S L_S \Phi$ nor $L_S L_S \sim \Phi$, i.e. that Φ is nominally consistent with **S**'s public beliefs.

(2) The *shallow game*. **S** only rejects Φ if $L_S \sim \Pi_i$ for some i. This obviously limits the depth of search and eliminates backtracking, though the game is not complete.

(3) The *deep game*. Even though $\sim L_S \sim \Phi$, it is possible that $\Delta_S \vdash_G \sim \Phi$. Another alternative to exhaustive search is use heuristics to irrevocably choose a single conjunct Π_i and accept the result of playing $G(\Pi_i)$. If this move does not result in a win, then assume that the other conjuncts, which looked less promising, will not be winners either.

The completeness of this strategy will naturally depend upon how good **S**'s choices can be. One can conceive of various strategies that MIN could use in choosing between conjuncts for further processing. Each is based on an attempt to estimate the relative size of the underlying model sets associated with each of the conjuncts.

(1) Conjuncts that are themselves conjunctions are more vulnerable than conjuncts that are atomic formulas, for example *produces(GEC, Nimrod)* & *produces(Boeing, AWACS)* has fewer models than *produces(GEC, Nimrod)*, while atomic formulas are more vulnerable than conjuncts that are disjunctions, for example *produces(GEC, Nimrod)* has fewer models than *produces(GEC, Nimrod)* v *produces(Boeing, AWACS)*.

(2) Closed formulas are more vulnerable than formulas containing free variables, for example *produces(GEC, Nimrod)* has fewer models than *produces(GEC, x)*.

(3) Closed universal formulas are more vulnerable than other closed formulas, since $(\forall x)(produces(GEC, x))$ has fewer models than *produces(GEC, Nimrod)*, which has fewer models than $(\exists x)(produces(GEC, x))$.

A game-playing strategy based on such heuristics may not be complete; however, it will make sensible use of the limited resources at MIN's disposal. To the extent that domain-specific heuristics are made available to an interpreter, one would expect its performance to improve on the results of purely syntactic strategies. The latter can be regarded as sensible default behaviours, to be employed in the absence of better information.

In addition to being interested in assertions, we are also interested in questions. In response to the question $\Phi_{(?,U,S)}$, it is reasonable to suppose that S should adopt the MAX role, in the sense that S will attempt to find a positive answer if possible. U is now in the role of MIN, as the consumer and critic of S's solutions.

Again, let us consider the high game for &, where $\Phi = \Pi_1 \& \ldots \& \Pi_n$. There is a slow strategy for playing (G.&), and a shallow game as before. For the question $\Phi_{(?,U,S)}$ to satisfy the felicity conditions, we demand that $\sim L_S L_U \Phi$ and $\sim L_S L_U \sim \Phi$. In addition, we require that $\sim L_U L_S \Phi$ and $\sim L_U L_S \sim \Phi$ and $\sim L_U L_S \Phi$, i.e. that S has not already answered U's question or failed to answer it.

In the case of $\Pi_1 \& \ldots \& \Pi_{n(?,U,S)}$, the deep game cannot simply consist of MAX choosing a single conjunct and attempting to evaluate it, no matter how good S's choice, because the answer must be sincere. If $\Psi_{(>,S,U)}$ is the answer to $\Phi_{(?,U,S)}$ then S must believe it to be so, as well as believing that Ψ, and S can only do this if it has found genuine support for Ψ in Δ_S. In the case where S accepts $\Phi_{(>,U,S)}$, the sincerity condition does not apply to S, but to U, so S can accept Φ, so long as $\sim L_S \sim \Phi$.

Thus S must process all the conjuncts in Φ, in order to answer $\Phi_{(?,U,S)}$ sincerely, and one can conceive of a number of MAX strategies that could be employed in ordering conjuncts for processing.

(1) Atomic formulas are cheaper to process than compound formulas and should therefore be evaluated first. Conjuncts that are conjunctions should be processed before conjuncts which are themselves disjunctions, since they have fewer models. If MAX is going to lose then he may as well lose sooner rather than later.

(2) Closed formulas are more vulnerable than formulas containing free variables, and the more distinct free variables a formula contains the less vulnerable it is. Thus *produces(GEC, Nimrod)* is easier to refute than *produces(GEC, x)* or *produces(x, x)*, which are easier to refute than *produces(y, x)*. The most vulnerable should be processed first, for the same reasons as given in (1).

(3) Open or closed atomic propositions that are "askable", i.e. that can be evaluated by asking the user, are cheaper to process than proposi-

tions that require inference. When playing MAX, the system should schedule the former before the latter. (When playing MIN, this strategy might give MAX two much initiative, for example in choosing values for variables that stop MIN from winning.)

Examples of these heuristics being deployed by a prototype are given in Section 4.2. No claims are made at the present time concerning their necessity or sufficiency. As noted earlier, domain-dependent strategies should enable an intrepreter to improve on these default behaviours, assuming that suitable means for representing and applying them can be found.

4   AN INITIAL IMPLEMENTATION

Section 4.1 outlines the prototype, while Section 4.2 gives examples of its use in conjunction with a knowledge base on personal finance. The sample dialogue is extremely primitive, but it may serve to illustrate some of the points made in earlier sections.

4.1   Game-Playing Procedures

The most natural style of programming for implementing a game-theoretic interpreter appeared to be the demonic style, whereby the high- and low-game rules associated with the logical operators of the language were coded as procedures. The high-game procedures were invoked as the main recursive loop of the interpreter unwrapped a complex expression until the atomic case was reached. Then the low-game procedures took over, in an attempt to evaluate the atom in the context of the current state of the knowledge base.

The specification of such an interpreter can be given in terms of a function *high-game*, which takes two arguments, a well-formed formula P of the logical language, and a *role* (either MAX or MIN):

$$\text{interpret}(P, \text{role})$$
$$\textit{if } \text{atomic}(P)$$
$$\textit{then } \text{low-game}(P, \Delta_S^P, \text{role})$$
$$\textit{else } \mathbf{G}_P(P, \text{role})$$

where *atomic* is a predicate that tests to see if P is an atomic proposition; *low-game* is a function that takes the atom, its conflict set, Δ_S^P, and the current role and initiates the low games; and $\mathbf{G}_P$ is the procedure that implements the high game for the logical operator governing P. Such procedures can be sketched in the following terms.

> and-high-game(P_1 & . . . & P_n, role)
> *if* $L_S L_U P_i$ *or* $L_S L_U \sim P_i$ *or* $L_U L_S P_i$ *or* $L_U L_S \sim P_i$ for any i
> *then* **complain**
> *else if* role = MIN
> > *then if* $L_S \sim L_U P_i$
> > > *then* **complain**
> > > *else if* $L_S \sim P_i$ for any i
> > > > *then* **false**
> > > > *else* high-game(P_i, role) for some i
> > *else if* $L_U \sim L_S P_i$
> > *then* **complain**
> > *else if* $L_S P_i$ for all i
> > > *then* **true**
> > > *else* min{high-game(P_i, role)} for all i
>
> not-high-game($\sim P$, role)
> *if* role = MIN
> *then* high-game($\mathbf{P}$, MAX)
> *else* high-game(P, MIN)

The procedure for playing (**G.&**) first plays the felicity game, complaining if the conditions described in Section 3.1 are infringed. If the associated speech act is felicitous then it adopts a different strategy depending upon the rule that the system is currently playing. In the MIN role, it will skim the conjuncts looking for one that can be shown to be false by look-up alone; this is essentially the shallow game for &. If this does not result in a win then MIN plays the deep game and picks a single conjunct for further processing. If the role is MAX then it skims the conjuncts to see if they are all known to be true; if not, it uses heuristics to order them and processes them all. The use of *min* assumes that **true**, **false** and the third truth value, **unknown**, are implemented as global variables bound to 1, 0 and 0.5 respectively.

The procedure for (**G.~**) simply reverses the roles, and invokes the interpreter on the proposition that was governed by negation. It should be noted that there are no heuristics for (**G.U**) at the present time. Thus both players backtrack over losing variable bindings, and (**F.T**) has to be modified as follows:

> (**F.T**)* If Ψ unifies with Φ then MAX wins,

since P may contain free variables. We shall see that this requires modifications to both (**G.U**) and (**F.E**) to preserve soundness.

Once the atomic case is reached, we need to replace Hintikka's truth rule
(G.T) with a function *low-game*, which takes as arguments the atom P, the
conflict set $\{Q_1, \ldots, Q_n\}$, and the system's current role. Conflict resolution,
with or without backtracking, constitutes what I shall call the *middle game*.
In the role of MAX, the system will prefer Q_i that can be used to verify P,
while in the role of MIN, it will prefer Q_i that can be used to refute P. The
MIN strategy can also be set to select only a single Q_i—the most complex
formula in $\{Q_1, \ldots, Q_n\}$—and pursue this without backtracking. The
rationale behind this choice is that this formula will place the most constraints upon P, rather in the manner of the "specificity" strategy found in
some production systems.

$$\text{low-game}(P, \{Q_1, \ldots, Q_n\}, \text{role})$$
$$\textit{if } \text{role} = \text{MIN}$$
$$\textit{then } \min\{\mathbf{F}_{Q_i}(P, Q_i, \text{role})\}$$
$$\textit{else } \max\{\mathbf{F}_{Q_i}(P, Q_i, \text{role})\}$$

In the above, $\mathbf{F}_{Q_i}$ denotes the low game associated with the logical operator
governing Q_i. If Q_i is atomic then $\mathbf{F}_{Q_i}$ is the truth game **(F.T)**, along the lines
of

$$\text{truth-game}(P, Q, \text{role})$$
$$\textit{if } P \text{ unifies with } Q$$
$$\textit{then if } \text{role} = \text{MAX}$$
$$\qquad \textit{then } \textbf{true}$$
$$\qquad \textit{else } \textbf{false}$$
$$\textit{else } \textbf{unknown}$$

Procedures for the other low games can be sketched in the following terms:

$$\text{and-low-game}(P, Q_1 \& \ldots \& Q_n, \text{role})$$
$$\textit{let } \text{result} := \mathbf{F}_{Q_i}(P, Q_i, \text{role}) \text{ for some } i$$
$$\textit{if } \text{result} = \textbf{true } \textit{or } \text{result} = \textbf{false}$$
$$\textit{then if } \min\{\mathbf{G}(Q_j): j \neq i\} = \textbf{true}$$
$$\qquad \textit{then } \text{result}$$
$$\qquad \textit{else } \textbf{unknown}$$
$$\textit{else } \textbf{unknown}$$

$$\text{not-low-game}(P, \sim Q, \text{role})$$
$$\textit{if } \text{role} = \text{MIN}$$
$$\textit{then } \mathbf{F}_Q(P, Q, \text{MAX})$$
$$\textit{else } \mathbf{F}_Q(P, Q, \text{MIN})$$

As described in Section 2, to win **(F.&)** a player must win a subgame on
one of the conjuncts, and then show that the other conjuncts are all true.

(F.~) performs role reversal once more. These procedures have been simplified in the above account, in that their counterparts in the actual code need to return unifiers and justifications.

Given that the implementations of **(G.U)** and **(G.E)** have no heuristics for choosing values for variables other than a backtracking search, the function

$$\text{some-low-game } (P,(\exists x)Q_x, \text{role})$$

must simply replace x with a new constant c, not appearing elsewhere, if it is to be sound. This arrangement allows $(\exists x)Q_x \vdash_G (\exists y)Q_y$, since MIN can no longer frustrate MAX by choosing a different individual, but it prevents $(\exists x)Q_x \vdash_G (\forall y)Q_y$ since **(G.U)** fails searches that bind universal variables to constants.

4.2   A Sample Dialogue

The program uses three representation languages at different levels in the system. The top-level user language is a notational variant of predicate logic; this is the language in which the user types input to the system and receives output. As an example, consider the following rule:

> **if** X dies intestate
> and X is married to Y
> and X has no issue and no near relations
> **then** Y takes the estate of X absolutely

In the user language, this is represented by the following formula:

> $@X@Y@Z[intestate\ X$
> $\&\ married\ X\ Y$
> $\&\ @W \sim [issue\ W\ X\ v\ near\text{-}relation\ W\ X]$
> $\&\ estate\text{-}of\ X\ Z$
> $\text{-}> takes\ Y\ Z\ absolutely]$

$@$ is the universal quantifier and $\%$ the existential, $\text{-}>$ denotes material implication, and $\&$, v and $\sim$ denote conjunction, disjunction and negation respectively. The usual precedence relations hold, whereby $\sim$ binds more strongly than $\&$ or v, which bind more strongly than $\text{-}>$.

At the level of stored data structures, such a proposition is represented by a frame with slots holding the LISP form of the proposition, the truth value of the proposition in Δ_S and Δ_U, plus a record of who has asserted, accepted, queried or rejected the proposition. In the present implementation, such a record is only kept for formulas of the propositional calculus. Given that felicity conditions use no more than table look-up, bound alphabetic variants cannot be detected.

An interactive dialogue with a personal finance knowledge base is given below that displays some of the control features described in Section 3.2. The language game shows an assertion being rejected, and the user being walked through an explanation. User inputs have been italicized for the sake of clarity; all else is system output.

-> (tag)
name of net? *demo*
—————————————————— old net demo ——————————————————
Ready > *sell-shares-in user Plessey*

The user starts the session by asserting that he will sell his shares in Plessey. The program sets out to show that this is not a good idea. This conclusion is then explained to the user, using the record of the interaction to edit the proof.

In the output of the trace package, indentations of the form = = = = etc. denote the recursive unwrapping of an input proposition as high games are played, while propositions preceded by – – – etc. are propositions in the knowledge base that are being considered as potential matches when the atomic case is reached.

```
= > user
      (sell-shares-in user Plessey)
= = sell-shares-in user Plessey
– –   @ Company
      (rerating-potential Company &
       shares-risen Company &
       steady sterling
       ->
       ~sell-shares-in user Company) . . . match
choice: (Plessey . Company)
```

The program adopts a minimizing strategy to the assertion by finding a rule that it can use to refute it. The rule states that you should not sell shares that may be rerated on the stock exchange, owing to an external event such as an imminent takeover bid, if the shares have just risen and sterling is steady. Having matched the input proposition with the consequent of this rule, the interpreter sets out to maximize the antecedent and derive a contradiction.

```
= = = shares-risen Plessey &
        steady sterling &
        rerating-potential Plessey
= = = = shares-risen Plessey
```

? shares-risen Plessey
Reply *yes*

= = = = steady stirling
? steady sterling
Reply *yes*

Note that, owing to an incomplete knowledge base, the system has to ask
the user whether Plessey's shares have risen and whether sterling is steady.
Note also that these conjuncts are processed before the issue of Plessey's
rerating potential is tackled, since the latter requires the application of
inference rules, as shown below.

```
= = = =  rerating-potential Plessey
- - - -    @ SmallCo
             (%BigCo
                (might-take-over BigCo SmallCo)
             ->
                rerating-potential SmallCo) . . . match
choice: (Plessey . SmallCo)

= = = = =    %Big Co
                (might-take-over BigCo Plessey)
= = = = = =    might-take-over BigCo Plessey)
- - - - - -    @Company
                 @Predator
                 (asset-rich Company &
                  profitable Predator &
                  illiquid stock-market
                 ->
                  might-take-over Predator Company) . . . match
choice: (Plessey . Company) (BigCo . Predator)

= = = = = = = asset-rich Plessey &
                  illiquid stock-market &
                  profitable BigCo
= = = = = = = = asset-rich Plessey
- - - - - - - -    asset-rich Plessey . . . match
= = = = = = = = illiquid stock-market
- - - - - - - -    illiquid stock-market . . . match
```

The knowledge base allows the system to conclude that Plessey is rich in
assets and that the stock market is illiquid. The interpreter then finds a
suitable company that might take over Plessey, namely GEC. Note that
asset-rich Plessey and *illiquid stock-market* are both processed before *profit-*

able BigCo, since they are easier to falsify, being closed formulas.

```
= = = = = = = =  profitable BigCo
– – – – – – – –        profitable GEC . . . match
```

surely not . . .

sell-shares-in user Plessey

Having found an argument against the assertion, the program walks through the justification, a premise at a time. The user has the option of typing *explain*, which gives a "canned text" rendering of the premise. Rejecting any of the premises would instigate the search for another refutation.

```
$35 @Company
        (rerating-potential Company &
        shares-risen Company &
        steady sterling
        ->
        ~sell-shares-in Company user)
```

Reply *explain*

It is worth hanging on to shares that have risen, so
    long as further gains are anticipated and sterling is
    steady

Reply *ok*

```
$13 @SmallCo
        (%BigCo
            (might-take-over BigCo SmallCo)
            ->
            rerating-potential SmallCo)
```

Reply *explain*

A takeover provides an excellent opportunity for
    shareholders to make a killing

Reply *ok*

```
$8 @Company
        @Predator
            (asset-rich Company &
            profitable Predator &
            illiquid stock-market
            ->
            might-take-over Predator Company)
```

Reply *explain*

At times of low trading on the stock market, a
    company with large assets will always be attractive
    to profitable predators

Reply *ok*

$63 asset-rich Plessey

Reply *ok*

$64 illiquid stock-market

Reply *ok*

$1 profitable GEC

Reply *ok*

Ready *ok*

$-------------$ end of demo $-------------$

Note that *shares-risen Plessey* and *steady sterling* are not cited in the proof. This is because these propositions were added to the user model δ_U when the user affirmed them in response to the system's queries. For the system to assert them now would infringe the appropriateness clause of the felicity conditions described in Section 3.1.

As the user is walked through the proof, δ_U is updated, to signify that **U** has accepted the premises that he has okayed, while the system model δ_S is also updated to signify that **S** has asserted the relevant propositions. Subsequent proof presentations then omit to mention premises that the system has already cited, unless the full proof is explicitly asked for. The idea behind this application of the felicity conditions is to have a default behaviour that gradually reduces the verbosity of explanations.

5   PROBLEMS AND PROSPECTS; RELATED WORK

An attempt has been made to lay some foundations for reasoning about knowledge and belief for advice-giving systems, in a manner that may ameliorate some of the epistemological problems noted earlier and still be computationally tractable. In the context of a consultation between a system, **S** and a user **U**, one can distinguish between **S** believes that *P*, **S** believes that ~*P*, **S** does not believe that *P*, **S**'s beliefs logically imply *P*, **S** believes that **U** believes that *P*, **S** believes that **U** believes that **S** believes that

P, S believes that S has told U that *P*, and so on. This kind of representation constitutes a first step towards being able to reason about the dialogue itself, as well as the domain of discourse. Such capabilities are at the heart of the overlap between knowledge-based systems and human–machine interaction (for a review see Jackson and Lefrere, 1984). Goal-directed dialogue is not just concerned with the truth or falsity of propositions according to some logic, but with additional concepts such as the acceptability of assertions and the appropriateness of speech acts generally.

5.1 Some Shortcomings of the Present Approach

It should be clear that the system as currently implemented has major shortcomings at the epistemological, logical and implementational levels, of which the following are just a few.

At the epistemological level, the record of previous games is a rather impoverished representation of what the user believes. Perhaps the system should be allowed to make default assumptions about typical users, and only revise these assumptions when necessary. Also the system contains no knowledge about how to develop a dialogue, i.e. there is no discourse model other than the felicity conditions.

At the logical level, there are no good heuristics for playing the quantification games, and so the system searches for variable bindings and backtracks over bad choices. It is felt that these games would benefit from the imposition of either restricted quantification or some more elaborate sortal structure onto the existing logic. Substantial gains ought to follow from this, both in terms of making certain kinds of semantic information explicit, and in terms of controlling inference (cf. Cohn, 1985).

At the level of implementation, some of the strategic knowledge that is at present hard-coded into the interpreter could be made more explicit by encoding some of the control information in the logical language itself. In other words, rather than modify and experiment with the flow of control by changing the LISP code for particular demons, the behaviour of the interpreter would be modified by loading different control theories. This would enhance both the modifiability and intelligibility of the system, though it might lead to a loss of efficiency.

In general, it is very hard to find domain-independent strategies to guide game choices, such as those required by (G.&), (F.&), (G.U) etc., for formulas of arbitrary complexity. Yet a game-theoretic interpreter is only as good as the heuristics that guide it, since the inference rules are neither sound nor complete, unless optimal choices are made by both sides or some form of backtracking is allowed in the implementation. Finding a suitable normal form might allow domain-free heuristics of the kind described earlier to be of more general use, but one suspects that domain-specific control knowledge will have to be applied at choice points for real improvement to be made (for more recent work on this problem see Jackson, in press).

In spite of these difficulties, none of which are trivial, it seems that viewing goal-directed dialogue as a language game may have some value in situations where various kinds of consistency need to be enforced in the course of an interaction. Needless to say, we shall never have complete methods for determining the consistency of first-order theories, since if this were so we should also have a decision procedure for the predicate calculus. Yet there are many applications where it is important to perform some such checks, for example when knowledge bases are subject to frequent updating by a variety of personnel. Game-theoretic semantics has the conceptual advantage that incompleteness, whether due to finitude of resources or undecidability, is more or less acknowledged at the outset. Encoding domain-specific knowledge about game choices might allow these simple semantic rules to be applied much more efficiently and effectively than at present.

5.2   Some Related Work

It is not the aim of this chapter to provide an alternative logic of knowledge and belief. Neither is this work intended as a correction of axiomatic epistemic logic—a task for which the author is ill-equipped. Rather the intention is to explore ways in which logic can be applied to advice-giving systems without making assumptions that violate common sense.

Nevertheless, there has been a growing literature on logics of knowledge and belief in recent years, which is worth examining as far as space allows. Although this work has yet to make an impact on expert-systems technology, its influence may be felt in the future. Only two aspects will be considered— distinguishing explicit and implicit belief, and some problems of complexity and control—since these are perhaps closest to the concerns of this chapter.

Levesque (1984) proposes two belief operators: B for explicit belief and L for implicit belief. Their semantics is given in terms of 'situations', which are like possible worlds, except that they may be incompletely specified and even incoherent. A situation may support P and/or its negation, or provide no support at all. P is explicitly believed if it is true in all situations the agent deems possible, and this semantic characterization turns out to be closely related to the notion of entailment in relevance logic. Such a characterization avoids an agent having to believe explicitly all the consequences of his beliefs, although implicit belief includes all propositional tautologies and is still closed under tautological consequence.

Using a limited form of inference, such as entailment, is a good way to reason about belief in better than polynomial time. However, it leaves open the problem of what to do if limited inference is not enough. It seems then that one only has recourse to methods that require exponential time in the worst case.

Game-theoretic semantics could perhaps provide a more graded approach that allowed a program to entertain beliefs in the absence of a complete proof. Using the riskier strategies (such as irrevocable choice in the high games, no backtracking in the middle game and shallow low games) in their various combinations, the prototype can accept assertions in time that grows linearly in such variables as the size of the formula, the size of formulas in the knowledge base, and the size of the knowledge base itself (or products thereof). To enable a system like the prototype to employ such ruthless heuristics in the answering of questions, one would have to define speech acts that had weaker sincerity conditions than assertion, such as "I *suspect* that *P*" and "I *suggest* that *P*". One could also usefully distinguish between "I *wonder* if *P*", "I *would like to know* if *P*", "I *must know* if *P*" etc., and have the system adopt different game-playing strategies accordingly. Enriching the pragmatics of the interaction language in this way would enable the system to respond more flexibly to user inputs.

Levesque's logic is propositional, owing to the obvious difficulties associated with quantifying into opaque contexts, and does not deal with multiple agents and nested beliefs. As we have seen, the treatment of quantification in the present work is limited to the non-doxastic component, and is sound only because the relevant inference rules are weak and their application restricted. Thus, given that quantifiers are never introduced or eliminated in doxastic theories, there is no danger of drawing unsound inferences, such as $L_a(\exists x)Fx \vdash_G (\exists x)L_aFx$.

Nested beliefs are dealt with by allowing the system to build a simple model of the user's beliefs inferred from his speech acts, and distinguish those propositions upon which system and user agree and disagree. The pool of previous game results represent common knowledge, not about the world, but about the players' beliefs. The tactic currently employed by the interpreter, in utilizing knowledge that is implicit in the conjunction of the system's beliefs and the user's, is to prefer propositions that the system believes when critiquing assertions in a MIN role, while preferring the user's view of the world when answering queries as MAX. The rationale behind this is straightforward: the system reserves the right to its own opinion, but there is no point in using propositions that the user believes to be false to construct a solution that the user will then reject. To cite such a proposition in the course of an explanation would in any case infringe the felicity conditions for assertion.

Deduction models of the beliefs of ideally rational agents (e.g. Konolige, 1985; Moore, 1985) are less attractive in the present context than Levesque's

logic, since they assume consistency and closure under tautological consequence. Further, the expressiveness of the underlying language must be
strictly curtailed if the introspection problem for ideal agents is to be
decidable. In languages containing quantifiers, the only solution appears to
be to abandon closure, perhaps by weakening the inference rules; thus
Konolige (1986) has recently suggested using unit resolution and rule-based
deduction for belief derivation.

The game-theoretic approach suggests another alternative, which is to
retain much of the power of the inference rules, but apply them under
heuristics that derive from the context of their application. If domain-specific
heuristics are available, then well and good; otherwise sensible default
behaviours should be supplied, as a function of pragmatic properties of the
interaction. The problem with this approach is that it is hard to prove any
interesting results about game-theoretic derivability, given the primacy of
the heuristic component.

The future for modal logics of knowledge and belief in the service of
expert systems is not altogether clear. The decision procedure for propositional S5 is NP-complete with a single agent, but adding other agents renders
the problem P-SPACE complete, while operators for common and implicit
knowledge require exponential time in the worst case (see e.g. Halpern and
Moses, 1985). Common and implicit knowledge may well be important in
systems with multiple knowledge bases, and they are certainly important in
advice-giving systems, where system and user need to be able to build on a
shared view of the world.

It could be that the complexity of deciding formulas that we are interested
in will be much better than the worst case, as Halpern and Moses suggest,
while limited inference of the kind described by Levesque and Konolige will
be sufficient for many problems. Nevertheless, there may also be some merit
in an approach based on language games, in which reasoning about belief
and reasoning about control are linked by pragmatic considerations, such as
felicity. For example, a closer analysis of quantification games might afford
insights into the problems associated with quantifying into opaque contexts.
Shared beliefs require a shared pool of individuals, and there are unwritten
rules concerning the felicitous introduction of individuals in an argument.
On the other hand, good conventions for establishing and choosing "typical"
individuals might enable us to convert decision problems in the predicate
calculus into weakly analogous but decidable ones that involve playing only
propositional games.

ACKNOWLEDGEMENTS

The author would like to thank Han Reichgelt, Frank van Harmelen,

George Kiss, Marco Colombetti and Jean-Phillipe Solvay for their comments on earlier papers and programs associated with this research.

REFERENCES

Austin, J. L. (1962). *How to Do Things with Words*. Cambridge, Mass.: Harvard University Press.

Chandrasekaran, B. (1983). Towards a taxonomy of problem solving types. *The AI Magazine* **4**, 9–17.

Cohn, A. (1985). On the solution of Schubert's Steamroller in many sorted logic. Proc. 9th Int. Joint Conf. on Artificial Intelligence, pp. 1169–1174. Los Altos, California: Morgan Kaufmann.

Halpern, J. Y. and Moses, Y. (1985). A guide to the modal logics of knowledge and belief: Preliminary draft. *Proc. 9th Int. Joint Conf. on Artificial Intelligence*, pp. 480–490. Los Altos, California: Morgan Kaufmann.

Hintikka, J. (1973). *Logic, Language Games and Information*. Oxford: Oxford University Press.

Hintikka, J. (1976). Quantifiers in logic and quantifiers in natural language. *Philosophy of Logic* (ed. S. Korner), pp. 208–270. Oxford: Basil Blackwell.

Hintikka, J. (1983). *The Game of Language*. Dordrecht: Reidel.

Jackson, P. (1987). A representation language based on a game-theoretic interpretation of logic. Ph.D. thesis, Computer Based Learning Unit, University of Leeds.

Jackson, P. (in press). On game-theoretic interactions with first-order knowledge bases. *Non-Standard Logics for Automated Reasoning* (ed. P. Smets). London: Academic Press.

Jackson, P. and Lefrere, P. (1984). On the application of rule-based techniques to advice-giving systems. *Int. J. Man–Machine Stud.* **20**, 63–86. Also *Developments in Expert Systems* (ed. M. J. Coombs), pp. 177–200. London: Academic Press.

Konolige, K. (1985). A computational theory of belief introspection. *Proc. 9th Int. Joint Conf. on Artificial Intelligence*, pp. 502–508. Los Altos, California: Morgan Kaufmann.

Konolige, K. (1986). *A Deduction Model of Belief*. London: Pitman.

Lemmon, E. J. (1965). *Beginning Logic*. London: Thomas Nelson.

Levesque, H. (1984). A logic of implicit and explicit belief. *Proc. 1984 Nat. Conf. on Artificial Intelligence (AAAI-84)*, pp. 198–202. Los Altos, California: Morgan Kaufmann.

McDermott, J. (1982). R1: A rule-based configurer of computer systems. *Artificial Intelligence* **19**, 39–88.

Moore, R. C. (1985). Semantical considerations on nonmonotonic logic. *Artificial Intelligence* **25**, 75–94.

Quine, W. V. O. (1974). *Methods of Logic*, 3rd edn. London: Routledge & Kegan Paul.

Searle, J. (1965). *Speech Acts: An Essay in the Philosophy of Language*. Cambridge: Cambridge University Press.

Shortliffe, E. H. (1976). *Computer-Based Medical Consultations: MYCIN*. Amsterdam: Elsevier.

3. Intelligent tutoring systems:
A tutorial survey

WILLIAM J. CLANCEY

Abstract. This survey of intelligent tutoring systems is based on a tutorial originally presented by John Seely Brown, Richard R. Burton (Xerox-Parc, USA) and William J. Clancey at the National Conference on AI (AAAI) in Austin, Texas in August 1984. The survey describes the components of tutoring systems, different teaching scenarios and their relation to a theory of instruction. The underlying pedagogical approach is to make latent knowledge manifest, which the research accomplishes by different forms of qualitative modelling: simulating physical processes; simulating expert problem-solving, including strategies for monitoring and controlling problem solving (metacognition); modelling the plans behind procedural behaviour; and forcing articulation of model inconsistencies through the Socratic method of instruction. Proceeding chronologically, examples of intelligent tutoring systems are described in terms of their internal knowledge representations and the evolving pedagogical theory. Although these programs are generally only research projects, examples of what they can do make abundantly clear the long-term scientific and software-engineering advantages of the new modelling methodology.

1 INTRODUCTION

What are intelligent tutoring systems? Why is it necessary to call them "intelligent"? Shouldn't every tutoring system be intelligent? This name in part reflects the history of the research (Sleeman and Brown, 1982; Wenger, 1986). The people who began this work—in particular John Seely Brown, Alan Collins and Ira Goldstein—wanted to contrast their work with traditional, computer-aided instruction, so they called their programs, based on artificial intelligence programming techniques, "intelligent CAI" (ICAI) programs. The name "intelligent tutoring systems" (ITS) means the same thing.

Perhaps the best reason for attributing intelligence to these programs is their ability to solve the same problems that they present to students. This capability greatly enhances student modelling and explanation. It provides an efficient foundation for explaining all of the details of solving a problem,

CURRENT ISSUES IN EXPERT SYSTEMS
ISBN 0-12-714030-1

not just what a teacher decided ahead of time might be useful. It also allows us to build a student modelling program that can solve problems in alternative ways. Obviously, to do this the modelling program first has to be able to solve the problem in at least one way.

Explaining how a problem is solved is by no means easy, and the idea of what constitutes an explanation has changed very much in the last ten years. In MYCIN, just saying what rules were used and printing them was an innovative accomplishment. We now call this an *audit-trail explanation*, similar to an inspectable record of financial transactions. The audit-trail explanation program can state every step, but does not necessarily know the rationale behind the steps. There is a difference between saying what happened and explaining why it was the right thing to do.

Another major characteristic of an ITS is the degree of individualized instruction it provides. Early CAI programs were contrasted with classroom teaching in terms of the individualized instruction they allow. An ITS provides improved individualized instruction by building a distinct model of what the student knows, as an interpretation of how he behaves (Clancey, 1986). Thus an ITS relates instruction to an understanding of the individual student's goals and beliefs.

Earlier CAI programs are sometimes described as branching programs. At each point, the program makes an evaluation as to whether the student's answer at some place in solving a problem is correct or wrong. The teacher builds in the program: if the student gives answer A go to this section, if the student gives answer B, go to this section. The program can only recognize these built-in answers. No coherent model of patterns in the student's behaviour is recorded. Of course, it is possible using conventional programming to build student models. For example, one could keep a history of all of the branches that a program made and have each new decision about where to branch based on the history of what branches have occurred before. This could be very complex, because one would have to anticipate all of the possible histories. The methodology of artificial intelligence provides an easier way.

Intelligent tutoring systems dynamically analyse the solution history and use principles to decide what to do next, rather than requiring situations to be anticipated by the author of the program. Also, the person who writes the traditional CAI program is not expressing his strategies of why the branching is occurring at any point. At each time, when he designs a new step in his program, he may be redundantly using the same ideas of how to teach. In intelligent tutoring systems we want to extract these principles so they can be applied automatically, as well as expressing them explicitly, so we know what they are.

A final point is that we shouldn't think of intelligent tutoring systems as being one kind of program with one kind of interaction with the student. There are really many different types of programs that have different capabilities. Some are completely reactive or passive in their behaviour—they wait for the student to do something and then respond. Others, like GUIDON, make an attempt to present new information in what is called *opportunistic tutoring* (Clancey, 1982). There is also a distinction between "coaching" and "tutoring". This was a point that Goldstein made in his early work (Goldstein, 1977). A coach is of course someone who watches and does not constantly interfere, but stays on the sidelines and lets one play the game. Then, perhaps when one asks for help or in a crucial moment of play, the coach interrupts and states an important lesson. This is a non-intrusive pedagogical strategy, based on the idea that people should just solve the problem and act on their own. An interruption will not give them the opportunity to develop skills to monitor their own problem solving, such as the capability to detect and back out of false starts.

1.1 Components of an ITS

Figure 1 is a diagram that I adapted from Goldstein (1978). I shall go over it in some detail because these components occur in most intelligent tutoring systems.

The central idea is that there is a knowledge base, some formal model, of how the problem is to be solved, which is in the kernel of the program. For example, suppose that the student's problem is to diagnose a patient, to see if the patient has a disease and to prescribe therapy. The problem might be, as we shall see in some other examples, a game that the student is playing. It might be a child's game, intended to teach mathematics. As the student is solving this problem, he might be receiving new information, and he is making certain solution steps that we shall call "moves" in general.

Suppose now that the student requests some patient data. The tutor is watching and passes on to a problem-solving simulator program (often called an *expert system*) all of the information that the student has received about the problem. If this were a game, such as a board game like chess or checkers, the tutor would tell the expert where all of the pieces are—the current configuration. The expert simulation program examines its knowledge base. This could include procedures, facts, plus maybe the rules of the game. The expert then generates the preferred behaviour of what to do next, possibly as a set of plausible alternatives. For medical diagnosis, this would be a set of good questions to ask about the patient, and maybe an indication of the expert's preferred next question. In a game, this would be the next move to make.

The idealized information is given to the modelling program, which

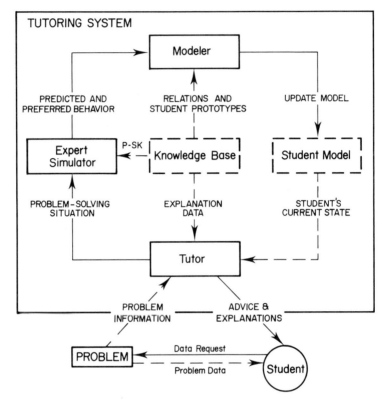

Figure 1   Components of an ITS (adapted from Goldstein, 1978).

combines it with some additional information, perhaps about different types of students and what students know depending on their background, maybe very complex patterns. (I am describing an idealized architecture that is more complicated than any existing ITS.) In addition to these prototypes or patterns of different types of students and student behaviour, there may be descriptions of typical misconceptions or incorrect knowledge. The modelling program may also be given knowledge about prerequisite ordering of facts and procedures—what does it make sense to know given what one already knows, what would it be difficult to understand given what one knows? (Wescourt, *et al.*, 1977; Goldstein, 1982).

The modelling program combines these patterns with the student's and expert's recent moves and rationalization for them, and updates the model of the student's goals, what he believes about the current problem, and what he knows in general. Thus the core of the student model, the result of relating student behaviour to the expert rationalization, is a description of what the student knows, expressed as a subset of the expert-knowledge base, with degrees of belief attached to each item. For example, GUIDON's model states what the student is believed to know about the current problem, his goal structure in requesting new data, and for each rule in MYCIN's knowledge base a certainty measurement indicating whether the student knows the rule. This *differential* or *overlay* model then is fed back to the tutor, which has to decide, given principles of teaching, what to say next. Should it make an interruption and give some advice, or just let the student continue to solve the problem on his own?

Note that the separate boxes in the figure correspond to separate parts of the tutoring system. This is our programming methodology: rather than writing one program that arbitrarily combines the knowledge, we abstract the components. This enables the expert simulator, modelling, and tutoring modules to operate upon different knowledge bases, as in GUIDON (see Chapter 4).

What is saved between sessions? There is also a cumulative record from one problem to the next of what the student knows. Maybe some future tutoring program will save certain things that it could not understand about a student's behaviour that, later on, it would be able to disambiguate. In fact, this conforms fairly well to the Schank model of memory that the exceptions are saved, and they help one to generalize concepts later on (Schank, 1981). Part of the problem of course is how much are we going to save; there is a space problem. This is why we need a combination of abstraction and good indexing.

Can we say more about Schank's method for remembering exceptions? The basic idea was called MOPS (memory organization packets). Janet Kolodner did the most relevant follow-on project in her dissertation research, involving memory organization for efficient retrieval and storage (Kolodner, 1983). She models how knowledge, as a memory of many specific facts, is organized. The program is thus able to answer questions about what happened in the past and what typically happens. The idea is that generalizations form a hierarchy of concepts.

The name of Kolodner's program was CYRUS. This was a model of Cyrus Vance who was the US Secretary of State at the time. She would feed the program stories of the travels of Vance and what he did on his various trips. Then one could ask the question: "When Cyrus goes to Egypt, will he visit the pyramids?" The program knows that this is a sightseeing event and looks at its memory to see where there were other sightseeing events. Is it common? Are there any times when Cyrus made a visit to a country but didn't do any sightseeing? The program would then say: 'Well, yes, Cyrus will probably visit the pyramids, because every time he has been in the Middle East, he has gone sightseeing." But if one asked about Asia, Cyrus might be uninterested in sightseeing in Asia, and the memory of exceptions would indicate that visits to Asia involve no sightseeing.

The basic idea is that a discrimination net organizes and filters events in memory. The program will notice that, up to a certain point, there have been several similar events, and an exception, a different specific event, is saved. If there are two exceptions, the program looks for similarities. The network, as a pattern of generalizations, provides an efficient way of saving exceptions: an exception is defined with respect to some pattern. This is related to other discrimination models of memory, such as that of Carbonell and Collins (1973).

I found this model to be very stimulating for thinking about teaching and learning. The most intriguing thing is that this is not how knowledge bases are typically organized. In fact, Janet Kolodner is now building an expert system using her model of memory and having the program record and consider exceptions as times when its heuristic generalizations might not apply. If the program has a record of all of the cases it has solved, and if generalizations constitute its rules for classifying each new experience, the program might notice that a new case is more similar to the exceptions than to the generalizations. It will now have an ability to say that it should be careful, that this case is something different than what it can understand, and maybe it should make an attempt to generalize the exception. Of course, it is a very difficult problem to start extracting medical knowledge in this way, and it requires knowledge of the mechanisms of disease; Kolodner has not considered causal representations. She is working in an area of psychiatry with a superficial theory of causal mechanisms, and this makes the simple classification approach tractable.

1.2   Teaching Scenarios

Figure 2 (following John Seely Brown) makes the point that teaching programs differ along a spectrum of learner control. Who is in charge of the interaction? In the case of a traditional program, what we call frame-based CAI, the branching type mentioned earlier, the program is constantly deciding what to do next. Again, this is a generalization and by no means describes every non-AI system. On the opposite side, a good example is the LOGO work of Papert and DiSessa at MIT, inspired by the Piaget exploratory school of discovery learning (Papert, 1980). The idea is to give the student a good environment to explore in which he can use his own innate curiosity, combining things in new ways to learn the underlying principles. If the environment is very rich, as in LOGO, with the concepts of recursion, iteration, modularity, hierarchy—which can be discovered as part of designing programs—the student may learn very general principles that can be of value to him.

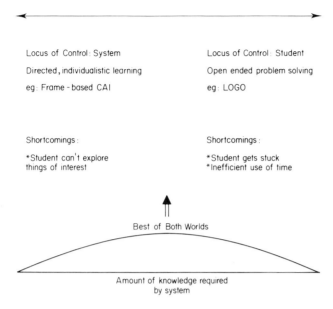

Figure 2   Learner control in computer-based teaching programs.

When we have extremes there are often disadvantages on each side. For example, if we do not allow the student the ability to move around as he wants, he cannot use his curiosity to explore new areas. The other extreme is that, if there is no initiative by a coach or the program, the student may get stuck or unable to progress. This may also be viewed as an inefficient use of the student's time. If someone would just say "Here is what I expect you to learn" then the student can say "I understand that already" or "Explain to me how this is different from something else." We can efficiently bring the student's conception of the world closer to what we think he should understand.

As we might imagine with these two alternatives, we want a combination. We want to give the student an ability to explore, but we also want some kind of an active agent, some kind of a coach perhaps, that watches the student and guides him, redirecting him at various times. John Brown points out here that in some ways this is the most difficult system to build because it requires the most knowledge. If the program is always in control, we need not understand what the student is saying to us when he wants to do something different, and we need not do something intelligent when he asks us for something different. In the case of a program that is not attempting to present something in some logical order, there are no large and complex student modelling, tutoring, system and explanation programs to build. We just design a good language, like LOGO, and a good set of problems. It is an interesting fact about LOGO that one observes the teacher going around and helping the students, or the students helping each other. Pedagogical control can be subtle to detect and describe.

Different forms of computer-based learning can be contrasted in another way. Early programs individualized instruction by *drill and practice*: I give you a problem and you solve it; I give you another problem and you solve it; and I keep selecting problems so that they get more difficult or they follow some logical sequence. This is a good idea, and it is something that we shall always want to do; sometimes one can select five good problems and if the student follows them, he will learn something. In the SOPHIE program John Brown and Richard Burton used a traditional CAI front-end to get the student familiar with the electronic circuit that they were going to learn how to diagnose. There can be a place for drill and practice.

Another perspective on computer-based learning might be called *intelligent machines*. GUIDON is a classic example, and there are perhaps six or seven similar systems from the 1970s. These problems exploit the idea of a mixed-initiative discourse to replicate many aspects of teaching. Through the use of general procedures, the program can respond flexibly to the student's initiative. Whenever the student says "help" to GUIDON, it uses its general procedures to provide help in any context. This was begun by Carbonell (1970) in the SCHOLAR program, which parsed natural language using a keyword parser, allowing the student to type in questions and respond.

It is an interesting historical point that from about 1979 to 1984 people stopped building these programs. The experience of building programs like GUIDON made us realize that we were trying to do everything at once. We did not have a good knowledge representation, and we did not really understand what kind of misconceptions the students have. The idea of modelling the student became the central idea. Almost every project from the late 1970s until today has started with this one problem: How do we write a program that can understand what the student is doing? There is no need to consider strategies for teaching if we do not understand what the student is doing. It was a logical step in the research to ignore the teaching problem and emphasize the problem of understanding.

The third form of computer-based learning involves the use of *simulation*. By the late 1970s, with LISP workstations and fancy graphics, it became possible to design new kinds of interaction in a teaching system. A good example is the STEAMER project. Here the idea is to use the program to give the student a realistic situation. STEAMER uses graphics and colour to show dials and process change, which is very similar conceptually to what happens in the world.

These three types of approaches—drill and practice, intelligent instructor, and simulation—can be combined, but they are useful extremes to consider.

1.3   Learning Scenarios For an Intelligent Tutor

Focusing now on the intelligent tutoring form of computer-based learning, we can further categorize learning scenarios by how the knowledge in the program is used. Here we have different pedagogical philosophies.

First, we have the *Socratic* approach, in which the teacher keeps asking questions and giving new cases to force the student to realize gaps and inconsistencies in his understanding. In GUIDON, using this pedagogical approach we would not spend two hours talking about one patient. Instead we would contrast cases, asking hypothetical questions and leading the student to see similarities and differences. This is the idea in the WHY program (Collins and Stevens, 1980). For problem-solving that is strongly based on precedent and particular experiences, such as law and medicine, this is obviously a good way to proceed.

In contrast, a *reactive environment* is used in SOPHIE. The student solves a problem, but the program does not interrupt. It reacts to the student and gives feedback. In *learning by doing*, the apprenticeship alternative, the teacher actively contributes. The teacher watches to see whether the student is making progress and checks his understanding. After classroom learning, medical students follow the physicians around the hospital and help them solve problems. The student takes a patient's history, and then the physician will ask "What do you think the problem is?" He will quiz the student to test his understanding and encourage him to consider alternatives. This is essentially the approach in GUIDON (see Chapter 4).

Learning while doing differs in a subtle way. Consider a job-performance aid, a tutor built into the machinery of the normal working environment. An example would be a copying machine that could watch what one is doing when making copies. Copying machines are complicated. If one wants to make reverse double-sided copies with collation, there might be more than one way to solve the problem. If we build a coach into the copying machine, the coach would observe what one does. Perhaps one never uses a certain combination of options. The tutor might know that people who know what they are doing use these options. Unless there is something special about one's task, one might not know how to use the machine effectively, and the program will interrupt to offer assistance. Thus a job-performance aid would help one learn during the normal course of business.

The examples illustrate how the research is proceeding: We are still discovering different ways in which instruction occurs and devising new opportunities for applying computers. Brown summarizes what we have learned by the aphorism that "teaching involves using knowledge, rather than just presenting it". Thus in GUIDON we give the student a problem to solve, rather than converting the knowledge base into a multiple-choice exam. In some sense, knowledge is inherently active. What it enables one to do is important, and this is what "learning while (or by) doing" seeks to exploit.

1.4A   Naive Theory of Coaching

Figure 3 shows Brown's model of coaching involving a computer-based coach with many different kinds of knowledge. It illustrates the lesson that we learned in GUIDON, that it is more than an expert system, to say the very least. Yes, the tutor does have expert problem-solving strategies, but it

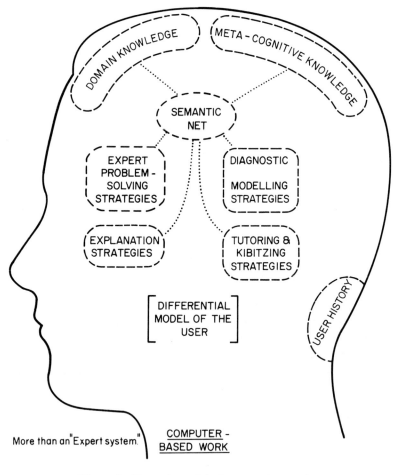

Figure 3   Brown's model of a computer coach.

needs knowledge about explanation, how to model the student and tutoring or kibitzing strategies (an interruptive strategy for probing the student's understanding and presenting information). From all of these, we contrast the model of the user, a differential model, in which difference in behaviour is explained in terms of a difference in knowledge.

One thing we have not considered here is *metacognitive knowledge*, such as knowledge about the mind, memory and learning. Schank's model of memory organization is one example: It describes how new experience is stored and generalized. When a problem-solver uses such knowledge to improve his problem solving or learning, we call such reasoning metacognition (Collins and Brown, 1987). Researchers take for granted that we also need a strong theory of how people learn in order to design an ideal tutoring program. Our study of misconceptions and student models in general is just the first step in this direction. Goldstein drew a box in his early diagrams that he called the *learning model*, corresponding to this idea. Nothing in our programs corresponds to it. However, Anderson has recently incorporated a learning theory in the design of his tutors for LISP programming and geometry (Anderson *et al.*, 1984a).

1.5   Making Latent Knowledge Manifest

An important theme behind ITS research is the attempt to make *latent knowledge* manifest. Latent knowledge has not been expressed or stated, but is implicit in the behaviour of a person or some physical process. By "manifest", we mean articulating it in words or making it visible in pictures. A simulation shows this is a simple way. We can simulate how a device works by using graphics and show the student step by step the mechanism and the interactions. The design and the process might be very hard to see from looking at the real device; graphically it can be simplified and idealized. This is the central idea in STEAMER. Another example is modelling the knowledge of an expert; we are taking the expert's knowledge and making it manifest. An expert might not be able to state what he does, but we look for patterns in his problem solving. We say "You have a procedure that you use. There is something you do that is regular." We make the procedure explicit.

John Brown also speaks of *reifying*—to make concrete or to make visible (Brown, 1983). For example, we can reify the space of possible ways of solving a problem. One strategy we might use for teaching is to show a student a graphic history of his various steps and compare alternative ways of solving the problem. Here is a simple example: we show the student a tree of rules and goals and show the student that if he had done things in a different order, it would not have been necessary to do as much work. This is one idea that we are pursuing in NEOMYCIN. Specifically, if the student asked a general question first, let us say about infection, rather than considering specific infections, he might save ten questions about specific infections by determining categorically that there is no infection. One way to show that is to lay out a kind of visible history and say "You went all of the way down here in all of these details, but if you had done it this way, you could have pruned the search earlier." This is what John Brown means by reifying the problem space.

Another example of latent knowledge is the idea of a *plan* behind a procedure. Several examples occur in the programming tutor. There is the superficial behaviour: What is it that the expert does? Behind that is a plan: Why is that a good procedure? To give an example from medicine again, I might ask, "Does the patient have a fever, has he lost weight, has he had a trauma, has he fallen?" This is my superficial behaviour, what you see me doing when I solve the problem. More abstractly described, my procedure is to reason categorically. I'm asking very general high-level questions before going down any path. We can now state the procedure separately, as an abstraction of the original questions. Obviously, the idea of reasoning categorically has nothing specifically to do with medicine. We could also ask why it makes sense to reason categorically. If the search space is organized hierarchically, it can be more efficient to start from the top and work down rather than to work from the bottom because you can eliminate possible paths. We call this description the plan behind the procedure.

Finally, the Socratic method is another way of making latent knowledge manifest. Asking the student questions makes him realize that there are things that are incomplete or contradictory in his knowledge. The Socratic teacher chooses examples that will force the students to realize a paradox in his behaviour and in his understanding, and leads him to express a question that will resolve that misunderstanding.

In building a teaching system, we are making different kinds of knowledge explicit: the domain knowledge, the method for explaining and the tutoring rules about interrupting and making presentations. We also make meta-cognitive knowledge explicit, knowledge about learning. To "teach" all of this to a computer involves theorizing, not just writing down what we all know for granted, but an abstraction process.

In building an expert system to be used for teaching, we learned that it is advantageous to work with good teachers. A good teacher has theories of knowledge organization and inference and learning. That is, he has knowledge about his reasoning, metacognitive knowledge, which he can impart to students to help them learn.

Similarly, because of our interest in making latent knowledge manifest, not every expert system makes a good tutoring system. In fact, we might ask whether any expert system makes a good tutoring system today. We need certain kinds of knowledge to be explicit and separate, which is the point of NEOMYCIN (Clancey and Letsinger, 1984), in which the diagnosis procedure is separated from the facts about disease. We may need alternative ways of solving problems, including the ability to understand misconceptions. We may need to justify the knowledge base to help the student understand why it is correct. In particular, to understand misconceptions, we need to understand why the preferred rules are correct.

2 SURVEY OF SPECIFIC SYSTEMS

2.1 SCHOLAR

The SCHOLAR program is the first attempt to use an AI representation as the basis of a teaching program (Carbonell, 1970). Carbonell saw the possibility of stating the teaching knowledge separately from the domain knowledge that was to be taught. So we have a semantic network for stating geographical facts, and we have a program for carrying out the interaction with the student. One of the later developments of SCHOLAR, work done by Collins, enabled the answering of questions that were not stored in the knowledge base. The program performs what is called "plausible reasoning" to infer what might be true, given certain assumptions about the world (Collins, 1978). It is a very interesting development, because people now understand this form of metacognition to be an important part of expertise. SCHOLAR is the first attempt to use AI for building a general system, allowing multiple use of the same knowledge, rather than encoding it as part of the teaching program.

Figure 4 shows part of an interaction with SCHOLAR, illustrating a mixed-initiative form that Carbonell and Collins sought to develop. The program asks a question "What is the language of Argentina?" The student answers "Probably Spanish." The program says "Very Good" and then asks another question. A transition-network parser is used here.

One can also see the student taking initiative, rather than answering the question that the program has asked. This clearly inspired Carbonell a great deal. In comparison with earlier AI programs, SCHOLAR allows the student to do whatever he wants at any point. The dialogue also illustrates retrieval of information from the semantic network. There is a hierarchy of countries and geographical areas, so it knows that Peru is located in South America. It has superconcepts and instantiations of them. Carbonell also used a clever kind of response: "Now answer the question you didn't answer before." This reminds me of how people were so excited about automatic spelling correction in early LISP programs, reminiscent of the joke about the dancing dog—it is superficial, but intriguing that it can be done at all.

What is the language of Argentina ?

** Probably Spanish

Very good. Approximately what is the area of Argentina ?

** Tell me something about Peru

Peru is a country.
It is located in South America.
The capital of Peru is Lima.
Now answer the question you didn't answer before

** The area of Argentina is 1 100 000 square miles.

Approximately true, but a more exact value is 1 200 000
The eastern bordering country of Peru is --- .

** Catholicism

Wrong. Catholicism is not a country but a religion.
The correct answer is : Brazil.
Where is Peru ?

** Is Asuncion hot ?

Since Asuncion is part of Paraguay, yes

** What is the most important difference between Peru and
Paraguay ?

The primary difference is : The population of Peru is larger by a

factor of 7.8.

Figure 4   Excerpt from a dialogue with SCHOLAR.

Carbonell also used a timer to see how long the student takes to solve the problem. The program interrupts after a while, and says "You are taking a long time."

When the student asks "Is Asuncion hot?", the program says "Since it is part of Paraguay, yes." This is an example of a fact that is not stored explicitly. The program knows that if a city is located inside a country, and the country has a climatic property like temperature or rainfall, then we can infer plausibly (with uncertainty) that the city has the same property. This does not always work, and it is not too hard to think of counterexamples where there are countries with coastal and mountain cities.

More complex examples are given by Collins. The student asks whether a particular country engages in a certain type of manufacturing or trade. The program has associated with it a number indicating how important each fact is, in this case importance of various trade facts related to each country. Let us say the question was "Does Brazil have oil wells?" The program would look at other countries and see that oil wells were mentioned, but not for Brazil, and that these wells were very highly ranked. So if a country has oil wells, it was rated at number 9, out of 10. So the program could infer that if Brazil had oil wells, and it were important for Brazil, it would be rated high, and would therefore be in the knowledge base. Assuming that one knows everything about the world to a certain point, a certain degree of importance, the lack of knowledge allows one to make an assumption about what is true. This is another form of metacognitive ability. We can say with some degree of belief that certain things are true or false, even if we have not learned them explicitly. We can infer them from general patterns of what we know. The idea was developed further to explain how we can answer so quickly that we do not know certain things. Collins also did some psychological studies with Quillian, measuring how long it takes people to answer certain questions, and used the results to support a model of memory.

2.2 WHY

WHY is the follow-on work to SCHOLAR, developed by Collins and Stevens (1980) after Carbonell's death. They changed the domain from purely factual reasoning of geography to casual reasoning of meteorology, opening up many new problems.

Figure 5 shows the program generating certain questions for the student: "Do you think the Amazon jungle has heavy or light rainfall?" Collins has made explicit the teaching rules for generating these questions. They are stated abstractly, referring to predictions, particular cases, prior causes, general rules, insufficient causes. This kind of terminology is a major advance. It inspired me in GUIDON to express teaching knowledge abstractly, separate from the medical knowledge (see Chapter 4).

Collins attempted to mimic the Socratic dialogues that we find in the writings of Plato. He also analysed teachers teaching law by the case method and looked at physicians teaching medicine. Notice the systematic logic behind these questions: "Why does the Amazon jungle have heavy rainfall?" The student has just said that he thinks it has heavy rainfall. The student replies "Because it has mountains nearby." This suggests that the student

Ask for a prediction about a particular case.

Do you think the Amazon jungle has heavy or light rainfall ?
** Heavy rainfall

Ask for prior causes

Why does the Amazon jungle have heavy rainfall ?
** Because it has mountains nearby.

Form a general rule for an insufficient cause

Do you think that any place with mountains has heavy rainfall ?
** Yes

Pick a counter example for an insufficient cause and
Ask for prior causes.

Southern California has mountains.
Why doesn't Southern California have heavy rainfall ?

Figure 5   Excerpt from a dialogue with WHY.

has a rule "if there are mountains then there is heavy rainfall." The program can look in the knowledge base to see if it is always true that mountains are correlated with heavy rainfall. The program observes that this is an insufficient cause in its model of rainfall. So it asks "Do you think any place with mountains has heavy rainfall?" This forces the student to realize that he has stated something that is not a necessary factor. Here the student says "Yes, of course." Now the program looks in the knowledge base and picks a counterexample. We have gone far beyond just retrieving facts, which occurs in SCHOLAR, to analysing the student's responses to see if he understands the particular model that we want to teach. Again, the idea of formalizing the questioning methods is a major accomplishment.

Collins and Stevens built in a tutoring plan that detects the facts that the student does not seem to understand. A teaching strategy then selects one of these misconceptions to work with. It says something like: "Deal with misconceptions before unnecessary factors." In this way, the program maintains a plan for its dialogue.

It is not clear how well WHY could understand the student's misconceptions. In their follow-up program, Collins and Stevens enumerate possible misconceptions to be recognized. After working with many students, they found patterns in what students tended to believe. The tutor checks to see if a student has these particular misconceptions. When I say "The program now sees that the student knows the rule", I do not know how explicitly this was modelled. In particular, it does not appear that WHY followed the student during long dialogues, characterizing model changes and consistency.

2.3   WEST

WEST is an example of a coach system (Burton and Brown, 1982). It is built on top of the game "How the West was Won". It is a child's game, a variation of a game also called "Shoots and Ladders" (Figure 6). There are sets of spinners or dials, and the student spins these to get three numbers, which he can combine using subtraction, addition and multiplication, or group the numbers using parentheses. The objective of the game is to get to the end first. One has the advantage of various ladders, which are shortcuts. So one wants to choose the mathematical operators that will allow taking the shortcuts. If one lands on a place where the opponent is located, that bumps the opponent back. Therefore it might be an advantage not to maximize forward progress, but to land where the opponent is in order to make him go back.

The game was originally available on the PLATO system. PLATO is the tutoring environment that was developed by Computer Development Cor-

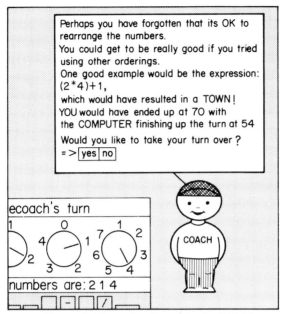

Figure 6 Example of coaching by WEST.

poration, CDC, in the 1960s. Given that this program was intended to teach mathematics, Brown and Burton decided that it would be good to add a coach to observe and critique the student's use of the various operators.

They developed a paradigm that they call *Issues and Examples*. They enumerated in the program all of the various kinds of operator combinations that a student should be able to use, called *issues*. For example, a student should be able to know that multiplication can be applied next to a parenthesis for example; this is legitimate syntax. Obviously the first thing that the student should know is that he can use any of these operators. To give a simple example, the program watches the student as he plays the game, maybe over several sessions, and after a while notices that there is a pattern, say, the student never uses parentheses. If the student used parentheses at various times then he might be able to play better. So, the program finds an opportunity to interrupt and says "You never use parentheses and if you used parentheses, as in this example, you would be able to land here and you would be way down here . . ." The student would see that using parentheses was to his advantage. This was the idea: the interruption should be well-motivated by something that the student will understand. One should not just say at some random time "You never use parentheses." Rather, one should pick a moment when the student will appreciate what parentheses are all about; this will help him remember. This is one of

WEST's kibitzing strategies concerning when to interrupt: pick a time when there is a good example of an issue that you want to bring to the student's attention.

The study of WEST was very complex and I strongly recommend that the reader consult Burton and Brown (1982) for further details. Burton and Brown's analysis of strategies is impressive. They found that there were students who were using the PLATO system with these colour graphics who enjoyed the game so much that they would keep trying to go back in order to make the game last longer. This raises a problem: the student modelling program that is looking at parentheses may be missing a more general plan. So Burton and Brown invented the idea of what they called a "tear" in the model: can one detect a time when one thinks one does not understand what the student is doing? For example, suppose that the student seems to be using parentheses sometimes, but not always, and one cannot understand the pattern. One way of understanding tear is that there are constant breaks in known patterns. It raises the larger issues of how to detect strategies, how to detect if a model is good or bad, and the meaning of the recognition of new strategies that were not built into the program.

The issues and examples paradigm is very useful for understanding how to build a tutoring or teaching system. The idea is very simple. One builds into the program concepts or rules (the issues) that one wants to teach the student—in this case the use of mathematical operators. Then one builds in recognizers (procedures) for detecting whether or not the student knows each issue. In GUIDON the issues are the EMYCIN rules, and the recognizers are replaced by a single general modelling program, which attempts to determine whether the student knows the rules used by the EMYCIN expert program. In contrast, in WEST each issue has a program for recognizing it, called a *specialist*.

Today in the United States there is increasing interest in applying some of these early ideas, especially programs like SCHOLAR and WEST. At San Francisco State University, and in several other universities in California, they are trying to teach high school teachers how to use this paradigm in their own areas of expertise. They are receiving computers from Hewlett-Packard, new LISP machines and networks. This is encouraging because it is something that researchers do not have the time to do—setting up projects to teach high school teachers what we did ten years ago and trying to make the ideas practical.

To summarize the research paradigm, we are stating teaching rules in an attempt to formalize principles. We have considered three examples. The WHY system illustrates the principle of constructing a counterexample for an insufficient factor. In GUIDON (see Chapter 4) we consider part of the procedure for completing a topic; GUIDON simply states a domain rule rather than belaboring the discussion. In WEST we consider the principle of illustrating an issue by an example that is dramatically superior to the move made by the student. I think this shows a science in a very early stage of writing down what is intuitively, in commonsense terms, believed by the researchers to be reasonable.

After this, we must represent this knowledge explicitly so it can be reasoned about by the programs and can be explained. Every complex system like GUIDON will have hundreds of teaching rules. They form another knowledge base, which we want to be easy to change. The program has to be able to explain its behaviour, easy to modify, and so on. Next, we must study this formalized knowledge and understand why there are good things to do. What is the underlying model of learning and of human reasoning that makes good teaching rules? For example, if we look at fifty GUIDON rules, we might find that they are inconsistent. Maybe we want to build different versions of GUIDON that systematically test alternative ways of teaching. For example, Collins studied Socratic tutoring in many different domains.

This is a good place to mention the work of Beverly Woolf. She went back to GUIDON, studied it in some detail, and restated the tutoring discourse according to natural language conceptions of patterns in a dialogue. She essentially tried to extract the strategies that were implicit in the alternative ways of tutoring that I had compiled in GUIDON's rules. Her program, the MENO-TUTOR, reasons in more layers of abstraction about what to do (Woolf and McDonald, 1984).

2.4   The WUMPUS Advisor

Goldstein and his colleagues developed a coach for the WUMPUS game, adapting it for teaching probabilistic reasoning to a student (Goldstein, 1982). In a manner similar to SCHOLAR, WEST, and GUIDON, Goldstein used production rules for stating teaching principles. Various rules produce explanations and select examples. In the game there are many caves, bats and pits. One moves through the caves to find one's way out or to find some treasure. When one arrives in a particular cave, one receives information about what might be nearby. One is told that it is cold or that one can hear certain sounds. One knows that the pits will have cold air coming from them, and so on. As one goes through this network of caves, one can collect evidence of what is nearby.

At one point the coach might interrupt and say, "Mary, it isn't necessary to take such large risks with pits. We have seen that multiple evidence is more dangerous than single evidence for bats . . ." Figure 7 shows part of WUMPUS's reasoning here. We want to teach the student the general rule

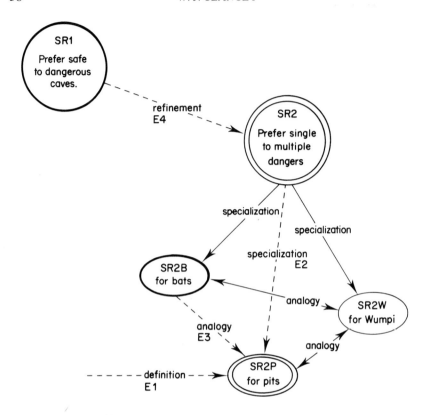

A dark outline signifies a rule hypothesized to be known by the player.
A double outline signifies a rule explained to the player.
A dashed link signifies that an explanation corresponding to that link has been generated.
E1 through E4 are the corresponding explanations in the text .

Figure 7   Knowledge structures used by the WUMPUS Advisor.

preferring single dangers over multiple dangers, and this becomes instantiated or specialized for three different types of dangers. Thus here a
previous explanation about how the rule applies to bats is referred to when
explaining its application to pits. Goldstein points out that the program
needs to keep records of what it has explained already so it has an
opportunity to draw an analogy. Note that in this formal domain, unlike in
medicine or meteorology, there is no underlying causal model, just axioms
describing how the world works. This greatly simplifies the modelling
problem.

2.5   TURTLE

The next three programs are concerned with teaching computer programming. We see a student's program and want to understand its design. What is the student's plan? Why is he using these steps in this way?

"Turtle" was one of Papert and DiSessa's constructions for teaching using LOGO (Papert, 1980). The instructions in the language are very simple—one can simply turn the turtle, one can move in a certain direction or one can have it lower its pen and draw as its moves. There is actually a mechanical device that draws on paper in the room; the student types in the program and the little robot turtle moves around. In this way the students can watch what their programs do, another example of reification. This was part of Papert's idea of an environment that would give students feedback.

The TURTLE system is extremely simple; it has the capability to only write four programs, and the solutions are canned (built into the program). The program is able to detect certain types of errors. It has prespecified hints that it prints out, which are intended to help the student (Figure 8).

```
          Task is to draw a well with a roof.

First step ? TOP
Next step ? DRAW 200
Next step ? BOX
Next step ? QUIT
OK, WELL is defined!

Let me see if I understand your program:
The function TOP draws the ROOF of the WELL-TASK.
The code : DRAW 200 draws the POLE of the WELL-TASK.
The function BOX draws the BASE of the WELL-TASK

Does that seem correct ?  YES

     After the student defines functions TOP and BOX

Did you intend to interface the function TOP to the step DRAW
200 by following the path C D ?  YES

Here is the interface you defined between the mainsteps in the
function TOP and the step DRAW 200 in WELL :

      TURN 180

Analysis:

Correct code          Commentary

TURN 180      Correct interface to turn through angle BCD
MOVE 50       Missing interface to move over segment CD
TURN 90       Missing interface to turn through angle CDE

 . . .

You provided no setup for the WELL-TASK.
```

Figure 8   Excerpt from a dialogue with TURTLE.

Here is how the program proceeds. The problem is to draw a well with a roof on it. We have a box, a square and then a pole. It is like a triangle on top of a box. Miller analysed in detail the various ways that people solve this problem. In the interaction the student says that his first step is to draw using another procedure. Then he wants to have the pen go 200 steps forward, draw a box, and then stop. This is his program for drawing a well with a roof. The program has to relate the terminology of the student's names for his programs to the internal names that the programmer has defined. This is a very interesting problem in programming tutors. The modelling program has to understand what the variables stand for. The program infers here that "Top" is the roof of the well and "Draw 200" is the pole and "Box" is the student's name for the base. This was done by building into the program various synonyms that people are likely to use.

Figure 8 shows a mapping between the student behaviour and the internal model of the task. It shows in a simple way the importance of being able to recognize alternative solutions, in this case by using something as trivial as different terminology. Next, the student defines these functions for Top and Box, and the program analyses where the pen moves around.

Next the TURTLE program points out that there is some basic step that has been left out. It says that no "Set-up" for the Well task has been provided. "Set-up" is a general programming concept. Before another procedure is called, the turtle has to be put into the right position to do the next procedure. This is a kind of initialization that makes the next procedure perform correctly. On looking at the picture, the roof might have been sideways, or maybe the pole might have the wrong angle. The program analyses what the drawing looks like and relates it to what the correct step should be. It points out that two steps were left out as part of this interface.

This is a very simple example of conveying to the student that programming has certain plans behind it, and there are certain recurrent operations in programming, in particular, performing a set-up as part of calling a subprocedure. The program has related the student's behaviour to the underlying model, isolated an error, told the student what the error is, and indicated what he should do differently. Note that there is no attempt to understand the student's error, why he did this, just what he did wrong and the correction that should be performed.

2.6   MENO

MENO (Soloway *et al.*, 1981) is the work of Elliot Soloway, who is now at Yale and did his thesis work at the University of Massachusetts in the late 1970s. MENO attempts to understand a student's programming bug, to articulate the misconception. It not only fixes the plan as in TURTLE, it also

A student's program...

```
1  PROGRAM AVERAGE 1 (INPUT, OUTPUT),
2  VAR
3      SUM, POSIDEN, COUNT : INTEGER;
4         AVE : REAL;
5  BEGIN
6         SUM : = 0 ;
7         COUNT : = 0 ;
8         READ (POSIDEN);
9         WHILE POSIDEN <> 9999 DO
10          BEGIN
11             SUM : = SUM + POSIDEN ;
12             COUNT : = COUNT + 1 ;
13             POSIDEN : = POSIDEN + 1;
14          END;
15          AVE : = SUM / COUNT ;
16          WRITELN ('THE AVERAGE IS', AVE)
17  END.
```

Figure 9   Program interpreted by MENO.

helps the student resolve his misconception. To summarize these levels: there is the surface behaviour of the program; there is the plan, which is the design; and there is the underlying misconception that generates the design that generates the program.

Figure 9 shows the input to the MENO program; it is a very difficult task to understand a program like this. It requires knowledge of the program that is to be solved and knowledge about alternative solutions. The purpose of this program is to compute an average. It initializes the sum and then counts how many numbers have been input. While the input is not equal to 999 (a *sentinel*, a strange number that would not be part of the input) we add the input to the sum and increment the count. Note that the student adds 1 to the input and then continues. This obviously takes a long time, but eventually we get to 999, exit the loop, and divide the number of times we have gone around into the sum.

The student has made a mistake of putting the READ statement outside of his loop. Why did he do that? Soloway and his collaborators have performed a very interesting analysis to get at the misconceptions.

Consider what MENO says to the student (Figure 10). First, like TURTLE, it finds a mapping between the student's names and the internal names of the program. It says "Positive identifier is the new value variable and count is the counter variable." There is a general plan that MENO has for doing averages. It does not have variable names like X, W, A, B, but it does have general names that correspond to the meaning of the variable: to get the new value, the counter, the running total, etc. Thus we are again relating the student's behaviour to the plan that is in the program. MENO has many plans for the problems that it solves. The program points out the bug: "You modified the new value variable by adding 1 to it whereas you should modify it by calling the READ-procedure."

MENO's analysis...

POSIDEN is the New Value Variable
COUNT is the Counter Variable
SUM is the Running Total Variable

You modified POSIDEN by adding POSIDEN to 1
whereas...
you should modify the New Value Variable by calling the READ
procedure: READ(POSIDEN).

Two misconceptions can be associated with this bug:

1. You might be thinking that the single call to the READ
procedure at the top of your program is enough to define a
variable which will always be read in from the terminal...

2. You might be thinking that POSIDEN is like COUNT... The
computer does not know to reinterpret + 1 in the former case
to be like a READ.

Figure 10   Excerpt from a dialogue with MENO.

MENO then goes further than TURTLE. It has a library of misconceptions, not generated by the program, but built in by Soloway. One possibility is that the student thinks that READ is like a declaration, and so, every time he mentions X, its value should be read. It is like saying that X is an integer, describing a property that should persist through the entire program.

Figure 11 shows the kind of analysis that is being performed. MENO builds a semantic net, a parse of the program, and then relates each of the variables and the operations to an internal model of the problem. Then it associates certain bugs with various plans. The analysis is not generative; the program cannot take an arbitrary program and understand it. It has to be an "Average program" or another one in the library. Explaining bugs requires a lot of creativity. The explanation of the bug as an alternative model is often as complicated and difficult as what one is trying to teach. People probably rely a great deal on experience and receiving information from students. It is not certain how many teachers could understand what the students are doing. We are certainly far from being able to write a program that could generate similar explanations for misconceptions, especially in domains like medicine or programming.

MENO was reimplemented by Lewis Johnson in his dissertation research as the PROUST program (Johnson and Soloway, 1984). Rather than matching bugs as specific segments of code, it constructs a complete parse of the code on different levels of abstraction. This provides a more robust, generative capability for understanding student programs and is the first step beyond the template approach of TURTLE and MENO. The misconceptions are still built in, but the program bugs are stated abstractly, rather than as specific lines of code to be matched.

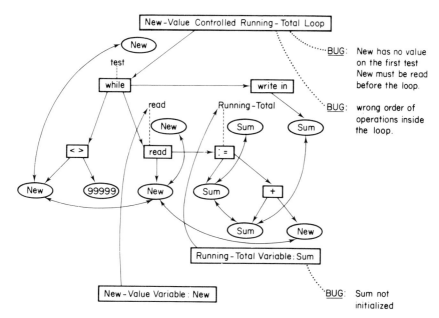

New-Value Controlled Running-Total Loop

BUG: New has no value on the first test New must be read before the loop.

BUG: wrong order of operations inside the loop.

BUG: Sum not initialized

Figure 11 Annotation of bugs in MENO's parse of a program (from Soloway *et al.*, 1982).

2.7 The MACSYMA Advisor

The MACSYMA Advisor (Genesereth, 1982) is very similar in style to the MENO system. We have the same problem of understanding a sequence of student behaviour. We want to extract the user's plan. MACSYMA, developed at MIT by Joel Moses, is a mathematical manipulation system for simplifying and combining equations. The problem is to take a user's sequence of interactions with MACSYMA and to provide help or consultation.

Figure 12 shows an example in which the user is surprised by an answer of zero. The user asks for help, indicating that there is a problem. The point is, when we type in commands to a program like MACSYMA, we have some kind of plan in mind, that is, a method or approach for solving a problem. In this case the user was trying to solve an equation (to determine values of X for which the formula gives an answer of zero). The MACSYMA Advisor has to examine the sequence of user actions, and, given the user's goal, infer his plan for using the MACSYMA program. The Advisor has a built-in library of different ways of using MACSYMA, somewhat similar to

```
(C7)  (A:COEFF(D6, X, 2),  B:COEFF(D6, X, 1),
       C:COEFF(D6, X, 0))$

(C8)  (-B + SQRT(B**2 - 4*A*C)) / (2*A);

(D8)              0

(C9)  HELP()$
```

USER: I was trying to solve D6 for X and I got 0.

ADVISOR: Did you expect COEFF to return the
         coefficient of D6?

USER: Yes, doesn't it?

ADVISOR: COEFF(exp, var, pow) returns the correct coefficient
of var^{pow} in exp only if exp is expanded with respect to var.
Perhaps you should use RATCOEFF.

USER: Okay, thanks. Bye.

Figure 12   Excerpt from a dialogue with the MACSYMA Advisor.

MENO's library of program patterns. The Advisor provides a remediation in terms of a correct set of steps of what to do, plus an explanation of the student's behaviour in terms of a misconception.

The user says "I was trying to solve equation that was stated in D6 for X and I got 0." At this point, the program determines that, if this is the user's goal and this is what he did, he must believe that the COEFF command or operator has a certain effect. The user has a misconception. He believes that COEFF returns the coefficient of a particular formula, but it returns the coefficient of X to the first power. The program goes on to say "If this is what you are trying to do, it's important that the expression be expanded with respect to the variable and you should use RATCOEFF to get the right result."

The important point is how the MACSYMA Advisor constructs this interpretation. Unlike the other programs that we have seen, where the misconceptions were pre-enumerated, the MACSYMA advisor has the capability of generating the misconception by an analysis of the student's plan. Consider Figure 13. At the top is the goal of solving the equation for X. At the bottom the user's superficial behaviour. In the middle is the interpretation of how this goal generates this sequence of behaviour, expressed as a hierarchical structure of subgoals and methods for accomplishing them.

To make the user's actions fit together in a coherent explanation, the

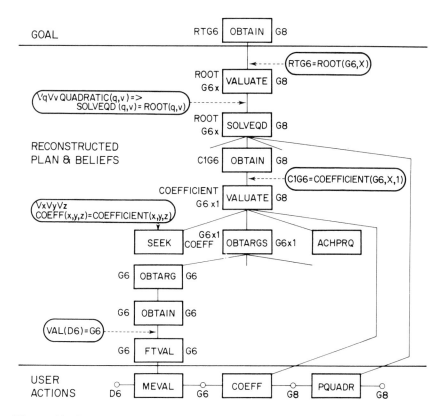

Figure 13 Reconstructed plan generated by the MACSYMA Advisor (from Genesereth, 1982).

program makes certain assumptions about the user's beliefs. The Advisor indicates the actual input and output for each operator and general constraints that the input and output must satisfy. Thus the interpretation of the user's misconception, as a model of his beliefs, is stated as both specific computation results and general facts about MACSYMA's operators.

In particular, the analysis shown here is made complete by assuming that the user believes that this particular operator, COEFF, returns a particular value that has a certain input and output. This assertion about COEFF is technically incorrect, but it makes the plan coherent; the user's sequence of behaviour is now understandable. Constructing such a plan is a complex search problem. The program generates multiple parses in both a bottom-up and top-down way. Having the behaviour constrains possible interpretations, and knowing the goal constrains the possible operations that are performed. Different template (canned) plans are used by the program to generate and to recognize the sequence of behaviour.

We see here the power of a logic formalism in which Genesereth expresses the various constraints on each of the operators and what the operators accomplish. Again, an appropriate language enables the writing of a program that can reason about the knowledge involved. If these operators were in LISP, the plan recognizer would not be able to reason about them. Note how far this is from the SCHOLAR system, which has only an idea of right and wrong answers. Here we generate a structural analysis of what the user believes, given his behaviour. I think this is one of the best examples of student modelling. It shows us how to generate misconceptions, rather than building them into the program. Contrast this with the work of Stevens and Collins, where the misconceptions about meteorology and heavy rainfall are pre-enumerated, so the program has only a fixed library of possible misconceptions. It helps of course to be working in a mathematical, closed domain. Genesereth has gone on to develop the ideas of the representation system that was used here, MRS, and to examine in more detail architectures for problem solving (Genesereth, 1983).

2.8 DEBUGGY

DEBUGGY is a program for modelling a student's knowledge of the subtraction procedure. It models incorrect procedures, to be contrasted with modelling (factual) misconceptions. DEBUGGY builds a procedure that describes how a student does subtraction, based on a set of example problems solved by the student.

Figure 14 shows the procedural network that is DEBUGGY's internal representation of an incorrect subtraction procedure (Brown and Burton, 1978). It shows a decomposition of the various steps. If for example, at one point, one wants to subtract a column from another, there are various alternative procedures to apply, depending on the current situation. Here the subprocedure "switch digits" has replaced "borrow and subtract". Brown and Burton were inspired by Sacerdoti's approach of using a procedural network to describe a plan.

The idea of DEBUGGY is that there are systematic errors that people make, and we can analyse the problems to detect these errors. It should be realized that there is a significant computational problem in generating this description from all of the possible alternative procedures DEBUGGY can

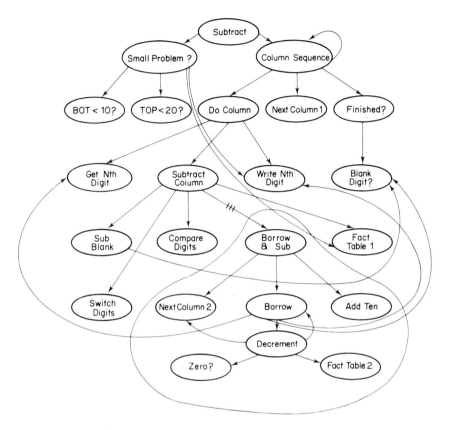

Figure 14   Example of a subtraction bug represented by a procedural net.

construct. Of the order of a hundred bugs were found to occur in students. There were thousands of students whose problems were examined.

2.9   Repair Theory

Recalling the distinction between describing student behaviour and the rationale behind this behaviour, Kurt and van Lehn's project was to understand where subtraction bugs come from. We start with the surface behaviour: the student cannot subtract from 0 or does not subtract from 0. We describe the procedure, and now we ask "Why does he do that?" Where did this bug come from? It is a model based on how people learn. In repair theory, rather than just recognizing the bugs, we try to understand the cause of the misconception. This is like taking the MACSYMA Advisor one more step. Suppose one has isolated a misconception, what is the reason for it? It is an attempt to understand learning problems. Recalling the MENO example, why does the student believe that READ is a kind of declaration? How can we explain why students have certain bugs and not others? We want a theory of where the bugs come from that allows us to generate the bugs and explain the systematic errors in more primitive terms.

The central idea in repair theory is that an incomplete correct procedure causes an impasse during problem solving, which is repaired by a general problem solver and critics. This is an interesting first-order theory, which seems to have a lot of power. In one sense, this is the idea of an *overlay model* again: the students know a subset of the correct procedure. But the next part is different. Suppose a student does not know what to do when there is a zero on top or when it is necessary to borrow (in a subtraction problem), but they do everything else correctly. Without a complete procedure, the student gets stuck. This is called an *impasse*.

For example, if one does not know what to do when the top number is smaller, one has to do something. One is supposed to write down some number when doing a subtraction, one cannot just leave a blank. Students know this, and so they need some kind of alternative way of acting. When they reach this impasse, they repair their procedure in some way. This is the origin of the name "repair theory". van Lehn assumes that people have general problem-solving methods that they will follow when they get stuck. They do not sit there paralysed: they do something. He wanted to study how a repaired impasse might generate bugs.

Figure 15 gives an example. Suppose we take the bug of not being able to borrow when the top digit is smaller than the bottom digit (not being able to subtract 6 from 3 here). This is modelled by deleting part of the procedure that allows us to behave when we reach that situation. It is a simple production-rule view of subtraction. There are situations and operations that can be performed. If one sees a large number on top of a small number, one just looks it up in a table. So if one sees 8 over 2, one can look it up: $8 - 2 = 6$.

But now one gets to $3 - 6$, and let us say that there is no table for that. One cannot write down -3. It is not permitted to write down a negative number here, but something must be written down. So it is time to borrow. But if we delete the knowledge about borrowing, there is an impasse.

van Lehn gives the general problem-solving strategies that he believes are sufficient to generate the observed bugs. First, skip the column—write down nothing. Some students do this. Secondly, quit, and stop the problem right there—do not write down any more numbers, but go on to the next problem. Thirdly (this is very creative), just turn the numbers around and subtract.

1. Delete rule of procedure:
   " borrow when top digit is too small "

2. Problem solving ends with an impasse:

   ```
      638
    - 462
    -----
       ?6      = > impasse occurs in second column
   ```

3. Different repair methods produce different procedural bugs:

REPAIR	BUGS
Skip	blank - instead - of - borrow
Quit	doesn't - borrow
Swap vertically	smaller - from - larger
Dememoize	zero - instead - of - borrow

Figure 15   Analysis of a bug provided by Repair Theory.

Fourthly, *dememoize*—just look up the answer in an idiosyncratic table of arithmetic facts.

These repair strategies will generate different bugs. We have the opportunity now of systematically deleting rules in the correct subtraction procedure, applying the problem-solving strategies and generating the bugs. We can go backwards from actual problems and determine how the people applied the strategies and so on. DEBUGGY discovered 89 different bugs in several thousand problem sets. Repair theory explains (generates) 21 bugs that have been observed. Also, interestingly, it generates 10 bugs that have not been observed but are at least plausible or possible. van Lehn uses the term *star bug* (from language theory) for a bug that we, for many reasons, believe could never occur. (This is from the idea of a sentence in a language that we should never expect anyone to utter.) Obviously we want the fewest number of star bugs; van Lehn takes this as a measure of quality of his theory that there is only one star bug. As for the ten originally unobserved bugs, he went back and found some of these in the problem sets. There are many detailed parts of this theory; it has recently been extended to explain the origin of the impasses in what is called *Step Theory* (van Lehn, 1983).

Finally, *bug migration* concerns changes in bugs over time. Using Repair Theory, van Lehn and Brown were able to make certain predictions, based on the idea that if the student has one bug, he might replace it by another one because his impasse stays the same. He still does not know how to borrow, but he might apply a different problem-solving strategy. One time he might leave it blank, and the next time he reverses the numbers. Thus, the bugs are related to one another, and van Lehn and Brown found a systematic change from, say, Friday to Monday when retesting the student. This also turns out to be an interesting concept, because, originally, we might have said the behaviour was random because the bugs seem to be changing. But a deeper analysis shows that there is some systematic pattern. van Lehn has written extensively about the problem of developing a principled theory (van Lehn *et al.*, 1984). I have gone into some detail with his work because, even though DEBUGGY and Repair Theory are not tutoring programs, they provide a good example of how AI methods are used to develop detailed models of human problem solving.

2.10 SOPHIE

SOPHIE is a very large, complex program of three different versions developed by Brown and Burton between about 1974 and 1978. Most of this work was done at Bolt, Beranek and Newman. SOPHIE stands for "Sophisticated Instructor for Electronics," but it was also the name of Richard Burton's dog. SOPHIE versions 1 and 2 did not contain an expert system in the sense that we define it today. At their core is a mathematical FORTRAN program that simulates how a particular circuit behaves under different loads. The simulator is used by the tutoring program to evaluate a student's diagnostic hypotheses. SOPHIE 3 is an attempt to formulate a procedure for doing diagnosis, an expert system, that the student can watch and emulate.

Recall that SOPHIE provides a reactive environment; it does not attempt to teach anything to the student in a systematic way. The student is given a version of the circuit with a bug in it, or a *fault*, as it is called in this context. He is to determine which component is faulty. The student makes measurements and then poses a hypothesis. He can ask questions about what could possibly be wrong, given the information is received.

Consider Figure 16. The program starts with a fault in the circuit. The student is told various readings, such as voltage. Burton developed a "semantic grammar" for parsing the student's input. This parser consists of a set of procedures corresponding to various phrases and expressions. The parser is capable of disambiguating pronouns and filling in omitted references (anaphora). The program has a fact table in which it looks up circuit information.

The student makes a measurement: "What is the voltage between R8 and Q1?" Later he poses a hypothesis: "Is it possible that Q6 is open?" The program has to disambiguate this discription, and then, using the simulator, determine if the hypothesis is consistent with the current setup of the circuit. It turns out that this is not the fault. The program points out that, if it were the fault, the measurements would have been different. To do this, it sets up

Welcome to SOPHIE, a reactive learning environment

The instrument has a fault and its present control settings are:

CC = 1, CR = HIGH, LOAD = 20, VC = 1, VR = HIGH *

\>\> What is the output ?
The output voltage is 11.7 volts.

\>\> What is it † in a working instrument ?
In a working circuit the output voltage is 19.9 volts.

\>\> What is the voltage between R8 and Q1 ?
The voltage at N1 is 47.6 volts

\>\> What is the base emitter voltage of the voltage limiting transistor ?
= transistor
The base emitter voltage of Q5 is -.037 millivolts.

\>\> Is it possible that Q6 is open ? ‡
Is the complete fault mode EB/EC/BC = OP/OK/OP what you intended ?
\>\> Sure

When the settings were:
CC-1.0, CR = HIGH, LOAD = 20, VC = 1.0, VR = HIGH
That fault conflicts with the following measurement. You observed that the
output voltage was 11.7 volts. § If Q6 had fault mode EB/EC/BC = OP/OK/OP it
would be 23.9 volts. In a working circuit it is 19.9 volts

That fault does not explain any of the symptoms you observed but it is
consistent with the values for the base emitter voltage of Q5 and the voltage at
N1. ‖

---

* Front - panel settings
† Uses model of dialogue for reasoning pronouns.
‡ Hypothesis.evaluation.
§ Constructs counterexample
‖ But also determines what is "good" with the hypothesis

Figure 16 Excerpt from a dialogue with SOPHIE (annotations added by John Seely
Brown).

the circuit again, using the student's fault and runs the FORTRAN simulation to determine how the circuit would behave given the fault that the student has stated. Using the FORTRAN simulation program in this way requires considerable intermediate knowledge structures and reasoning to set up meaningful boundary conditions for the hypothesized situation. This integration of multiple knowledge representations is a major contribution of SOPHIE research: the FORTRAN program simulates the circuit; a semantic network describes the components of the circuit; and semantic parsing procedures disambiguate student input.

The program comments that, even though the student's hypothesized fault is incorrect, it is consistent with two of the values that the student received. We have seen this tight logical analysis of consistent, necessary and sufficient factors in several programs (WHY, GUIDON, WUMPUS Advisor).

The student could also ask "What are all of the things that could be wrong?" This has to be answered with respect to the current known measurements. The program has to run multiple simulations, setting up the circuit in different ways to determine all possible faults that could account for the behaviour that has been observed so far. This is also a very complicated type of analysis.

While SOPHIE has no teaching knowledge in it, it provides a laboratory workbench, a kind of smart tool. In any lab, we could take a faulty circuit and have the student try a diagnosis. But here using the computer with a simulation, the student can pose hypotheses and ask for alternative analyses.

We can summarize the type of inference that SOPHIE can perform as follows.

(1) *Hypothetical question answering*: What happens when the circuit is changed in a certain way?

(2) *Hypothesis evaluation*: Could the circuit be faulty in some way?

(3) *Hypothesis generation*: What could be wrong, given the information known so far?

(4) *Redundancy checking*: Does a particular measurement add any new information given the set of possible faults and what has been observed so far? (Is the student testing a useful hypothesis or is he just randomly making measurements?)

It is possible to apply these ideas to a tutor built upon NEOMYCIN. But imagine the difficulty of answering the question "What if the patient didn't have a fever? What if the patient's fever were 110?" Imagine the complexity of the model of the body and the kind of computations that would be necessary to deal with any question of this form. The power of SOPHIE comes from the complete simulation model, which makes certain assumptions, of course, about how the circuit works and what the current environment is. In medicine we cannot perform this hypothetical generation and question answering. We cannot say everything that could be wrong. We have a model, but we do not have a basis for performing experiments for determining how the patient would behave under different environmental loads.

This is a subtle point. The problem arises not just because we have represented a small part of the space of possible diseases in NEOMYCIN. Diseases in medicine are different from faults in a circuit. Diseases in medicine are not faulty components, they are interactions that the "device" has with the world that cause the components to fail. You cannot possibly enumerate all of the world knowledge that could cause all the possible diseases that are or could be observed.

As an example consider a disease like tennis elbow. Suppose someone plays tennis and gets a sore arm and he comes and says "Something is wrong with my arm." One needs to know to tell him to stop playing tennis. Just having a model of the body says nothing about tennis. One needs to know all of the ways that people interact with the world. SOPHIE's form of electronic diagnosis has nothing to do with how the circuit interacts with the world. If the fault is caused by a room that is too warm or because somebody dropped the power regulator before they installed it, SOPHIE would not know about it. To restate this, a disease in medicine is not a component fault, but what caused the fault in the world. (This is reminiscent of the difference between a procedural bug (DEBUGGY) and the problem-solving and learning process that generated this bug (Repair and Step Theory).)

There is a lot more to say about SOPHIE; for further details see Brown *et al.* (1982), which explains the work of de Kleer, which came later, involving an expert system that could perform and describe the diagnostic process.

2.11 STEAMER

STEAMER teaches how to operate a steam plant in a ship (Hollan *et al.*, 1984). The use of graphics coupled to a mathematical simulation program and semantic network descriptions allows the program to provide a high-fidelity conceptual model of how the steam plant works. STEAMER is the work of Stevens, Forbus and several people of the Naval Personnel and Research Development Center, including Jim Hollan and Mike Hutchins. The project was originated by a psychologist, Mike Williams, who had experience on a ship teaching and learning steam-propulsion plant operation.

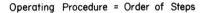

Operating Procedure = Order of Steps

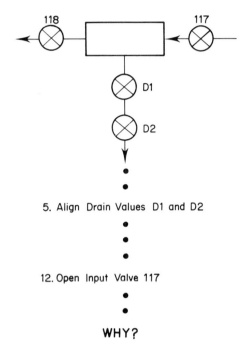

Figure 17   Schematic from STEAMER with steps in operational procedure.

The project was designed to be put into the field as a prototype within a few years; today STEAMER is being used to train new recruits. In general, the military is excited about automating teaching because of their high turnover and the great deal of technical expertise to be learned in many different areas.

The major difficulty here is to understand the rationale for why the procedures for running the steam plant are correct, particularly to facilitate remembering and modifying them. Valves, pipes and wires are arranged in a complicated jumble inside a ship. When a student is brought on board, it is very hard for him to understand how things are connected to one another. Graphics provide an easy way of visualizing the information. One can look at the lubricating system and one can look at the steam system. This graphics system is connected to the underlying simulation program, using the idea of active images or "active values" in the LOOPS programming system, developed at Xerox-Parc. The program sends a message to a particular concept or a unit, say one that corresponds to a valve. The valve instance is then responsible for setting itself on the screen to reflect its value.

Figure 17 shows part of the teaching problem in STEAMER. The procedure says "Step 5, align the drain valves D1 and D2." Much later, it says "Open valve I17." This is what one is supposed to do. The rationale for this procedure is not explicit—why should one do step 5 at all? Why should one do it before step 12? We want to teach the rationale as well as the procedure: whenever steam is admitted to a chamber, one must align the drains first. If one does not, the water that is left in the chamber will mix with the steam, and high-energy water pellets will be thrown downstream.

STEAMER research included new work in explanation. Using the description of the current state of the plant, the program generates explanations of what is happening. For example, it can describe a feedback process. There has been some consideration of the problem of packaging the text and presenting overviews, as well as going through causal detail. There is some natural-language work, but the research has emphasized causal modelling.

3   CONCLUSION

How well do these programs perform? Is anybody using them? Some of them have been tested, but there is no system that has in any significant way replaced the traditional methods of teaching. These are mainly pilot studies that demonstrate plausibility. STEAMER might be the closest to a system that has replaced some traditional teaching and maybe greatly augmented what can be taught. DEBUGGY has been used for thousands of students—but as data collection to verify the model, not interactively. MENO is being used at Yale, for teaching introductory programming. The WEST system was used as an exploratory system for a couple of months in an elementary school. SOPHIE was used experimentally for a few years over a computer network within the United States. Recent programs by Anderson and Reiser are effectively teaching LISP and geometry (Anderson *et al.*, 1984b; Anderson *et al.*, 1985).

In short, education has not been turned upside down. The process of developing these ideas and getting the programs to be used is very slow. I believe that professional educators in the schools today, not the researchers who developed the programs, will be the people who eventually take these ideas and apply them.

So what is all this worth? How would we compare the state of CAI and ICAI today? There is a mixture of goals and accomplishments. I think if we did a very simple analysis of the best traditional programs today, we should find that they are much better than almost any of the ICAI tutoring systems.

They are better when viewed in terms of being operating, portable programs that students can actually learn from. Many hours of work were put into designing CAI programs, with a lot of handcrafting of the design to make them useful. I know a physician at Stanford who has been cranking out CAI programs for probably 20 years. He felt embarrassed when he saw what we were doing. He felt that we were coming from another planet and believed that now all of his work was obsolete. I told him that was not true at all. He is teaching students today with his programs, and it might be ten years before we have anything to give him. That was in 1977. His programs still work, and they are teaching many students every year. ICAI is still mainly a lot of promises.

On the other hand, these promises are profound and are changing not just how we think about teaching, but our understanding of what needs to be taught. We should remember that CAI systems do not have a systematic conceptual representation of what is being taught. The person who designs the traditional system is not provided with a language that allows him to write down what he knows in a structured, reusable way. Very little cumulative science or engineering is occurring. Each CAI author is building in his knowledge and not effectively sharing it with other teachers except to say "Here is my program, you can learn from my example." The field will advance much more quickly if people could share their knowledge of learning and pedagogy, and develop formal theories. While WEST, WHY, GUIDON and other ICAI programs take many years to develop, ICAI researchers can now say "Here is my set of rules: use them in your system." The idea of shared knowledge bases is something that excites me a great deal when I consider where we might be in ten or twenty years, after collecting and abstracting knowledge in tutoring and expert systems.

ACKNOWLEDGEMENTS

This paper is an edited version of a presentation given in the University of Namur, Belgium in May 1985 as part of the program for the International Professorship in Computer Science (Expert Systems) sponsored by the Belgian National Foundation for Scientific Research and IBM. I sincerely thank my friend Axel van Lamsweerde for his hospitality during my stay and for his arduous efforts to produce a transcript of this presentation. While the original transcript has been edited a great deal, this paper is intended to reflect the extemporaneous nature of an oral presentation, rather than a scholarly work. I have however added citations to bring the material up-to-date. As indicated in the text, much of the material was prepared by John Seely Brown and Richard R. Burton, or in collaboration with them.

Much of what I know about Intelligent Tutoring Systems comes from working with John and Richard.

My research is sponsored in part by ONR (contract N00014-85-K-0305) and by a grant from the Josiah Macy, Jr. Foundation. Computational resources have been provided by the Sumex-Aim National Resource (NIH grant RR00785).

REFERENCES

Anderson, J. R., Boyle, C. F., Farrell, R. and Reiser, B. (1984a). Cognitive principles in the design of computer tutors. *Proc. 6th Ann. Conf. of the Cognitive Science Society, Boulder, June 1984*, pp. 2–10.

Anderson, J. R., Farrell, R. and Sauers, R. (1984b). Learning to program in LISP. *Cogn. Sci.* **8**, 87–129.

Anderson, J. R., Boyle, C. F. and Yost, G. (1985). The geometry tutor. *Proc. 9th Int. Joint Conf. on Artificial Intelligence, Los Angeles, August 1985*, Vol. 1, pp. 1–7.

Brown, J. S. (1983). Process versus product—a perspective on tools for communal and informal electronic learning. *Education in the Electronic Age, Proc. Conf. Sponsored by the Educational Broadcasting Corporation, WNET/Thirteen, July 1983*.

Brown, J. S. and Burton, R. B. (1978). Diagnostic models for procedural bugs in basic mathematical skills. *Cogn. Sci.* **2**, 155–192.

Brown, J. S., Burton, R. and de Kleer, J. (1982). Pedagogical, natural language, and knowledge engineering techniques in SOPHIE I, II, and III. *Intelligent Tutoring Systems* (ed. D. Sleeman and J. S. Brown), pp. 227–282. New York: Academic Press.

Burton, R. B. and Brown, J. S. (1982). An investigation of computer coaching for informal learning activities. *Intelligent Tutoring Systems* (ed. D. Sleeman and J. S. Brown), pp. 79–98. New York: Academic Press.

Carbonell, J. R. (1970). Mixed-Initiative Man–Computer Instructional Dialogues. Tech. Rep. 1971, Bolt Beranek and Newman.

Carbonell, J. R. and Collins, A. M. (1973). Natural semantics in artificial intelligence. *Proc. 3rd IJCAI, Stanford, August 1973*, pp. 344–351.

Clancey, W. J. (1982). GUIDON. *The Handbook of Artificial Intelligence* (ed. A. Barr and E. A. Feigenbaum), pp. 267–278. Los Altos, California: William Kaufmann.

Clancey, W. J. (1986). Qualitative student models. *Ann. Rev. Comp. Sci.* **1**, 381–450.

Clancey, W. J. and Letsinger, R. (1984). NEOMYCIN: Reconfiguring a rule-based expert system for application to teaching. *Readings in Medical Artificial Intelligence: The First Decade* (1978) (ed. W. J. Clancey and E. H. Shortliffe), pp. 361–381. Reading, Mass.: Addison-Wesley.

Collins, A. (1978). Fragments of a theory of human plausible reasoning. *Proc. 2nd Conf. on Theoretical Issues in Natural Language Processing, TINLAP, July 1978*, pp. 194–201.

Collins, A. and Brown, J. S. (1987). The computer as a tool for learning through reflection. *Learning Issues for Intelligent Tutoring Systems* (ed. H. Mandl and A. Lesgold). New York: Springer.

Collins, A. and Stevens, A. L. (1980). Goals and Strategies of Interactive Teachers. BBN Tech. Rep. 4345, Bolt, Barenek and Newman.

Genesereth, M. R. (1982). The role of plans in intelligent teaching systems. *Intelligent Tutoring Systems* (ed. D. Sleeman and J. S. Brown), pp. 137–155. New York: Academic Press.

Genesereth, M. R. (1983). An overview of meta-level architecture. *Proc. Nat. Conf. on Artificial Intelligence, August 1983*, pp. 119–124.

Goldstein, I. P. (1977). The Computer as Coach: An Athletic Paradigm for Intellectual Education. AI Memo 389, AI Lab., MIT.

Goldstein, I. P. (1978). Developing a computational representation for problem solving skills. *Proc. Carnegie-Mellon Conf. on Problem Solving and Education: Issues in Teaching and Research, 9–10 October 1978*.

Goldstein, I. P. (1982). The genetic graph: a representation for the evolution of procedural knowledge. *Intelligent Tutoring Systems* (ed. D. Sleeman and J. S. Brown), pp. 51–77. New York: Academic Press.

Hollan, J. D., Hutchins, E. L. and Weitzman, L. (1984). STEAMER: An interactive inspectable simulation-based training system. *The AI Magazine* 5(2), 15–27.

Johnson, W. L. and Soloway, E. (1984). Intention-based diagnosis of programming errors. *Proc. Nat. Conf. on Artificial Intelligence, Austin, August 1984*, pp. 162–168.

Kolodner, J. L. (1983). Maintaining organization in a dynamic long-term memory. *Cogn. Sci.* 7, 243–280.

Papert, S. (1980). *Mindstorms: Children, Computers, and Powerful Ideas*. New York: Basic Books.

Schank, R. C. (1981). Failure-driven memory. *Cogn. Brain Theory* 4, 41–60.

Sleeman, D. and Brown, J. S. (eds.) (1982). *Intelligent Tutoring Systems*. New York: Academic Press.

Soloway, E. M., Woolf, B., Rubin, E. and Barth, P. (1981). Meno-II: An intelligent tutoring system for novice programmers. *Proc. 7th Int. Joint Conf. on Artificial Intelligence, Vancouver, August 1981*, pp. 975–977.

Soloway, E. M., Rubin, E., Woolf, B., Bonar, J. and Johnson, W. L. (1982). Meno-II: An AI-based Programming Tutor. Tech. Rep. CSD/RR 258, Yale Univ.

van Lehn, K. (1983). Human procedural skill acquisition: Theory, model, and psychological validation. *Proc. Nat. Conf. on Artificial Intelligence*, Washington, DC., August 1983, pp. 420–423.

van Lehn, K., Brown, J. S. and Greeno, J. (1984). Competitive argumentation in computational theories of cognition. *Method and Tactics in Cognitive Science* (ed. W. Kintsch, J. Miller and P. Polson), pp. 235–262. Hillsdale, N.J.: Lawrence Erlbaum Associates.

Wenger, E. (1986). *AI and the Communication of Knowledge: An Overview of Intelligent Teaching Systems*. Los Altos, California: Morgan Kaufmann.

Westcourt, K. T., Beard, M. and Gould, M. (1977). Knowledge-Based Adaptive Curriculum Sequences for CAI: Application of a Network Representation. Tech. Rep. 288, Stanford Univ., Inst. for Mathematical Studies in the Social Sciences.

Woolf, B. and McDonald, D. D. (1984). Context-dependent transitions in tutoring discourse. *Proc. Nat. Conf. on Artificial Intelligence, Austin, August 1984*, pp. 355–361. Menlo Park, California: American Association for Artificial Intelligence.

4. From GUIDON to NEOMYCIN and HERACLES in twenty short lessons*

WILLIAM J. CLANCEY

Abstract. This chapter reviews the research leading from the GUIDON rule-based tutoring system, including the reconfiguration of MYCIN into NEOMYCIN and NEOMYCIN's generalization in the heuristic classification shell, HERACLES. The presentation is organized chronologically around pictures and dialogues that represent conceptual turning points and crystallize the basic ideas. The purpose is to collect the important results in one place, so they can be easily grasped. In the conclusion, some observations about research methodology are made.

1   ORIGINS

The idea of developing a tutoring program from the MYCIN knowledge base was first described by Ted Shortliffe (1974). In fact, it was the mixed-initiative dialogue of the SCHOLAR teaching program (Carbonell, 1970) that inspired Shortliffe to produce the consultation dialogue of MYCIN. He conceived of it as a question–answer program in SCHOLAR's style, using a semantic network of disease knowledge. Shortly after I joined the MYCIN project in early 1975, Bruce Buchanan and I decided that developing a tutoring program would be my thesis project.

The GUIDON program was operational in early 1979. This review describes the key ideas in GUIDON and the important developments of the following six years as research continued under funding from the Office of Naval Research (ONR), the Defense Advanced Research Projects Agency (DARPA), and the Army Research Institute. The first three years were covered briefly in an earlier report (Clancey and Buchanan, 1982). In general, only publications from this project are cited; many other references appear in the cited publications.

* This chapter originally appeared in *AI Magazine*, **7**(3) 40–60, Conference edition, 1986. Reprinted with permission.

2 OVERVIEW: INTRODUCTION TO THE PROGRAMS

Figure 1 shows the relationship between programs we have constructed in the past six years, including MYCIN and EMYCIN, which served as the foundation.

The medical consultation system, MYCIN, was generalized to EMYCIN (van Melle, 1979). The tutoring system, GUIDON, was designed to work with any EMYCIN knowledge base (Clancey, 1979a, 1982).

NEOMYCIN, another medical diagnosis program (Clancey and Let-singer, 1984), expands MYCIN's disease knowledge to include competing alternatives; for example, diseases that might be confused with meningitis. This provides an opportunity for teaching diagnostic strategy. MYCIN's strategy of exhaustive, top-down refinement is sufficient for the small set of diseases it knows about, but it is unrealistic for medical diagnosis in general. Using NEOMYCIN, we can convey the more complex processes of forming hypotheses, grouping competitors, discriminating among competitors, and reasoning causally. A second important idea in NEOMYCIN, distinguishing it from other expert systems, is that the inference procedure for diagnosis is

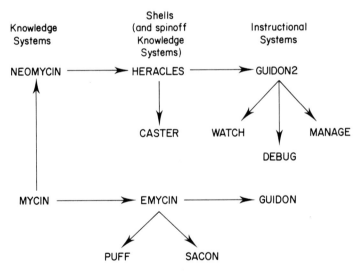

Figure 1   A map showing the evolution of research. NEOMYCIN, a reconfiguration of MYCIN, is also a medical consultation program. Research from both programs follows a parallel path: generalizing the system into a knowledge system shell, applying the shell to develop knowledge systems in other domains (PUFF, SACON, CASTER), and developing an instructional system compatible with any knowledge system developed from the shell. This chapter describes the key ideas in GUIDON and the upper path of research.

represented in a well-structured language, separate from the medical knowledge. This facilitates explanation and student modelling.

HERACLES is the generalization of NEOMYCIN, standing for Heuristic Classification Shell (Clancey, 1985). By analogy with EMYCIN, we might say that HERACLES is "NEOMYCIN without the knowledge," but there is a big difference. We retain NEOMYCIN's diagnostic procedure; it is reused and adapted in new applications.

GUIDON2 is a set of tutoring systems that work for any HERACLES knowledge base; it is currently being developed with NEOMYCIN. In the GUIDON2 family of programs, we are exploring different forms of student and teacher initiative (Clancey, 1984a).

3 GUIDON: "TRANSFER OF EXPERTISE"

In GUIDON (see Figure 2), we held the MYCIN knowledge base constant and considered the additional knowledge about teaching that would provide a good tutoring system. We were especially interested in teaching from different knowledge bases using one program. This exciting idea was motivated by the EMYCIN design that allows putting in a different knowledge base and carrying on a consultation in a different domain. GUIDON's teaching knowledge is separate from the medical knowledge; therefore it is reusable and adaptable to new applications. This is a significant advance over traditional computer-assisted instruction methodology that requires writing a new program for each case to be discussed. We now have two kinds of generality. First, this tutor can discuss any case that MYCIN can solve. Secondly, we can swap in a different knowledge base and discuss cases in another domain. The separation of the knowledge base from the procedures that interpret it is the important idea.

4 DISCOURSE PROCEDURES: ALTERNATIVE DIALOGUES AND TRANSITIONS

Another successful aspect of GUIDON's design is the representation of the tutoring knowledge. This knowledge can be shown as a transition diagram, where each node represents a situation within a tutoring dialogue (see Figure 3). The program has a list of rules for reasoning about what to do at each step. For example, when GUIDON detects that a goal under consideration has been determined (from MYCIN's point of view), it selects from three alternative transitions: presenting a conclusion, presenting a summary, and asking the student to make a hypothesis (Clancey, 1979b).

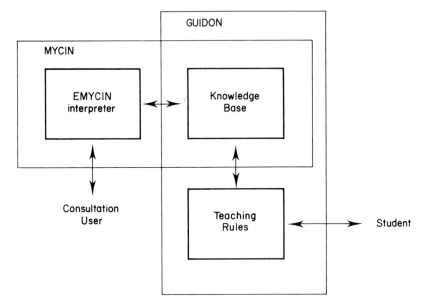

Figure 2   Guidon teaches from MYCIN's knowledge base. The MYCIN knowledge base, combined with an interpreter for applying rules and interacting with a user, forms a consultation program. The same knowledge base is interpreted by teaching rules for interacting with a student in a case-method dialogue, constituting the GUIDON instructional program. MYCIN's rules are ranked, relating them to years of medical experience (for modelling the student and selecting new material for the student to learn). Additional annotations indicate subtype and causal relations among rule clauses and relate the rules to a general description of the infectious process, which is used by GUIDON to provide more concise explanations of MYCIN's reasoning. Within a few limits, GUIDON can discuss any case that MYCIN or any EMYCIN program can solve. In conventional computer-assisted instruction, a new program is written for each case.

Each of these transitions is encoded by rules called tutoring or t-rules, numbering about 200. We built the system very much like a traditional expert system, running cases and incrementally modifying the t-rules. When the program said something inappropriate, we modified t-rule conditions to change when that kind of remark would occur. Similarly, GUIDON sometimes missed an opportunity to say something interesting. For example, if a fact can be inferred by definition, there is no need to go through a long dialogue, gathering data and forming hypotheses and so on; we added t-rules to deal with this case, leading the program to give MYCIN's conclusion or to ask for the student's conclusion, depending on the model of what the student knows and the goals for the dialogue.

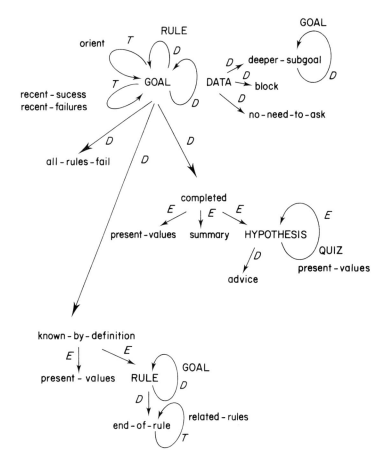

Figure 3   Dialogue transition diagram. Each node stands for a situation in a case-method dialogue, represented in GUIDON as a stylized procedure of ordered rules or a rule set, totalling 200 rules in 40 situations. For example, in pursuing a goal explicitly agreed upon by student and program, the student can request more case data. GUIDON can recognize the data as relevant to a subgoal, provide it as a set of related information (block), or determine that there is no need to ask (perhaps because the requested data can be inferred from known information). Arrows that loop back indicate that a situation may occur iteratively or recursively. For example, several related rules might be presented after a given rule is discussed. The italicized labels indicate the basis for a transition: Economy, Domain logic and Tutoring goals.

This works rather well, though it lacks a theoretical foundation. Arbitrary strategies are encoded in the tutoring rules. Building on the t-rule idea, Beverly Woolf has added a hierarchical structure to the alternative dialogues, couched in the terminology of discourse analysis. This represents in a more principled way the choices the program is making. (See Woolf and McDonald (1984).)

5   OVERLAY MODEL: EVALUATING A STUDENT HYPOTHESIS

Perhaps the most interesting reasoning in GUIDON involves evaluating a student's partial solution (see Figure 4) (Clancey, 1979c). In this example, the student says that the organisms causing the infection could be *Diplococcus, Pseudomonas,* or *Neisseria.* The program looks at MYCIN's rules and sets up a consistent mapping. It uses double evidence, a history of interaction with the student, and a measure of rule difficulty to construct a consistent model.

For example, suppose the student mentions *Neisseria.* If MYCIN's rules argue for and against this hypothesis then the student might know the positive evidence, but not the negative evidence. GUIDON concludes in a similar way that *Pseudomonas* is believed by the student because the patient is burned—but not because of the white blood count (WBC) or because the infection occurred in the hospital (nosocomial)—given that the student did not mention the two other diagnoses associated with this evidence (*E. coli* and *Klebsiella*). It is a straightforward, logical analysis, demonstrating the value of production rules for indexing how facts are concluded and used in a program.

6   THE SACON TUTORIAL:
EXPERIMENTING WITH OTHER KNOWLEDGE
BASES

Figure 5 shows an excerpt from a dialogue with GUIDON using the SACON knowledge base. It graphically demonstrates the value of keeping GUIDON's tutoring knowledge general. The same tutoring program can interpret SACON's rules and discuss a structural analysis problem with a student.

This interaction plausibly captures some of the behaviour that we would like to see in a teaching program. It was produced entirely by t-rules that were written for medical examples and then just plugged into SACON. It

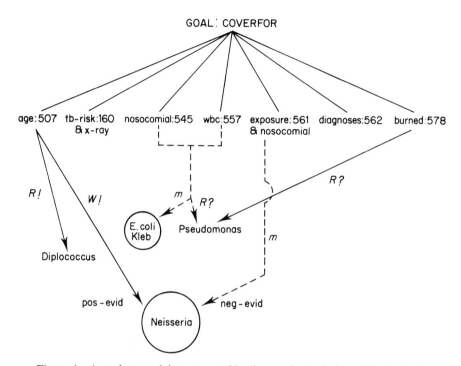

Figure 4 A student model constructed by the overlay technique. The student states that the organisms causing the infection might be *Diplococcus, Pseudomonas* or *Neisseria*. MYCIN rules that conclude about the organisms causing the infection are shown with associated patient data. For example, rule 507 states that if the patient is between 15 and 55 years old then *Diplococcus* and *Neisseria* are organisms that therapy should cover. Circled values are missing from the student's hypothesis (for example *E. coli*) or wrongly stated (for example *Neisseria*). Dotted lines lead from rules the student probably did not use. m = evidence link that the tutor believes is unknown to the student. R and W = links to the right and wrong values the tutor believes are known by the student; ! = a unique explanation; the tutor knows of no other evidence at this time. ? = questionable, the tutor is uncertain about which evidence was considered by the student. For example, R? means that the student stated this value, it is correct, and more than one MYCIN rule supplies evidence for it.

We must now determine whether the shape of the floor section
(SUB-STRUCTURE-1) is one of : the surface shapes.

Here is some relevent data you could have asked for : the
geometry of the floor section is planar, the modelling
dimensionality of the floor section is 2, and continuum is one
of the constructions of the floor section.

What does this tell you about the shape of the floor section?
** HELP

Can you conclude that the shape of the floor section is
(select from the following):

       1) beam — suggestive evidence (.62)

       2) semimonococque — suggestive evidence (.62)

       3) not shell — strongly suggestive evidence (-.95)

       4) plate — with certainty (1.0)

** 4
Yes, that's right (see RULE100).

Figure 5   Excerpt of GUIDON tutorial using SACON knowledge base. GUIDON
encounters an incomplete subgoal in a rule that it is trying to discuss with the student.
A t-rule in the procedure for discussing an incomplete subgoal finds that the subgoal
can be inferred by a definitional rule and then invokes the procedure for discussing
definitional rules. GUIDON gives the student new information (the geometry,
dimensionality and construction of the floor section), and then asks him if he can now
infer the shape of the floor section. The student asks for help, and GUIDON converts
the question into a multiple choice. Reasoning about the current problem state, text
generation and quiz construction and evaluation are all accomplished by general
t-rules that were originally developed in the context of a medical-diagnosis dialogue.

took about an hour to make it all work, with a few modifications to cope with syntactic variations in SACON's rules. For further discussion and an example from PUFF see Clancey (1979a, 1982).

7 INADEQUACY OF MYCIN: IMPLICIT, NONPSYCHOLOGICAL STRATEGY

We now consider the analysis that led to NEOMYCIN. What problems arise in using MYCIN for teaching?

Figure 6 shows an excerpt from an experiment with GUIDON; this was a pivotal example for me. GUIDON indicates that the age of the patient, 34,

```
What are the organisms which might be causing the infection ?

>> NEISSERIA - MENINGITIDIS


What facts about this case tell you that Neisseria – meningitidis

is one of the organisms which might be causing the infection ?

>> AGE

>>


-> The fact that the age of Pt538 is 34 years is not evidence for the

conclusion that Neisseria - meningitidis is one of the organisms which

might be causing the infection.


Do you have a question ?

**
```

Figure 6   Problematic excerpt of GUIDON tutorial using MYCIN knowledge base. The student offers to state a partial solution (student input follows ">>"). The program responds by rephrasing the current topic as a question, "What are the organisms which might be causing the infection?" When the student says *Neisseria*, GUIDON checks and finds that MYCIN has made no conclusion at all up to this point. A t-rule prompts the student to justify his hypothesis. The student says that he is considering the age of the patient. It is a lost cause for the student, however; whatever he says next, GUIDON will reply, "No, that's not sufficient", because MYCIN has made no conclusion. At the final prompt, the student can review the available data and MYCIN's reasoning, if desired. In fact, the student's hypothesis is reasonable, but GUIDON would need to know how MYCIN's rules are constructed and a different model of reasoning to understand why the student did something different.

is not evidence for *Neisseria*. However, a rule in the knowledge base says "If the age of the patient is between 15 and 55 then Neisseria is one of the organisms." I was rather surprised. This rule is consistent with the student's hypothesis and justification.

The problem is that some of the information in the premise of this rule is still unknown, so MYCIN cannot apply the rule. Specifically, there is no indication that the age of the patient is causally related to *Neisseria* and that the age would be sufficient in itself to suggest this conclusion. GUIDON has no way of knowing that one of the clauses is more directly associated with the conclusion than any other clause. To make this clear, consider another rule: "If the age of the patient is greater than 17 and the patient is an alcoholic then *Diplococcus* might be causing the infection." Considering this rule and knowing only that the patient is 34 would not make one think of *Diplococcus*. Here the age clause controls the application of the rule, preventing the program from asking whether a child is an alcoholic. The causal relation is between alcoholism and *Diplococcus*.

The student's knowledge and the procedure being used are very different from MYCIN. The student has probably formed a hypothesis just from learning the age of the patient and some tentative information (not shown in the excerpt) that suggests meningitis. MYCIN will only conclude *Neisseria* when, from its point of view, it has exhaustively considered the evidence for meningitis and considered whether it is bacterial and so on. MYCIN does a top-down search through the set of diseases, but the student has "triggered" meningitis from just partial information, with no direct evidence for an infection or bacterial infection at all.

To respond properly to the student, we would have to represent the association between age and *Neisseria* explicitly and separate out the search procedure. However, to recognize what strategy the student is following, we would have to encode a different strategy, expressing why it makes sense to think about *Neisseria* just knowing the age and some tentative evidence for meningitis. The very idea of a hypothesis is foreign to MYCIN.

8   THE IDEA OF STRATEGY: FROM "TRACING A PARAMETER" TO "FOCUSING ON A HYPOTHESIS"

Figures 7 and 8 illustrate that at a certain level MYCIN's reasoning is arbitrary, lacking the focus on hypotheses we find in people. People group their questions logically; they do not jump around without reason. However, MYCIN does not focus on a particular hypothesis as it goes down through its (implicit) tree of diseases. When it considers types of meningitis or organisms, the types are considered arbitrarily, based on the order in which

32) Does J. Smith have a history of NEUROSURGERY ?

** NO

33) Does J. Smith live in a crowded environment ?

** NO

34) Do you suspect recent alcoholic history in J. Smith ?

** NO

35) Is the meningitis a hospital - acquired infection ?

** YES

36) Is J. Smith's clinical history consistent with EPIGLOTTITIS ?

** NO

37) Is J. Smith's clinical history consistent with OTITIS - MEDIA ?

** NO

38) Has J. Smith ever undergone splenectomy ?

** NO

39) Is J. Smith a burn patient ?

** YES

Figure 7   Sequence of data requests from MYCIN consultation.

rules were entered into the program. The program proceeds systematically from infection to meningitis to bacterial meningitis to organism, but the process is unordered at each level of refinement with regard to children. This is because the goals that MYCIN pursues are always more general than the conclusions in the rules being applied. In order to teach a procedure to a student and to recognize what the student is doing, we need a program that will deliberately focus on particular diseases and that will be able to articulate its focusing principle.

This analysis of MYCIN was directly inspired by a study of strategy by Brown (Brown *et al.*, 1977). He points out that a problem solver does not apply algebraic operators randomly when simplifying an equation; there is some logic behind each choice, describing a line of reasoning. Applying this analysis to MYCIN, I understood for the first time how a strategy reasons about operators or problem-solving methods, focusing their application. In MYCIN, a rule corresponds to an operator, and problem solving involves some strategy for selecting which rule to apply. Specifically, the diagnostic reasoning is usefully controlled by *focusing* data requests and hypothesis testing.

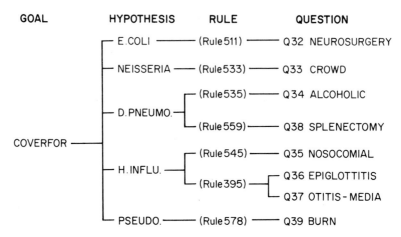

| GOAL | HYPOTHESIS | RULE | QUESTION |

Figure 8   Relating MYCIN's data requests to organism hypotheses. MYCIN's questions, shown in Figure 7, have been reordered according to the hypotheses that motivate them. For example, question 33 about living in a crowded environment is asked in order to apply rule 533, which concludes *Neisseria*. All of the questions pertain to the same goal—determining what organisms therapy should cover—but the rules conclude about different organisms. Neither the sequence of rule applications nor the questions are sorted by organism. Questions 34 and 38 pertain to *Diplococcus-pneumoniae*, with three intervening questions pertaining to *Hemophilus-influenzae*. Thus, in pursuing a goal, MYCIN's reasoning is unfocused at the level of possible values for the goal—in this case organisms that might be causing the infection.

From this perspective, it can be seen that describing strategy only in terms of domain rule ordering, as in Davis's original conception of metarules, is inadequate. The problem is that there is an implicit, undisciplined mapping between medical knowledge and MYCIN's parameter-value language. For example, if MYCIN's diseases were all represented by individual parameters (rather than by a general parameter called "coverfor" with organisms as values) then the normal back-chaining process would make the reasoning focused. Thus a strategy can be implicitly encoded in the relation between parameters and their values. Recalling the age–alcoholism example, a strategy is already implicitly coded in the ordering of rule clauses. Before metarules can be written to systematically control domain rules according to a hypothesize-and-test strategy, conventions must be established for distinguishing between data and hypothesis parameters and consistently encoding causal and subtype relationships among them.

9 THE TETRACYCLINE RULE: STRUCTURE, STRATEGY AND SUPPORT

This brings us to about 1980, when I studied MYCIN's 400 rules to determine how they might be reconfigured for use in teaching. Up to this point, in constructing GUIDON, only limited annotations had been added to the original rule set. Now any change at all would be allowed.

Early on, I developed a framework that turned out to be very useful in protocol analysis. In this framework, explanations are analysed according to *knowledge roles*; how knowledge is used in relation to other knowledge (Clancey, 1983a) (see Figure 9):

the *heuristic rule*: a relation between data and diagnoses, and therapies;

structure: subsumption relations among data, diagnoses, and therapies;

strategy: the procedure for applying rules;

support: the justification for rules.

As an example of structural knowledge, one might think of "SSS" when trying to remember this framework.

To understand the different kinds of knowledge here, suppose that one has a patient who is four years old. One would probably say "Well I'm not going to prescribe tetracycline." However, that is not a very good model of how a physician reasons; this would be a strange conclusion to make right at the beginning. Just as there is a logic for requesting data and for focusing on hypotheses, there is a logic for making assertions given available information. All together, we call this logic the *inference procedure*. (In the literature, it is also called *control knowledge* or, more specifically, *diagnostic strategy*. To emphasize the reasoning about control alternatives, the term managerial strategy or metastrategy is also used, particularly in the education literature (Schoenfeld, 1981).)

By strategy, I mean the general goal that leads the physician to remember a heuristic rule. For example, when is it important to remember not to prescribe tetracycline? Obviously the physician must take this into account when prescribing therapy.

By structural knowledge, I mean the relations by which heuristic rules are indexed and subsequently controlled. In general, this involves categorizing the facts the rules use (for example, patient factors) and the facts they conclude about (for example, therapies).

By support knowledge, I mean the justification for the rule. Why would one not prescribe tetracycline to someone less than seven years old? Here we

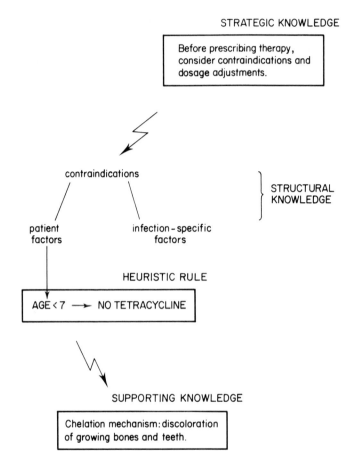

Figure 9   Analysis of knowledge relating to MYCIN's tetracycline rule. The rule states, "If the patient is less than seven years old then remove tetracycline from the list of drugs under consideration." Relation of age to other contraindication factors (such as whether the patient is pregnant), justification for the rule, and time when it would be considered are relevant to explaining this rule, but are not represented in MYCIN. Making explicit this structural, support, and strategic knowledge enhances our ability to understand and modify MYCIN.

have a chemical process, a chelation mechanism, that results in the molecule binding to the growing teeth and bones, and a social consideration that attests that people do not want to have discolored teeth. This is a very interesting justification, because it shows that giving tetracycline might save the patient's life, even though it might have an undesirable side effect. This is important to know if tetracycline is the only drug available. It is a nice example of why it is useful to know the justification of a rule—so that one can violate the rule and know what the consequences will be.

Generally, this figure suggests a framework for understanding an expert's explanations. When I ask a physician who is solving a problem "Why did you ask that question?" I classify the answer into one of these categories. If the physician tells me "Well I'm not going to prescribe tetracycline because the age is less than seven," I am being told what assertions were made from given information (that is, a heuristic rule). If I ask the physician why, and I get an explanation having to do with chelation, then I am being given the justification for the assertion (that is, support). If the physician says "This is just one of the contraindications I'm going to consider," then I am being told about the organization of his knowledge, the categories used for focusing (that is, structure). Finally, if the physician tells me when contraindications are considered and how each type is considered, then I am getting the inference procedure (that is, strategy). I tried to consistently apply this analysis when working with physicians, particularly to focus their explanations on strategy and avoid the bottomless pit of support explanations.

NEOMYCIN research focuses on representing strategy and structure, because this is the deficiency of GUIDON we most want to improve. We also sense that structure and strategy are at the top of a pyramid of knowledge and are more limited in nature. A research effort focused on them is attractive because this knowledge conceivably might be carefully and exhaustively explored.

10   THE BECKETT TAPES: AN ARTICULATE TEACHER

In 1980, Reed Letsinger and I worked with Tim Beckett, M.D., who was recommended by Ted Shortliffe and who turned out to be a rather fortunate choice. Beckett was known at Stanford for being a good teacher. He could articulate general principles for reasoning very well. He did not just say what it is one should ask about or what one's conclusions should be—he was able to speak in general terms about how one should think.

We taped interviews and classroom interactions, and transcribed and studied them (Clancey, 1984b). In one interaction, Beckett interrupts a student who is examining a patient played by another student:

> When you ask these questions about whether gargling makes it better or worse, or whether it's better certain times of the day, are you thinking about how that's going to help you move down different diagnoses? . . . ask a couple of general questions maybe that could lead you into other areas to follow up on, rather than zeroing in.

Note the absence of medical terms in his strategic advice. Again:

> We're talking at the top of infections, but before we go down infections, are
> there any other things you can think of? The mistake you don't want to make
> is leaving out the important things on top.

We repeatedly heard these general statements—move down different diagnoses, ask general questions, do not leave out important things on top. These were the strategic gems—better than I could have expected—that would allow us to construct NEOMYCIN. Essentially, I saw the opportunity here for a program that would talk procedurally about these operations: moving down different diagnoses, asking general questions, not leaving out important things at the top. This procedure is separate from the medical knowledge, describing how the medical knowledge is searched. That is, the statement of strategy does not directly mention domain terms; it is abstract.

In Beckett's explanations, we see regular switching back and forth between the concrete situation and a generalization:

> Ask it very generally, like "Have you had any major problems, or are you on
> any medication?" Those types of general questions are important to ask early
> on because they really tell you how soon you can focus down.
>   You have to think of some of the common things, but at the same time you
> have to think of some of the serious things that may not be common. What is a
> serious infection that can get in your throat?

This last example shows most clearly my model of inference in NEOMY-CIN.

Refining the diagnosis and thinking of some of the common things, the physician looks into the domain model and asks, "What is a serious infection that can get in the throat?" and "What are some of the common things that could cause it?" This is how the metarules in NEOMYCIN work.

As confirmation of the potential effectiveness of Beckett's approach, we analysed his best student's reasoning. The student obviously followed the procedure Beckett articulated in class. Of course, not all students would necessarily find Beckett's teaching approach to be useful, but we had an existence proof and clear statements of at least one diagnostic procedure, so we wrote the approach down.

About this time, we also had the first glimmer of how an explicit procedure could help a student learn relevant medical knowledge. When I had Beckett present problems to me, I often lacked the medical knowledge to carry out the procedure. However, knowing the procedure, I found that I could ask reasonably intelligent questions: "I know I should be thinking about some of the serious and common causes of this disease, but I don't know what they are." This has evolved into our version of explanation-based learning (see

Section 20 below). We also applied the procedure to an analysis of Beckett's interruptions of students: given this model of his reasoning, could we use it to infer his strategy for interrupting students and providing assistance? The most telling example, occurring just before Beckett asks the question about sore throats shown here, is analysed in Clancey (1984c).

11   NEOMYCIN: SEPARATING THE MEDICAL KNOWLEDGE FROM THE DIAGNOSTIC PROCEDURE

Figure 10 shows the architecture of NEOMYCIN, illustrating the idea of separating the diagnostic inference procedure (control knowledge) from the medical knowledge. Crucially, both are represented in well-structured languages so that they can be reasoned about by the explanation, knowledge-acquisition, and student-modelling programs (Clancey 1983b).

Davis's conception of metarules for expressing strategy inspired this design. However, TEIRESIA's metarules compose domain facts with procedure, just like MYCIN's rules (Clancey, 1983a). NEOMYCIN's metarules mention no domain terms. Moreover, they constitute a coherent procedure that completely controls every data request and every inference; so there is no back-chaining of rules at all.

As is apparent in Beckett's generalizations, we can think of this procedure as "asking questions of the domain model". The language of relations used in metarules corresponds to the propositions in the knowledge base. These

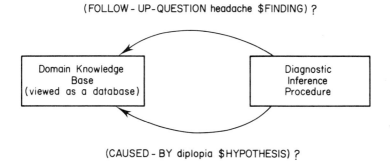

Figure 10   Architecture of NEOMYCIN. An inference procedure queries the knowledge base, relating findings and hypotheses to one another in order to make a diagnosis. For example, given that the patient has diplopia (double vision), the program asks the knowledge base what could cause it. One or more hypotheses might be returned, which the inference procedure will proceed to discriminate, test and refine, making further inquiries about disease and symptom relations.

relations impose a classification on domain terms. This is what I called structural knowledge in the tetracycline analysis.

Given a hypothesis, the program asks, "What is a common cause of this disorder?" The program then looks up this relation in the knowledge base. In this sense, the inference procedure is interpreting the domain model. If we compiled the procedure—instantiating and composing it with respect to a particular knowledge base—we should get something very similar to MYCIN's rules. In making this abstraction, stating these general rules, I am not claiming that people reason through general statements every time or even realize that these patterns exist. In particular, reasoning categorically probably involves automatic processes of memory. Some distinctions, such as considering causal prerequisites of diseases before effects, might be regularities that the physician does not consciously realize (Clancey, 1984c).

I now believe that these domain relations are in large part what we want to teach students, as generalizations, to help them learn about new diseases. In describing how to focus reasoning, we are indirectly saying how knowledge should be practically organized. For example, we say "You should think in terms of common causes and serious causes." That is much more informative than saying, "You should form a hypothesis" or "You should reason forward." We hypothesize that the procedure is automatic once you have the knowledge. A medical student might not have to be told to refine hypotheses, but he† has to be taught the subtypes of fungal meningitis.

12   THE DISEASE TAXONOMY: SEARCHING AN ABNORMAL PROCESS CLASSIFICATION

There are several dimensions for describing NEOMYCIN's reasoning: psychological aspects of memory and attention, AI representation and control techniques, and aspects of medical causal reasoning. Figure 11 provides one perspective in which these dimensions come together.

The main part of the knowledge base is a taxonomy of diseases or, more generally, a classification of abnormal processes. Each disease describes a process, something that has happened to the patient in the past, accounting for the set of observed manifestations. In general, there can be many different taxonomies, orthogonal and tangled.

How do we know that a given taxonomy is complete? This important question did not explicitly arise in MYCIN research because we did not isolate the disease taxonomy as a separate object of study. We now hypothesize that the physician's classification, particularly its level of specificity, depends on how it will be used. The physician is not involved in

---

† Masculine expressions in this chapter are used as generic terms—no bias is intended.

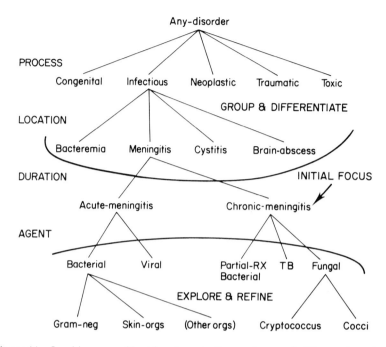

Figure 11   Looking up and looking down in diagnostic search. Disease knowledge is represented as a taxonomy of processes. At the highest level are internal aberations in structure building or maintenance (for example congenital diseases) and processes involving environmental interaction (for example infection, trauma). Processes are specialized here by location, temporal extent, and specific agent. The taxonomy is overprinted to show hypothetically how it might be searched. Initial information—chief complaints—triggers some hypothesis, shown arbitrarily here in the middle of the disease taxonomy. Two operations follow: (1) looking up, thinking of the high-level categories and discriminating among them (GROUP-AND-DIFFEREN-TIATE) and (2) looking down to refine hypotheses when distinctions are important for selecting therapy (EXPLORE-AND-REFINE). This is to be contrasted with an exhaustive, top-down search, which a large knowledge base makes impractical.

scientific research here; what goes into the taxonomy is based on distinctions useful for selecting therapy. For example, NEOMYCIN makes no attempt to determine precisely which type of viral meningitis the patient has. The reason is that they are all treated in the same way—with a lot of aspirin and orange juice—and it is irrelevant to resolve the cause any further. Thus, NEOMYCIN's disease taxonomy deliberately remains a partial model of abnormal processes within this area of medicine.

Another part of the knowledge base, the causal network, is discussed in the context of CASTER (see Section 19 below).

Diagnostic Task Tree

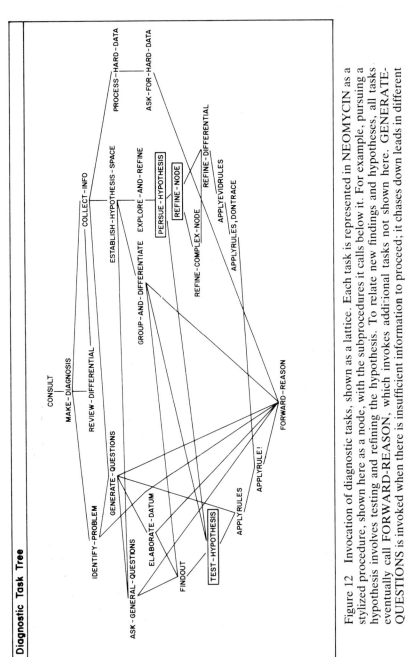

Figure 12 Invocation of diagnostic tasks, shown as a lattice. Each task is represented in NEOMYCIN as a stylized procedure, shown here as a node, with the subprocedures it calls below it. For example, pursuing a hypothesis involves testing and refining the hypothesis. To relate new findings and hypotheses, all tasks eventually call FORWARD-REASON, which invokes additional tasks not shown here. GENERATE-QUESTIONS is invoked when there is insufficient information to proceed; it chases down leads in different ways, thus explaining its central position. Note also that FINDOUT calls TEST-HYPOTHESIS so that domain rules will be selected deliberately, replacing the back chaining of EMYCIN. Using this representation for explanation and student modelling requires additional knowledge about task preconditions and postconditions and how metarules controlling task invocation are ordered.

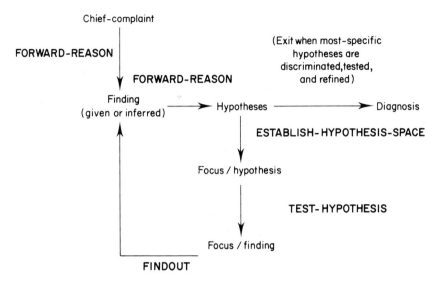

Figure 13 Predominant focus shifts in Diagnosis. This diagram simplifies the dynamic flow of control between tasks, revealing how findings and hypotheses are related. New findings suggest new hypotheses and support existing hypotheses (FORWARD-REASON); a decision is made to focus on a particular HYPO-THESIS (ESTABLISH-HYPOTHESIS-SPACE); a decision is made to focus on a particular finding (TEST-HYPOTHESIS); the implications of the new information are considered, and so on. In contrast, MYCIN does not change its goals on the basis of new data or deliberately order the goals and data it will pursue. Accomplishing this by abstract metarules (not specifying domain terms) requires explicitly representing relations between findings and hypotheses, on the basis of which they will be selectively considered. Tasks (appearing in bold italics) can be related to Figure 12, which shows the subtasks they invoke. In practice, ESTABLISH-HYPOTHESIS-SPACE is only invoked if there is reason to stop pursuing the current HYPOTHESIS. Criteria for applying domain rules in FORWARD-REASON are complex. For example, new findings are related to hypotheses "in focus"; if a new HYPOTHESIS "explains" the known findings at least as well as existing hypotheses, it is considered; new hypotheses are related to previously known findings, etc. The program stops when its differential, the list of most-specific hypotheses under consideration, has been discriminated, tested and refined.

13   THE DIAGNOSTIC PROCEDURE: SEARCH OPERATORS AND CONSTRAINTS

The overall diagnostic strategy or inference procedure is a program consisting of a set of subprocedures as shown in Figure 12.

Each procedure is represented as a set of ordered and controlled conditional statements called *metarules*. Rules provide a uniform, well-structured language. Although experienced programmers can read a LISP encoding of the diagnostic procedure easily enough, it is difficult to write a program that can understand arbitrary LISP code. Too much of the design is implicit and not available for explanation. Therefore we devised a highly structured representation, organized around the idea of rule sets, with every "loop" encoded as a separate task (subprocedure) and the control of rules stated declaratively (simple versus iterative, try-all versus stop-on-success). Each task has a typed focus (argument), local variables, and an explicit "end condition" (equivalent to the "while" or "until" condition of a loop). Making every program statement a rule facilitates interpreted control, annotation and record keeping.

The overall design is similar to LOOPS, which evolved at the same time as NEOMYCIN. However, NEOMYCIN's metarules use variables, rather than domain terms. Also, the end condition, inherited by task invocation, enables a procedure anywhere on the current stack to regain control, either because its goal is completed or there is reason to reconsider how its subgoals are being accomplished. Figure 13 shows the flow of control in terms of focus changes.

In writing down the diagnostic procedure as rules, we are following the same methodology used in developing MYCIN and GUIDON. With the knowledge expressed in a disciplined way, it now becomes possible to study patterns and to consider how the knowledge could be derived. Such implications are too numerous to recapitulate here. The interested reader will find the metarules listed in Clancey (1984c), with a discussion of the procedure in terms of *operators* and the cognitive, social, mathematical, and case population *constraints* implicit in the rules. The next section considers the procedure as a *grammar*.

14   IMAGE AND ODYSSEUS: PARSING THE DIAGNOSTIC PROCESS

Given the abstract nature of the tasks and metarules, they can be viewed as a kind of grammar for parsing a problem solver's sequence of requests for data. Such an analysis is shown in Figure 14, the picture I had in the back of

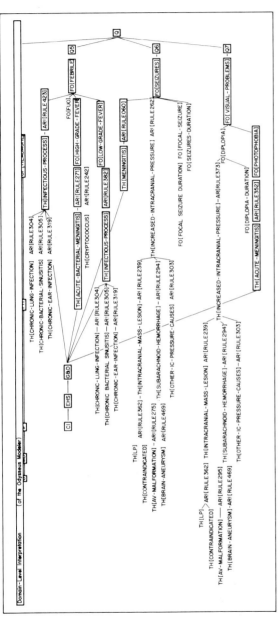

Figure 14   ODYSSEUS's parse of a student's data requests. Given a sequence of requests for patient data, listed on the right side of the figure (Q5, Q6, Q7), the program indicates all of the alternative justifications for why a question might have been asked. For example, the student's query about seizures (FINDOUT/Seizures, Q6) might have been asked to determine whether the disease is caused by an Intracranial Mass Lesion, Subarachnoid Hemorrhage, and so on. The program indicates by boxing nodes, combining its bottom-up analysis with a top-down parse, that this question relates to meningitis (TEST-HYPOTHESIS/Meningitis), as part of the process of discriminating hypotheses (GROUP-AND-DIFFERENTIATE). Thus the problem state (hypotheses under consideration) and the tasks interact to explain finding requests in terms of a logic for focusing on hypotheses and findings. Note that by the same analysis the question about a fever (Febrile, Q5) has three consistent interpretations. This kind of analysis is not possible using MYCIN because, first, its reasoning did not involve "looking up" from "triggered hypotheses" and, secondly, its inference procedure is represented behaviourally as specific productions. A functional representation, as diagnostic tasks, relates surface behaviour to abstract goals, which can be accomplished in multiple ways.

my mind in about 1980 when I wanted some way for GUIDON to reason about what a student was doing. An interpretation of a student's partial solution provides a good basis for assisting him when he does not know what to do next. Such an interpretation is also a source of information for relating a student's explicitly stated diagnosis to a model of his domain knowledge. As a contextual analysis, it potentially shortens the interactive dialogue that might be necessary to confirm the student's understanding.

Bob London, David Wilkins and I have been developing student-modelling programs with the common goal of using NEOMYCIN's diagnostic procedure to interpret a sequence of student requests for data. London has followed a top-down approach in the IMAGE program (London and Clancey, 1982); Wilkins's ODYSSEUS program uses exhaustive, bottom-up reasoning (Wilkins et al., 1986). Evaluation of these alternative approaches is in progress.

Figure 14 shows a parse of reasoning produced by the ODYSSEUS program. We are testing this program with "synthetic" students, systematically varying NEOMYCIN and comparing ODYSSEUS's interpretation with the known variations in the knowledge base. Another application is to give ODYSSEUS a sequence of data requests and to have it determine what knowledge base changes would be required to produce this sequence, consistent with the inference procedure. We believe that the simple classification nature of the inference procedure makes this approach plausible. We are developing this capability for a tutoring program called GUIDON-DEBUG (Clancey, et al., 1986). The same program could be used for knowledge acquisition.

15   NEOXPL: STRATEGIC EXPLANATION

Using NEOMYCIN's well-structured representation, Diane Hasling, Glenn Rennels and I (1983) reformulated MYCIN's WHY/HOW explanations in terms of metarules and tasks. Figure 15 shows how procedural information is available prosaically (by asking WHY) or through the task stack.

Although our WHY/HOW system goes up the goal stack in a way similar to MYCIN's explanation program, this new program takes advantage of the structured representation to be more selective about what it says. In particular, it looks at the focus of a task to determine whether to mention the task as it goes up the stack. A focus can be one of three basic terms—a finding, a hypothesis or a domain rule—or a list of these. If the focus is a rule or list of rules, the explanation program skips over the task (for example, APPLYRULES). The task is mentioned if its metarule establishes a new focus, such as going from a list of hypotheses to a single hypothesis

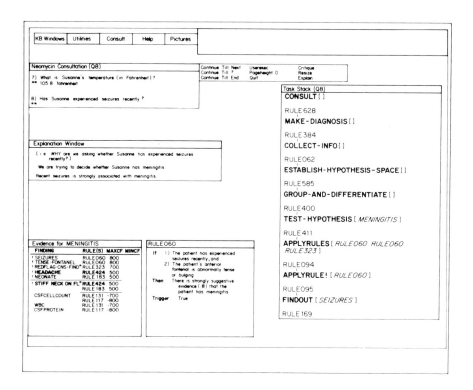

Figure 15 Multiple views of the diagnostic process: question, evidence relation, task stack, metarules, and prosaic condensation. When NEOMYCIN asked about seizures (question 8), the user selected a subitem in the KB WINDOWS menu, which caused the *task stack*—the current line of reasoning—to be displayed. The rule above a task is the metarule that invoked it; thus rule 400 selected meningitis as a focus, invoking TEST-HYPOTHESIS with it as an argument. Selecting meningitis in this window caused the table in the lower left to be displayed. Here bold type indicates positive findings and successfully applied rules. Underlined items correspond to negative findings and failed rules. Thus the patient is not a neonate; rule 424 succeeded. Arrows preceding a finding indicate that the finding is in a triggering relation with the hypothesis. For example, the headache volunteered in the chief complaint caused the program to try to apply rule 424. When the user selected EXPLAIN in the menu adjacent to the consultation typescript, the program summarized the line of reasoning, skipping over "uninteresting" tasks.

(GROUP-AND-DIFFERENTIATE) or from a hypothesis to a rule (TEST-HYPOTHESIS). This turns out to be a good explanation heuristic. A new explanation system under development uses the propositional encoding of the metarules (described later) to select particular rule-premise clauses to mention.

16   MRS/NEOMYCIN: FROM FINDINGS AND HYPOTHESES TO RELATIONS

Student modelling, debugging and explanation require that our programs reason about the premises of metarules, particularly to determine which domain facts matched and why rules failed. Originally, metarule premises were encoded in LISP. In a hybrid system called MRS/NEOMYCIN, Conrad Bock and I represented metarule premises in MRS, a logic-programming language that provides a framework for multiple representations of knowledge and control of reasoning (Genesereth and Smith 1982). Bock also recoded the interpreter in MRS rules, and placed a simple deliberation-action loop at the top (Clancey and Bock 1982). Unfortunately, recoding the interpreter slowed down the program by an order of magnitude and made the procedure too obscure to read or maintain. In the current version of the program, we retain the original interpreter and use a variant of MRS as a specification language for metarule premises, which are compiled into LISP. This provides the well-structured, uniform language our modelling and explanation programs require without sacrificing runtime efficiency. Figure 16 illustrates how MRS is used in the metarules and definitional rules for relations.

Figure 16   Propositional representation of a metarule. This is one of six metarules for accomplishing the task PROCESS-FINDING, which is invoked whenever a new finding becomes known. The metarule detects that this finding is serious and has to be explained (a red-flag finding), or it is something that's not currently explained by the set of possibilities under consideration. The program gathers up the *trigger rules*—automatic inferences—and tries to apply them. The idea is that if the finding does not always have to be explained and it is explained by hypotheses that were already triggered, one should not trigger a new hypothesis. For example, if the patient has a headache, and other evidence suggests meningitis, which would explain the headache, there is no need to consider other explanations of the headache. Intermediate relations, such as EXPLAINEDBY, are defined by other rules (simplified here). All pattern variables in these rules are instantiated as domain rules or terms. All expressions are implicitly universally quantified.

TASK: PROCESS-FINDING
FOCUS: $FINDING

Metarule

IF: (AND (OR (FINDINGTYPE $FINDING REDFLAG)
               (NOT (DIFF. EXPLAINED $FINDING)))
          (MAKESET (TRIGGERS? $FINDING $RULE)
               RULELST))
THEN: (TASK APPLYRULES RULELST)
*If the finding must always be explained or
it is not currently explained by the differential,
then trigger hypotheses that explain it.*

Definitional relation rules

IF: (AND (DIFFERENTIAL $HYP)
          (EXPLAINEDBY $FINDING $HYP))
THEN: (DIFF. EXPLAINED $FINDING)
*A finding is explained by the differential
if it is explained by some hypothesis in the differential.*

IF: (OR (CAUSED-BY $F $H)
        (AND (TYPE $H $PARENT)
             (EXPLAINEDBY $F $PARENT)))
THEN: (EXPLAINEDBY $F $H)
*A finding is explained by a hypothesis
if it is caused by the hypothesis or by some more general category.*

Figure 16

Primitive relations are compiled as direct LISP operations, using explicit declarations about how propositions are represented in the LISP-encoded knowledge base. For example, a **TYPE** proposition is represented as a property list structure, so the compiler substitutes a **GETPROP**, an **ASSOC**, or more complex loop construction, depending on what terms are known when the proposition is encountered in the metarule. In encoding propositions in standardized LISP structures, distinguishing between the language for expressing knowledge and how it is stored in the computer, we are exploiting the multiple-representation aspect of MRS, which is one interpretation of its name. A number of elegant patterns in the metarules made the compiler easy to write (Clancey and Bock, 1987). Figure 17 summarizes how rules, tasks, and relations are encoded as EMYCIN rules and parameters and how these entities are related. Our success in building HERACLES on top of EMYCIN demonstrates the generality of the original parameter-rule representation language. It is closer to a typical frame language than is commonly realized.

The most exciting result of this reformulation is what it reveals about the relational nature of the knowledge base. It is now evident that the metarules are selecting foci (findings, hypotheses, domain rules) on the basis of how they are related to one another. These relations can be either static (for example, red-flag finding, one that needs to be explained) or dynamic (for example, hypothesis in focus). The knowledge base can be viewed as a database, defined in terms of these three primitive terms and relations among them. Writing a new metarule tends to require defining a new preference relation for discriminating among findings, hypotheses, and domain rules. That is, each new relation further classifies the primitive terms in a way useful for controlling reasoning. For example, the metarule shown in Figure 16 required the new relation, "a finding that needs to be explained". As this example shows, the meaning of a relation is tied to how the relation is used. This is particularly clear for relations such as follow-up question and trigger rule.

A detailed analysis shows that the metarules are collecting, sorting, and filtering domain terms and rules on the basis of their applicability as operands (foci) for the operators (subtasks) that will accomplish the current task. For example, metarules for TEST-HYPOTHESIS collect, sort, and filter potential findings to support a hypothesis. Refining a hypothesis means collecting, sorting and filtering its causes and subtypes (for example, distinguishing between common and serious causes). Generally, the domain relations classify NEOMYCIN's experiential knowledge of predefined disease models (see Section 18 below) according to how they are triggered, tested, discriminated, and refined by operators (tasks) for constructing a problem-specific, historical accounting of the disease process (see Section 20 below).

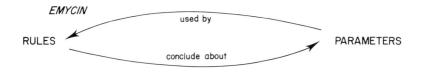

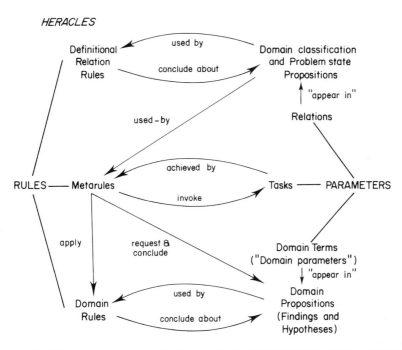

Figure 17   How control knowledge is encoded in HERACLES. HERACLES is implemented as a specialization of EMYCIN. The original conception of domain parameters and rules is shown above. In HERACLES parameters are specialized as domain relations, control tasks and domain terms, conditionally inferred and invoked by rules. We use "relation" in the mathematical sense to refer to both predicates and functions. "Finding" and "hypothesis" formally classify the domain terms (for example meningitis), and informally are used to refer to propositions in a situation-specific model; so we say that "the patient has meningitis" is a hypothesis. Tasks are accomplished by an interpreter that applies metarules. Propositions used by metarule premises (such as (EXPLAINED-BY $F $H) appearing in Figure 16) can be inferred definitionally by rules or can be inferred by procedural attachment (for example accessing LISP structures). These propositions are both static and dynamic. They classify domain propositions and domain rules, as well as characterizing the problem-solving state (such as whether a hypothesis is in the differential or whether a task has been done yet). Additional relations that classify tasks are used by the task interpreter (not shown here). Metarule actions apply domain rules, requests (from the user) or conclude domain propositions, or invoke other tasks. In particular, the task FINDOUT uses all of these methods to infer domain propositions. In HERACLES all domain rules are applied directly by metarules rather than by back-chaining. Only domain rules mention domain terms directly; other rules use variables.

NEOMYCIN has about 170 relations in its control vocabulary. They appear in the 75 metarules, grouped into 29 tasks. In HERACLES, the generalization of NEOMYCIN, the knowledge engineer can modify these metarules, defining new relations for describing his domain.

17   GUIDON-WATCH: REIFYING THE PROCESS

The availability of graphics has changed how we can illustrate reasoning, and is shaping our ideas of what we'd like to show. As a first step toward implementing a new instructional program on top of NEOMYCIN, Mark Richer and I (1985) used the Interlisp-D window and menu features to construct a complex interactive system for browsing the knowledge base and watching reasoning. This includes the dynamic task tree (similar to Figure 14) and the task stack (see Figure 15). Our work has been directly inspired by Brown's emphasis on reifying or making concrete the reasoning process (Brown, 1983).

Figure 18 shows how the disease taxonomy is overprinted to reveal the pattern of NEOMYCIN's reasoning. In GUIDON-DEBUG, now under development, it is possible to roll back the consultation display to show any window at the time any given question was asked. This is a debugging facility we could hardly have imagined even five years ago.

18   HERACLES: FROM DISEASES TO STEREOTYPES

In late 1983 I began to consider how NEOMYCIN might be generalized. What kinds of problems can be conveniently solved by an architecture consisting of a classification network and a separate, abstract control strategy? In particular, to what problems can the same diagnostic strategy be applied? It was obvious from the start that the procedure had nothing

---

Figure 18   Overprinting a classification network to show how it is searched. Nodes blink and are boxed to make visible the "looking up" and "looking down" process of diagnosis. Numbers indicate the relative certainty of conclusions; the cumulative certainty factor (CUMCF) includes hierarchical propagation. Heavy-bordered boxes indicate the program's *differential*—the most specific cut through the taxonomy and causal network. The differential is printed in the lower-right window with indenting to show specialization by process subtype and cause. When a hypothesis is selected, the evidence window can be displayed, indicating which findings and rules have been considered and the outcome of each consideration. Dozens of other windows are available, including different views of causal networks and the history of task invocation.

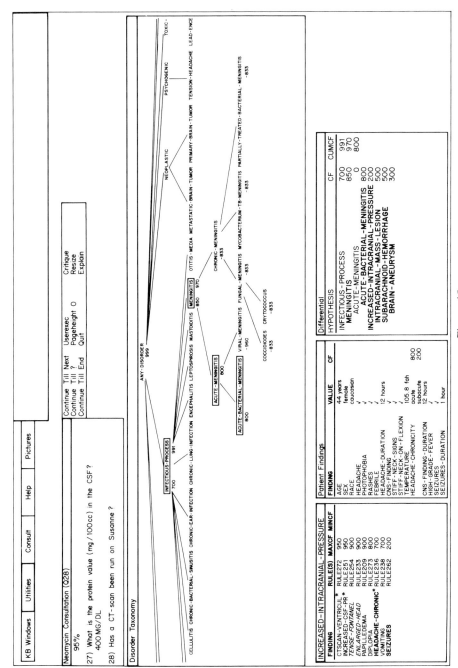

Figure 18

specifically to do with medicine; was it more general than diagnosis? In attempting to teach the NEOMYCIN approach to AI students, I found that it was possible to redescribe other knowledge bases in its terms. For example, in terms of the mapping between models of situation descriptions and selected solutions, "people are to diseases" as "meals are to wines". I had also recently reread Rich's (1979) work on user modelling, intending to apply this to our explanation program. I recognized that it fitted the same pattern—models of people related to a taxonomy of books. Finally, I recalled that Rubin (1975) and Aikins (1983) emphasized that diseases are described (in knowledge bases) as stereotypes. The general model of heuristic classification fell into place: some problems can be solved by selection, heuristically relating a classification of problem data to a classification of known solutions (Clancey, 1985).

To my chagrin, this new model required a reconceptualization of parts of NEOMYCIN. We began to consider the diseases as stereotypes, we introduced qualitative abstraction of numeric data where it had been omitted in MYCIN, and we realized that our representation of diseases as classes is inadequate given what is required in general and what is evident in other programs (for example, allowing for multiple inheritance). We call the reconceptualized framework HERACLES. It is not a completed tool but an idea that continues to evolve.

Figure 19 illustrates the heuristic classification analysis of SACON, a program that many of us knew about and talked about for five or six years, but that few understood until its knowledge base was portrayed in this way. The purpose of SACON is to select a configuration of programs in a structural-analysis software package developed by the Marc Corporation. These programs can analyse an object for structural failure in many ways, some of which are unnecessarily accurate and time-consuming. An expert can tell you which of the programs should be run to analyse a particular structure, and that is SACON's task. Imposing a type of classification on SACON's concepts, and labelling inferences as abstractions, heuristics and refinements, we find a previously hidden secondary structure, which helps us to understand what SACON does.

Studying and generalizing knowledge-based programs, we can go quite a bit further. First, we can realize that as stereotypes the classifications are models of systems: specifications or descriptions of systems and plans for assembly or modification of systems. Secondly, the classification sequences, relating one model to another, are regular and limited in nature, constituting tasks. A model of the system being monitored is related to a plan for controlling its behaviour. A diagnostic model of a faulty system is related to a repair plan. A specification is related to a design and then to an assembly

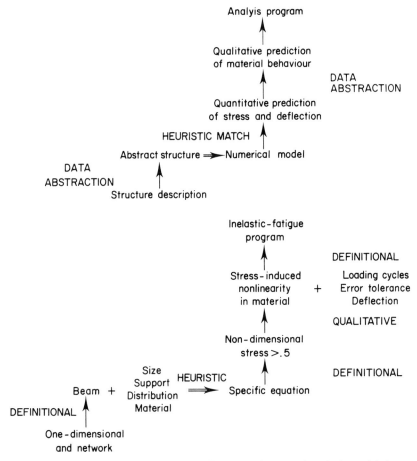

Figure 19   Inference structure of SACON. An abstract description of inference chains is shown above a particular sequence of associations. SACON abstracts the given structure and relates this abstraction to half a dozen rules of thumb that make a quantitative prediction of the structure's behaviour under stress. Specifically, the fact that the structure is a beam is combined with information about its size, support and load distribution in order to select a numerical equation, which computes stress and deflection. These predictions are abstracted, and definitionally related to the structural analysis program. Specifically, the characterization of stress, combined with information about loading and error tolerance, is classified as a particular kind of "analysis" for which the program is specialized. The SACON program selects from about 30 different program combinations. This corresponds to the number of organisms in MYCIN, and is probably good to remember when considering whether the heuristic classification method is appropriate for solving a problem.

plan. Finally, the idea of systems, tasks and common sequences is independent of how the solutions are computed each step along the way. Either heuristic classification or some constructive method (perhaps involving nonmonotonic reasoning, hypothetical worlds, and so on) might be used. It is important to remember that this inference structure shows the pattern of inferences that map given information to final solutions, and makes no claims about the process or order in which the inferences are made. Further examples and extensive discussion appear in Clancey (1985, 1986).

19   CASTER: FROM DISEASES TO ABNORMAL SUBSTANCES AND PROCESSES

In addition to the disorder taxonomy (Figure 11), a knowledge base for diagnostic problems constructed in HERACLES might include a causal–associational network. Disorders in this network are descriptions of internal states in the system being diagnosed. Figure 20 shows such a network for CASTER, a knowledge system for sand-casting diagnosis.

Tim Thompson and I (1986) developed this program in order to better understand the distinction between the pathophysiological states of the causal net and the *aetiologies*, or final causes, of the disorder taxonomy. This distinction was emphasized in the CASNET program (Weiss *et al.*, 1978); our interest was to apply the ideas to a nonmedical problem.

What did we learn from the CASTER experiment? First, for diagnosing malfunctions in some manufacturing process, it is useful to organize the disorder taxonomy according to each stage in the overall process (pattern design, melting, and so on). In contrast, the top level of NEOMYCIN's taxonomy corresponds to defects in the neurological system, viewing it as an object, not a process: assembly flaw (congenital), environmental influence (infection, toxicity, trauma, psychological load) or degeneration (vascular disorder, immunoresponse, muscular disorder). In both of these physical systems, externally observable manifestations are explained in terms of internal system behaviour, tracked back to faulty structures and malfunctions of subsystems. These are in turn explained by the aetiologies, processes in which the system interacted with its environment, bringing it to its current state. In medicine, these aetiologies include congenital problems (caused by the mother's lifestyle or her environment), psychogenic problems (emotional overload), trauma (structurally damaging the body), toxic environment, and so on. In the human body, internal systems generate new subsystem structures, so developmental and degenerative processes are also important aetiologies. We believe that this analysis can be generalized to cover all physical systems.

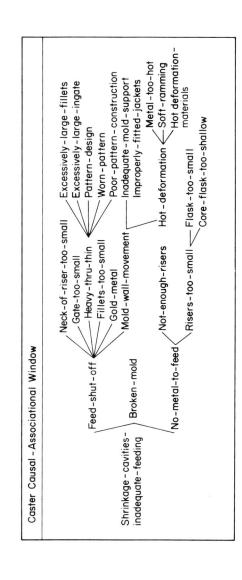

Figure 20 CASTER's causal–associational network for shrinking defects in cast iron. This simplified network relates structural failures (for example mold-wall movement) to functional failures (for example inadequate mold support). These are all internal to the system and often cannot be observed directly. Reasoning proceeds as follows. Given some surface fault, such as shrinkage cavities in the cast iron, we reason backwards to possible causes: (1) feed of metal shut off; (2) a broken mold (leak); and (3) absence of metal to feed. Gates, risers and fillets refer to structures for shunting metal and venting gases. Terminal nodes, on the right-hand side, track the problem back to some problem in the iron-casting process (pattern design, mold formation, metal melting, and so on), thus relating system behaviours to external causes (the designer's assumptions, previous treatment of the sand, contamination of the metal supply, and so on). We believe that analysing such networks, relating them to the well-defined structure and function of the sand-casting system, will help us to redefine in a principled way the causal relations given to us by experts in other domains, such as medicine. Working in multiple domains proliferates metaphors and helps us to develop more general theories about expert knowledge.

A second interesting result is the set of heuristics we discovered for constructing a well-formed causal network (Clancey, 1984d). These heuristics include asking the expert about categories of states; asking about unobservable states that track back to different aetiologies; distinguishing clearly between substances and processes, particularly, never causally linking substances directly; and working backward from repairs to causes. This last point emphasizes that the purpose of the causal–associational and etiologic taxonomy is to make choices about repair, a point I emphasized above in Section 12. Uncertainty in diagnostic reasoning need only be resolved to the extent that it makes a difference in distinguishing among repairs.

Our heuristics can be viewed as criteria for critiquing a behavioural causal model. Can we formalize these constraints so that they can be taught to a student? Viewing a diagnosis as a model is the first step.

20   THE SITUATION-SPECIFIC MODEL: FROM A DIAGNOSIS TO AN EXPLANATION

This lesson might be the most important. It is the idea that a diagnosis is not the name of a disease but an *argument* that causally relates the manifestations that need to be explained (because they are abnormal) to the processes that brought them about (See Figure 21). A number of ideas come together here:

   (i) Diseases are processes (see Sections 12 and 19 above). Thus a diagnosis is a network causally linking manifestations and states to processes.

  (ii) A causal explanation applies the general concepts and links in a knowledge base to construct a case-specific model (Patil *et al.*, 1981). Thus the network linking manifestations and diseases is a model of a particular sequence of events in the world (also called a *situation-specific* model).

 (iii) Diagnostic operators examine and modify the differential (most specific diseases under consideration), linking and refining them. Thus, HERACLES tasks are operators for constructing a situation-specific model (similar to ABEL's diagnostic operators (Patil *et al.*, 1981)).

  (iv) A causal explanation has the structure of a geometry proof: It must account for all of the findings and must be coherent and consistent. Thus, the situation-specific model must be a connected graph with one process at the root (assuming a single fault).

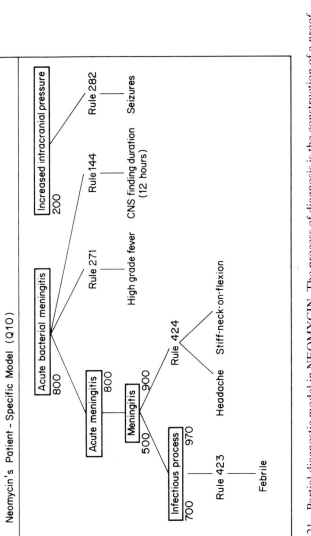

Figure 21   Partial diagnostic model in NEOMYCIN. The process of diagnosis is the construction of a *proof tree*, relating the findings and disorders that could have caused these findings. At some intermediate state when solving the problem, the network is disconnected and partial. The patient has seizures; what could have caused that? There is some support for Acute Bacterial Meningitis and Increased Intracranial Pressure, but these two hypotheses have not been related. Is there some underlying cause (process) that could account for all of the manifestations? Diagnostic operators can be viewed as graph-construction operators, focusing on particular nodes and trying to grow the graph down to support possible explanations or refining it upward to more specific explanations. A final situation-specific model is a connected network, with some root process that we say explains the internal states (such as Increased Intracranial Pressure), which in turn explain the observed findings. This graph, as an argument having the structure of a proof, is the diagnosis, not the term Acute Bacterial Meningitis.

The evolution of these ideas is intriguing, revealing how our computational tools and the use of the computer as a modelling medium changes how we think. Sometime in 1985 it occurred to me that we could extend the windows offered by GUIDON-WATCH to include a graph showing how the final diagnosis related to the known findings. When I saw the way Anderson replaced a linear-geometry proof by a graph (using the same Interlisp-D graphics package), the analogy between a causal explanation and a proof became concrete (Anderson *et al.*, 1985). Thus the example from another domain showed how Patil's idea of a patient-specific model could be useful in teaching, and the availability of the graphics package encouraged us to create the picture to see what it would look like.

It is astounding to realize how many hundreds of expert systems are cranking out diagnoses with neither the programs nor their designers ever explicitly considering a diagnosis as a coherent causal model. They do not even check to see if all of the findings are covered by the final diagnosis. Our language is too loose: the program prints out the name of a disorder, and we say "The program has made a diagnosis." However, where is the explanation argument?

For the purpose of teaching, this graph could perhaps be the best way to reify the process of diagnosis. For several years, inspired by Brown's emphasis on "process versus product" (possibly derived from Dewey, 1964), I have been searching for some written notation that we could use, something analogous to algebra, to make visible what the operators of diagnosis (NEOMYCIN's tasks) are doing. The analogy with geometry turns out to be stronger than the analogy with algebra, because each inference itself relies on a proof, analogous to the causal arguments behind each link of the situation-specific model. In algebra the inference rules are all axioms.

Giving this window to the student, we might have him carry out the diagnosis by posting his hypotheses and linking them to the known findings. At each step along the way, there are visible problems to be solved. The student can see that he is trying to construct a logically consistent network. Behind each request for data is an operation for making the network hang together—explaining the findings that need to be explained and refining the hypotheses that need to be made more specific. An instructional program is now being developed based on this idea. Called GUIDON-MANAGE, it has a student "manage" the diagnosis by explicitly applying strategic operators.

This is an amazing change. Ten years ago I thought I was trying to teach parameters and rules, and now I am saying that I want to teach the student to be an efficient model builder. What can we tell the student that will help him critique the model that he is constructing? For example, we shall say "All the important findings need to be explained." Observing that he has failed to do something that needs to be done, we shall tell him about the operators, so he can step back and say "Well, what knowledge might I be missing that prevented me from carrying out that task?" So debugging by explanation of failure—proceeding from model constraints to operators to knowledge relations—is the approach that we are following. This leads to an interesting model of learning (Clancey *et al.*, 1986).

21 METHODOLOGICAL LESSONS

To summarize ongoing projects mentioned or alluded to here, we are currently doing the following:

developing instructional programs based on NEOMYCIN;

studying learning in the setting of debugging a knowledge base;

reimplementing the explanation program to use the logic encoding of the metarules (stating this program in the same task-metarule language so that it might reason about its own explanations);

generalizing our graphics package using object-oriented techniques;

applying the student-modelling program ODYSSEUS to knowledge acquisition;

preparing HERACLES for use by other people.

I am going to jump up a level here to consider some methodological lessons we can draw from this research.

Figure 1 provides a simplified summary of how the various programs and research ideas are connected. We observe two examples of a specific expert system being generalized, with the resulting shell used to construct other specific systems and a tutoring shell. Is there any logic in this sequence that might reveal something about learning in general or at least about how we learn by constructing programs?

In the section names in this chapter I have indicated the sequence of terminological changes ("from . . . to . . .") that seem to mark each major change in my understanding.

The renaming that occurred in moving from "clinical parameter" to "model" is dramatic. None of the intermediate concepts (hypothesis, relation, process, and so on) is new, but it is interesting to note how they are retained and how they build upon one another as the knowledge structures are reinterpreted from different perspectives.

Thus in HERACLES today we have parameters, terms, hypotheses, diseases, processes, stereotypes and models. All of these remain true descriptions of what is in our program. The perspective changes, broadening from *language terminology* (parameters, terms) to *reasoning phenomenology* (hypotheses), *domain ontology* (disease process taxonomy); and, finally, *epistemological distinctions* (stereotypes, models). With the heuristic classification perspective at the top—couched in terms of systems, tasks, and models (Clancy, 1986)—previous terminology is retained for describing the program at different levels.

Looking closely at the sequence of research itself, there are some clear patterns:

abstracting or generalizing terminology to incorporate another specific domain (for example, moving from disease to disorder process);

separating a domain model (what is "true") from the inference process (what to do) by identifying and justifying procedural sequences (for example, defining relations for ordering MYCIN's rule clauses and, later, defining relations for ordering NEOMYCIN's metarules);

justifying domain relations in terms of underlying constraints and patterns (for cxample, a theory for generating appropriate follow-up questions or trigger rules or a theory for generating a causal network in terms of faulty structures and malfunctions).

Figure 22 summarizes the overall pattern. The point of the analysis phase is to detect patterns that we want to model explicitly and that have been mapped into the language in an implicit and perhaps undisciplined way. Thus findings and hypotheses, causality and subtype, and disease knowledge and procedures are not distinguished in MYCIN. Findings and hypotheses are both represented as parameters. Cause and subtype are represented by sequences of clauses in rules, or in the relation between a parameter and its values (for example, parameter—"the kind of Meningitis"; value—"Bacterial"). Focusing procedures are also encoded by rule clause ordering.

There is apparently no end to this criticism; the same game can be played with NEOMYCIN. For example, in attempting to improve the explanation program we find that the use of terms in NEOMYCIN's original metarules is ludicrously undisciplined; they are used like arbitrary program variables, with no apparent connection between $HYP and $CURFOCUS. Interpreting this representation for diagnosis causes no difficulties, but the explanation program needs to know that the metarules refer to the same kind of entity, a hypothesis.

This analysis suggests that detecting patterns of statements in some language, articulating a new classification model, and defining a new procedure by which the statements are to be interpreted are intricately related. Recalling the analysis of metarules (Section 16 above), we observe that each

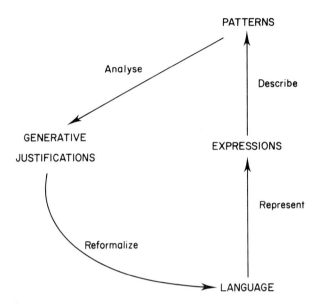

Figure 22   Methodology for improving computational models. In the process of knowledge representation, we write statements in some language; we organize what we have written down, describing and classifying patterns; we explain the patterns in terms of primitive relations; and we define a new language that enables us to state these primitive relations explicitly and generate the original patterns. For example, clause correlations in MYCIN's rules are now reformulated in tasks, metarules, and domain relations. Another cycle occurs when we study these metarules and articulate the constraints behind their design. Similarly, patterns in NEOMYCIN's disease taxonomy and CASTER's causal network are articulated by characterizing diseases as processes and states as abnormal structures and malfunctions. These new perspectives—the search for patterns and their articulation in a new language—all arise in an attempt to formulate some generative rationale for constructing similar structures in new domains as well as to evaluate existing networks for consistency and completeness. A generative theory of a representation facilitates teaching people how to use the representation, reformulating it for efficiency, and constructing explanation programs and knowledge-acquisition tools.

new purpose for interpreting a representation requires new distinctions— new relations—to classify existing domain terms, rules, and relations among them. Thus the compiler needs to know which domain relations are predicates and which are functions (in the mathematical sense). ODYSSEUS needs to know when metarules can be reordered. The teaching program needs to know why metarules are ordered a certain way. In classifying the relations and terms, we are constantly asking "Which things can be procedurally operated upon in the same way?"

Winograd reached the same conclusion in his analysis of how language arises. The need to take action reorients us to the world, forcing us to make new distinctions. The relevant properties attributed to an object are determined by the role the object plays in an action: "This grounding of description in action pervades all attempts to formalize the world into a linguistic structure of objects, properties, and events" (Winograd and Flores 1986). Indeed, by this analysis the world and its objects exist only in language, mediated by action.

The expert-system methodology of writing down knowledge in some structured way so that it can later be studied and better formalized is a remarkable, exciting turning point in epistemological practice. We try to understand why a relation holds by abstracting it and then trying to find similar relations in the knowledge base. If a pattern holds, we restate everything more abstractly. Why is it correct to say that "broken mold" causes "inadequate feeding"? What other causal links in the network connect the same kind of concepts, leaving out the same kind of details? Do all links in the network connect structures to functions? Is there any reason why they should?

Having written a model down, the most powerful tools of language come into play:

> it is possible to reflect on what was said, to ask why it is true, to develop a better understanding or theory;

> an incremental critique and transformation process becomes possible— the best way to build anything so that it is reliable and useful (Petroski, 1985).

Computational languages provide a way of writing things down so that the model is executable, the very thing we need for modelling processes. AI research is exploring how to model physical, inferential, communicative, motoric and perceptual processes using qualitative (principally nonnumeric, relational) representations (Clancey 1986). Graphics provide a medium for visualizing processes, so we can understand the complexity of the systems we construct (Hollan *et al.*, 1984; Clancey, 1983c; Richer and Clancey 1985), and even start to ask new questions as icons and graphs become part of our language for stating theories. The marriage of qualitative modelling and graphics in the 1980s, made available on cheaper, more powerful machines, provides a sharp stimulus to AI research and a good reason to be optimistic about the progress to come.

ACKNOWLEDGEMENTS

This chapter was originally prepared as a final ONR technical report for the period 1979–1985. The GUIDON project was first funded jointly by

Marshall Farr at ONR and Dexter Fletcher at DARPA. Other tutoring programs in the ONR/ARPA family at that time included WHY, WEST and SOPHIE. Avron Barr, John Seely Brown, Ira Goldstein and Keith Wescourt helped us to define the initial proposal, conveying the problems and methods then current in the research community. Bruce Buchanan was principal investigator, shaping the clarity and style of the first proposal and continuing today to serve as advisor on the project.

I sincerely thank the students and programmers who have made so many significant contributions to the NEOMYCIN and HERACLES programs (chronologically): Reed Letsinger, Bob London, Conrad Bock, Diane Warner Hasling, David Wilkins, Glenn Rennels, Mark Richer, Tim Thompson, Steve Barnhouse, Arif Merchant, David Leserman and Naomi Rodolitz. Victor Yu, M.D. helped me understand MYCIN in the early years. I am especially grateful to the late Tim Beckett, M.D. for showing me what a good physician teacher can do. Curt Kapsner, M.D., John Macias, and Bevan Yueh have enthusiastically collaborated in our recent work.

The project was funded jointly by ONR and the Army Research Institute during the period 1981–1985 (ONR contract N00014-79C-0302). Computational resources have been provided by the Sumex-Aim National Resource (NIH grant RR00785). Organization and maintenance of computer resources in the Knowledge Systems Laboratory is managed by Tom Rindfleisch. Continuing research is supported in part by ONR contract N00014-85-K-0305 and by a grant from the Josiah Macy, Jr., Foundation.

This chapter is based on a talk I gave at the Computer Science Colloquium at Carnegie-Mellon University on 19 November 1985. I thank David Evans for arranging to have the talk taped and Rene Bornstein for her accurate transcription. Many useful revisions were suggested by Steven Barnhouse, Ted Crovello, Bod Engelmore, and Mark Richer. Special thanks to Susan King for TEXing the final copy.

REFERENCES

Aikins, J. S. (1983). Prototypical knowledge for expert systems. *Artificial Intelligence* **20**, 163–210.

Anderson, J. R., Boyle, C. F. and Yost, G. (1985). The geometry tutor. *Proc. 9th Int. Joint Conf. on Artificial Intelligence, Los Angeles, August 1985*, Vol. 1, pp. 1–7. Los Altos, California: William Kaufmann.

Brown, J. S. (1983). Process versus product—a perspective on tools for communal and informal electronic learning. *Education in the Electronic Age.* New York: Educational Broadcasting Corporation, WNET.

Brown, J. S., Collins, A. and Harris, G. (1977). Artificial intelligence and learning strategies. *Learning Strategies* (ed. H. O'Neill). New York: Academic Press.

Carbonell, J. R. (1970). Mixed-initiative man–computer instructional dialogues. Tech. Rep. 1971, Bolt Beranek and Newman.

Clancey, W. J. (1979a). Transfer of rule-based expertise through a tutorial dialogue. Ph.D. thesis, Stanford University.

Clancey, W. J. (1979b). Dialogue management for rule-based tutorials, *Proc. 6th Int. Joint Conf. on Artificial Intelligence, Tokyo, August 1979*, pp. 155–161. Los Altos, California: William Kaufmann.

Clancey, W. J. (1979c). Tutoring rules for guiding a case method dialogue. *Int. J. Man–Machine Stud.* **11**, 25–49. Also in *Intelligent Tutoring Systems* (ed. D. Sleeman and J. S. Brown), pp. 201–225. New York: Academic Press, 1982.

Clancey, W. J. (1982). GUIDON. *The Handbook of Artificial Intelligence*, 267–278. Los Altos, California: William Kaufmann.

Clancey, W. J. (1983a). The epistemology of a rule-based expert system: a framework for explanation. *Artificial Intelligence* **20**, 215–251.

Clancey, W. J. (1983b). The advantages of abstract control knowledge in expert system design. *Proc. Nat. Conf. on Artificial Intelligence, Washington, D.C., August 1983*, pp. 74–78. Menlo Park, California: American Association for Artificial Intelligence.

Clancey, W. J. (1983c). Communication, simulation and intelligent agents: implications of personal intelligent machines for medical education. *Proc. AAMSI-83*, pp. 556–560. Bethesda: American Association for Medical Systems and Informatics.

Clancey, W. J. (1984a). Teaching classification problem solving (abstract). *Proc. 6th Ann. Conf. Cognitive Science Society, Boulder*, pp. 44–46. New York: Cognitive Science Society.

Clancey, W. J. (1984b). Methodology for building an intelligent tutoring system. *Method and Tactics in Cognitive Science* (ed. W. Kintsch, J. Miller and P. Polson). Hillsdale, N.J.: Lawrence Erlbaum Associates.

Clancey, W. J. (1984c). Acquiring, representing, and evaluating a competence model of diagnosis. HPP Memo 84-2, Stanford University, February 1984. To appear in *Contributions to the Nature of Expertise* (ed. M. Chi, R. Glaser and M. Farr).

Clancey, W. J. (1984d). Knowledge acquisition for classification expert systems. *Proc. ACM Ann. Conf.* October 1984, pp. 11–14. New York: Association for Computing Machinery.

Clancey, W. J. (1985). Heuristic classification. *Artificial Intelligence* **27**, 289–350.

Clancey, W. J. (1986). The science and engineering of qualitative models. KSL Rep. 86–27, Stanford Univ.

Clancey, W. J. and Bock, C. (1982). MRS/NEOMYCIN: Representing metacontrol in predicate calculus. HPP Memo 82–31, Stanford Univ.

Clancey, W. J. and Bock, C. (1987). Representing control knowledge as abstract tasks and metarules. *Computer Expert Systems* (ed. M. J. Coombs and L. Bolc). New York: Springer-Verlag.

Clancey, W. J. and Buchanan, B. G. (1982). Exploration of problem-solving and tutoring strategies: 1979–1982. Tech. Rep. STAN-CS-82-910, HPP 82-8, Stanford Univ.

Clancey, W. J. and Letsinger, R. (1984). NEOMYCIN: Reconfiguring a rule-based expert system for application to teaching. *Readings in Medical Artificial Intelligence: The First Decade* (ed. W. J. Clancey and E. A. Shortliffe), pp. 361–381. Reading, Mass.: Addison-Wesley.

Clancey, W. J., Richer, M., Wilkins, D., Barnhouse, S., Kapsner, C., Leserman, D., Macias, J., Merchant, A., Rodolitz, N. (1986). Guidon-Debug: The student as knowledge engineer. KSL Rep. 86–34, Stanford Univ.

Dewey, J. (1964). The process and product of reflective activity: Psychological process and logical form. *John Dewey on Education: Selected Writings* (ed. R. D. Archambault), pp. 243–259. New York: Random House.

Genesereth, M. R. and Smith, D. E. (1982). Meta-Level Architecture. HPP Rep. 81–6, Stanford Univ.

Hasling, D. W., Clancey, W. J. and Rennels, G. R. (1983). Strategic explanations in consultation. *Int. J. Man–Machine Stud.* **20**, 3–19. Also in *Development in Expert Systems* (ed. M. J. Coombs), pp. 117–133. London: Academic Press.

Hollan, J. D., Hutchins, E. L. and Weitzman, L. (1984). STEAMER: An interactive inspectable simulation-based training system. *AI Magazine* **5**(2), 15–27.

London, G. and Clancey, W. J. (1982). Plan recognition strategies in student modelling: prediction and description. *Proc. 2nd Nat. Conf. on Artificial Intelligence, Pittsburgh*, pp. 335–338. Menlo Park, California: American Association for Artificial Intelligence.

Patil, R. S., Szolovits, P. and Schwartz, W. B. (1981). Causal understanding of patient illness in medical diagnosis. *Proc. 7th Int. Joint Conf. on Artificial Intelligence, August 1981*, pp. 893–899. Los Altos, California: William Kaufmann.

Petroski, H. (1985). To Engineer is Human: The role of failure in successful design. New York: St. Martin's Press.

Rich, E. (1979). User modelling via stereotypes. *Cogn. Sci.* **3**, 355–366.

Richer, M. H. and Clancey, W. J. (1985). GUIDON-WATCH: A graphic interface for viewing a knowledge-based system. *IEEE Comp. Graphics Applics* **5**(11), 51–64.

Rubin, A. D. (1975). Hypothesis formation and evaluation in medical diagnosis. Tech. Rep. AI-TR-316, Artificial Intelligence Lab., MIT.

Schoenfeld, A. H. (1981). Episodes and executive decisions in mathematical problem solving. Tech. Rep. Hamilton Coll., Maths Dept, 1981.

Shortliffe, E. H. (1974). MYCIN: A rule-based computer program for advising physicians regarding antimicrobial therapy selection. Ph.D. thesis, Stanford University.

Thompson, T. and Clancey, W. J. (1986). A qualitative modelling shell for process diagnosis. *IEEE Software* **3**(2), 6–15.

van Melle, W. (1979). A domain-independent production rule system for consultation programs. *Proc. 6th Int. Joint Conf. on Artificial Intelligence, August 1979*, pp. 923–925. Los Altos, California: William Kaufmann.

Weiss, S. M., Kulikowski, C. A., Amarel, S. and Safir, A. (1978). A model-based method for computer-aided medical decision making. *Artificial Intelligence* **11**, 145–172.

Wilkins, D. C., Clancey, W. J. and Buchanan, B. G. (1986). An overview of the ODYSSEUS learning apprentice. In *Machine Learning: A Guide to Current Research* (ed. T. M. Mitchell, J. G. Carbonell and R. S. Michalski), pp. 369–373. New York: Academic Press.

Winograd, T. and Flores, C. F. (1986). *Understanding Computers and Cognition: A New Foundation for Design.* Norwood, N.J.: Ablex.

Woolf, B. and McDonald, D. D. (1984). Context-dependent transitions in tutoring discourse. *Proc. Nat. Conf. on Artificial Intelligence, Austin, August 1984*, pp. 355–361. Menlo Park, California: American Association for Artificial Intelligence.

5. Qualitative prediction:

The SPARC/G methodology for inductively describing and predicting discrete processes

RYSZARD MICHALSKI, HEEDONG KO and KAIHU CHEN

Abstract. Qualitative prediction is concerned with problems of building symbolic descriptions of processes, and using these descriptions for predicting a plausible continuation of these processes. It stresses the qualitative form of prediction, as it does not seek precise characterization of future events, but rather a specification of plausible properties and constraints on the future events. An important aspect of qualitative prediction is that only a partial knowledge of the process is available; therefore the construction of a description must necessarily involve inductive inference. It also involves deductive inference to relate the observed process to the concepts contained or derivable from the system's background knowledge.

This chapter describes a domain-independent methodology, SPARC/G, for a simple form of qualitative prediction, where processes are sequences of discrete events or objects that are characterized by finite-valued attributes. Building a description of a process employs general and domain specific knowledge, and involves a new type of inductive learning called *part-to-whole* generalization. The key idea behind the methodology is the use of multiple description models, and model-oriented transformations of the input sequence. Each description model constrains the syntactic form of candidate descriptions, and in this way greatly reduces the total search space. A model is instantiated to a specific description by defining various parameters. A description is considered plausible if it fits a transformed input sequence well, according to the requirements of the model.

The methodology is illustrated by several example problems, such as discovering a secret code for a passage through a sequence of channels, determining preconditions for actions in a blocks world, learning a robot action sequence, predicting the motion of an oscillating spring, and discovering rules in the card game ELEUSIS that models the process of scientific discovery.

1 INTRODUCTION

1.1 What is Qualitative Prediction?

Events in our world tend to be highly interdependent. This interdependence

CURRENT ISSUES IN EXPERT SYSTEMS
ISBN 0-12-714030-1

makes it possible to make predictions about the future on the basis of our knowledge of the past. In fact, the whole purpose of building and maintaining knowledge is to be able to predict and/or influence the future. If our world were a sequence of completely unrelated random scenes, and therefore our knowledge of the past were of no use to interpret or predict future events, there would be little reason for storing any knowledge. As the construction and usage of knowledge is a primary function of intelligence, the need for intelligence would cease also. The above agrees with the observation by Rivest (at a seminar at the Artificial Intelligence Laboratory, MIT, Fall 1985) that "the purpose of intelligence is to predict the future."

The relationship between future and past is usually imprecise and uncertain. Also, it is typically very complex and multifactored. An important way to capture this relationship is to build descriptions or models that are qualitative, i.e. that characterize processes in terms of causal relationships, trends and dependencies. In qualitative prediction the main stress is on building descriptions from partial knowledge of a process. Therefore the major type of inference involved here is inductive. This is different from the approaches in De Kleer and Brown (1984) and Forbus (1984), which are deductive in nature. Inductively derived descriptions may range from statements of "surface" properties (e.g. observable physical properties) to causal explanations and abstract relationships characterizing the process.

The most widely researched type of inductive learning has been concerned with discovering a general description of a class of objects, given selected instances of the class. For example, given instances of cancerous and noncancerous cells, the task is to determine a general rule for discriminating between these two types of cells (Michalski, 1983). This type of inductive learning is called **instance-to-class** generalization.

The inductive learning involved in qualitative prediction is different from such instance-to-class generalization. It involves a form of the **part-to-whole** generalization. To explain the latter type of induction, let us consider a few examples. Suppose that a palaeontologist has excavated bones of a prehistoric animal, and from his information he then hypothesizes the entire skeleton of the animal. As another case, consider an archaeologist who is given an incomplete set of pieces of a broken ancient sculpture, and has to reconstruct the original. In such cases we do not have independent examples of some class of objects, but rather interdependent parts of one structured object. The task is to hypothesize a description of the whole object.

Clearly, the above problems fit the general notion of inductive generalization, but are not the **instance-to-class** generalization problems. In **instance-to-class** we are given instances that are **independent** members of a class; any possible relations among training instances are considered irrelevant. In **part-to-whole** generalization, the inputs are descriptions of **parts** of a structured object, and relations among the parts are of primary importance.

A very simple form of the **part-to-whole** generalization problem occurs in IQ tests where the task is to predict a plausible continuation of a sequence of numbers or letters. The given sequence can be viewed as a part of an unknown complete sequence. The task is to hypothesize the remaining part of the complete sequence on the basis of the known parts of the sequence.

Suppose that instead of letters or numbers, we have snapshots of some process occurring in time. Assume also that our background knowledge contains sufficient information for characterizing the relationships between these snapshots. The task is to determine a description of the process that not only accounts for snapshots seen so far but also suggests a plausible continuation of this process. Suppose further that the description sought is not quantitative but rather qualitative. Instead of precise prediction of the future process, which may not be possible, one desires only a general characterization of the properties that the future events are expected to satisfy. In this exploratory paper we assume that a process is represented by a sequence of events, called an **episode**:

$$E = \langle e_1, e_2, e_3, \ldots, e_k \rangle.$$

It is also assumed that each event can be satisfactorily characterized by a vector of values of certain attributes:

$$x_1(e_j), \quad x_2(e_j), \quad x_3(e_j), \quad \ldots, \quad x_n(e_j),$$

or briefly,

$$x_1, \quad x_2, \quad x_3, \quad \ldots, \quad x_n,$$

We shall also assume that attributes $x_1, \ldots, x_n$ have domains that are known *a priori* (value sets):

$$D(x_1), \quad D(x_2), \quad D(x_3), \quad \ldots, \quad D(x_n).$$

Each $D(x_i)$ is the set of all values an attribute can possibly take for any event in the given or future episodes. These value sets, their structure (which defines the type of an attribute), the constraints on the relationships among attributes, and knowledge of the application domain, constitute the *background knowledge* of a qualitative prediction system.

Given an episode E and the background knowledge, the task is to induce a description that characterizes the given episode, and predicts plausible future events; i.e. $e_{k+1}, e_{k+2}, \ldots$ Such a description is called a *qualitative prediction rule* (QPR). It is not required that a QPR specify precisely what event will follow, but merely that it constrain the type of events that may follow. When constraints are sufficiently strong that only one event may satisfy them at each place then the QPR is a deterministic prediction rule; otherwise, it is a nondeterministic prediction rule. Discovering such qualitative prediction rules is called a nondeterministic prediction problem (NDP).

An example of an NDP problem is to discover the secret rule in the card game ELEUSIS. The rule, known only to the dealer, describes a sequence of cards that are *legal*. Players attempt to play one or more cards that correctly extend the sequence. To do so, they have to infer the secret rule or its approximation from the cards observed so far. Dietterich (1980) describes a method and a program for discovering such rules which in some instances outperformed human players. Another paper (Michalski *et al.*, 1985); describes the SPARC/E program that discovers rules, and plays the Eleusis game as an autonomous player using the rules discovered. The methodology underlying the SPARC/E program was subsequently generalized and described by Dietterich and Michalski (1985). This paper further expands and extends the method, and presents results of various experiments with an implemented program, SPARC/G (which stands for "Sequential Pattern Recognition/General). These results demonstrate the performance and generality of the method.

Three main topics are discussed in this chapter. First, various models for expressing descriptions are defined, and algorithms for constructing descriptions based on these methods are detailed. Secondly, a program that implements the methodology is described. Finally, several example problems are used to demonstrate the strengths and weaknesses of the methodology.

1.2   Relationship to Time-Series Analysis

There are parallels between this approach and the regression and spectral methods in time-series analysis (Box and Jenkins, 1976). Regression methods attempt to explain the behaviour of a particular variable in terms of the behaviour of a set of independent variables using a polynomial regression function. Spectral analysis attempts to describe the behaviour of a particular variable by analysing its frequency spectrum. In our approach, we use three description models. Our decomposition model corresponds to the regression polynomial. Our periodic model is a symbolic counterpart of the spectral method. However, our third model, the disjunctive model, seems to have no counterpart in classical time-series analysis. The major differences between the proposed approach and time-series approach can be characterized as follows.

(i) In the proposed methodology, each event in the process can be characterized by a large number of attributes. The attributes may have different types: numerical, nominal, cyclic or structured (where the value set is a hierarchy).

(ii) The prediction for the next events is qualitative and nondeterministic; the system constructs a symbolic description that characterizes the set of plausible next events.

(iii) The background knowledge of the program contains constructive induction rules that generate new attributes not present in the initial data.

We assume that the input information about a given process, and the information derivable from the program's background knowledge, are sufficient for predicting a plausible continuation of the process.

2   INDUCING GENERAL DESCRIPTIONS FROM EPISODES

This section presents the theoretical background and basic algorithms underlying the SPARC/G methodology.

2.1   Events and Episodes

The goal of the SPARC/G methodology is to construct a description of an observed process that permits one to predict qualitatively plausible future events. The desired description should be conceptually simple, and consistent with the information known about the process and the system's background knowledge. To develop such a description, "snapshots" of the process are taken. In each snapshot, we measure the state of the process in terms of various attributes believed to be relevant ("attribute" and "variable" are used interchangeably throughout).

A collection of measurements of the process in one snapshot is called an **event**. A sequence of events in chronological order is called an **episode**.

2.2   Representation of Events

A simple representation of an event is just a list of values of some attributes. A more elaborate representation would be in the form of graphs or predicate logic expressions. Here, we use a representation based on VL_1 (the Variable-Valued Logic 1: Michalski, 1974). Each event is represented by a conjunction of relational statements called **selectors**. Each selector describes some measurements taken from the original process. Conjunctions of selectors are called VL_1 **complexes**, or simply **complexes**. Formally, a **selector** consists of an attribute name, a set of values called a **reference**, and a relation between the attribute name and the set of values. It is written as

[attribute relation reference]

For example, the relation

$$[\text{suit} = \text{clubs v diamonds}]$$

states that the attribute **suit** may take on the value **clubs** or **diamonds**.

Each attribute is assigned an explicit set of values called its **domain**. All legal values in the reference of a selector must be taken from the domain. Four types of attributes are distinguished: linear, nominal, cyclic and structured. Both linear and cyclic attributes have integer values. Nominal attributes have nonordinal values. For example, the domain of the nominal attribute **suit** is {clubs, diamonds, hearts, spades}. A **complex** (a conjunction of selectors) is written by placing selectors adjacent to each other. For example, the complex [suit = clubs v diamonds][value < 3] describes the set of cards {AC, 2C, AD, 2D}. A structured attribute represents a value hierarchy that is built on top of existing attributes, and can be either linear or nominal. For example, the structured attribute **color** (of cards) can be defined using attribute **suit**, such that [color = red] is defined as [suit = hearts v diamonds], and [color = black] is defined as [suit = clubs v spades].

2.3 Representation of Episodes

Subscripts are used to indicate the relative ordering between events. Attributes with subscript 0 refer to the current event of interest. A subscript 1 refers to the event immediately preceding the current event of interest; a subscript 2, to the event before that, and so on. For example, the complex [color1 = red][value0 > 6] states that the color in the preceding event was red and the value in the current event is greater than 6. We also introduce difference and sum attributes. The attribute dvalue01 is defined as value0 − value1. The attribute svalue01 takes on value0 + value1.

2.4 Lookback and Periodic Descriptions

Statistical prediction methods specify possible next values of some attributes along with a probability of each value. The method described here differs from such methods in that it specifies a symbolic description characterizing all possible next events. There are two basic types of descriptions used to characterize a sequence and predict its future course: **lookback** descriptions and **periodic** descriptions. A lookback description is a function F of the lb most recent events, where lb is the lookback parameter. This function predicts the next event, or a set of plausible next events (the nondeterministic prediction) in terms of the properties of the lb past events. Thus, given an episode

$$E = \langle e_1, e_2, e_3, \ldots, e_n \rangle,$$

we have

$$F(e_{i-lb}, e_{i-(lb-1)}, \ldots, e_{i-2}, e_{i-1}) = \{e_i\},$$

where $\{e_i\}$ is the set of plausible next events.

An example of a lookback description with $lb = 4$ is the function

$$x_i = x_{i-1} \cdot x_{i-2} - x_{i-3} \cdot x_{i-4}, \qquad \text{where } x_0, x_1 = 1, x_2 = 2, x_3 = 3,$$

that describes the sequence

$$\langle 0, 1, 2, 3, 6, 16, 90, \ldots \rangle.$$

A *periodic description* characterizes a sequence by observing a regularity that binds the events at some fixed distance from each other (the period length) throughout the whole sequence. The relative position of an event within the same period is called a **phase**. For example, the sequence

$$\langle a, b, c, \quad b, c, d, \quad c, d, e, \quad d, e, f, \ldots \rangle$$

is characterized by a periodic description of period length 3, in which letters of the same phase grow alphabetically.

2.5   Description Models

Inductive learning is the process of generating hypotheses that are plausible in explaining the observed events and useful in predicting the unobserved. One approach to induction is to identify one or more description models that constrain the form of hypothesized descriptions. Inductive learning then becomes a two-step process of first instantiating the model to generate a specific description, and then evaluating the plausibility and utility of the resulting description. Simple forms of such techniques have long been used in traditional regression analysis, where a typical model is a regression polynomial, and statistical tests are used to test the fit between the data and the instantiated model.

Examples of symbolic description models are the decision tree used by Hunt (1966), and the disjunctive normal form used by Michalski (1969, 1971, 1974). Such models carry a good deal of implicit problem-specific knowledge. It is important that a general inductive tool permit dynamic specification, modification and manipulation of the models.

Our method uses three description models.

(1) *Periodic conjunctive model.* This model specifies that the description must be a periodic description in which each phase is described by a single complex. For example, the rule

$$\text{Period ([color0 = red], [color0 = black])}$$

describes an alternating sequence of red and black cards. Furthermore, we can imagine a periodicity within the phase, in which case we have an embedded periodic rule. For example, suppose that the first phase of the above rule is another periodic sequence of face and nonface cards. This is represented as

Period ([color0 = red][Period ([face0 = true], [face0 = false])],
[color0 = black])

(2) *Lookback decomposition model.* This model specifies that the description must be a lookback description in the form of a set of if–then rules:

$$[\text{color1 = red}] \rightarrow [\text{value0} < 5]$$
$$[\text{color1 = black}] \rightarrow [\text{value0} \geqslant 5]$$

The left-hand sides, or condition parts of the rules refer to no more than *lb* (the lookback parameter) events prior to the event to be predicted (subscripts 1, 2, etc.). The right-hand sides provide predictions for the next events in the sequence given that the condition part is true. The decomposition model requires that the left-hand sides be disjoint so that only one if–then rule be applicable at one time.

(3) *Disjunctive normal form (DNF).* This model requires only that the description of the sequence must be a disjunction of VL_1 complexes. For example, the DNF expression

$$[\text{dsuit01 = 0] v [dvalue01 = 0}]$$

states that either the suit of the current card must be the same as the suit of the previous card, or the value of the current card must be the same as the value of the previous card.

From a logical standpoint, any decomposition rule or periodic rules can be written in disjunctive normal form. The periodic and decomposition models are useful not because of their theoretical expressiveness or power, but because of their assistance in locating plausible descriptions quickly. Depending on the number of descriptive attributes used, the space of all DNF descriptions could be immense and thus difficult to search. Therefore, this is a "catch-all" model, used after the other models have failed.

2.6 Descriptions Based on Segmentation

Often sequences of events are best described in a hierarchical fashion as series of subsequences. For example,

$$S = \langle 3, 4, 4, 5, 5, 5, 6, 6, 6, 6, 7, 7, 7, 7, 7 \rangle$$

is best described as a sequence of subsequences. Each subsequence is a string of identical digits. The length of each subsequence is one longer than its predecessor. The digit used in the subsequence is one larger than the digit used in the previous subsequence. In our method, this is indicated by a two-part description in which one part defines the segmentation condition, and the second part defines the relations among segments:

> *Segmentation condition:*
> String: [dvalue01 = 0]
> *Intersegment relation:*
> [dvalue01 = +1][dlength01 = +1]

The segmentation condition defines subsequences of events with constant value (dvalue01 = 0). The intersegment relation defines relations among the segments in the new sequence. For example, dvalue01 and dlength01 refer to the values and lengths of the segments. In our example the sequence is **segmented** into strings of maximal length satisfying this segmentation condition. This yields a new sequence

$$S' = \langle (3,1), (4,2), (5,3), (6,4), (7,5) \rangle.$$

In the original episode S each event of the episode is an entity with only one attribute, the value. In S' each event is related to a subsequence of events in S. Some of the attributes of S may also be used in S', while some others are newly created for S'. For example, the second event in S' has value 4 because all the corresponding events in S have value 4. Events in S' have a new attribute, length, indicating the number of events corresponding to this event in S.

Any description model listed in Section 3.3 can be applied to a sequence after it has been segmented. The discovery of such segmented descriptions requires both the discovery of the segmentation condition and the formulation of the description of the segmented sequence. In the current implementation, the system is equipped with a repertoire of segmentation conditions. A segmentation condition is chosen if its application produces a sufficient (according to a user defined criterion) number of elements in the transformed sequence.

3   THE ALGORITHMS UNDERLYING THE SPARC/G PROGRAM

3.1   Input Representation

The input episode is represented as a list of events. Each event in the list is represented by a set of attributes which are defined by the user. In addition, each event is marked as a positive or negative event of the episode. Let us use a very simple example (Figure 1) to illustrate the workings of SPARC/G. Each event in the episode is characterized by its texture, orientation (in degrees) and size. The representation (what is actually used by the program) is shown in Table 1.

Figure 1   Sequence of geometric shapes.

Table 1   Input VL_1 events.

Event	txtr0	orient0	size0
1	blank	45	small
2	striped	90	big
3	blank	135	small
4	solid	180	big
5	blank	225	small
6	striped	270	big
7	blank	315	small
8	solid	0	big
9	blank	45	small
10	striped	90	big
11	blank	135	small
12	solid	180	big

3.2   Data Transformations

The first step is to use constructive induction rules to derive additional attributes that may be useful for creating descriptions of the episode. Such rules are a part of the program's background knowledge, supplied by the user. New attributes are defined in terms of existing attributes, which in turn may be derived from previously defined attributes. The new attributes

Table 2   Augmented VL_1 events.

Event	txtr0	orient0	size0	shaded0
1	blank	45	small	false
2	striped	90	big	true
3	blank	135	small	false
4	solid	180	big	true
5	blank	225	small	false
6	striped	270	big	true
7	blank	315	small	false
8	solid	0	big	true
9	blank	45	small	false
10	striped	90	big	true
11	blank	135	small	false
12	solid	180	big	true

augment the current event descriptions. Here, a new attribute **shaded** is added that has two values: true and false. The value **false** characterizes a blank texture and the value **true** characterizes any other texture. If the generated attributes pass a preliminary relevance test, they are used to augment episode representation. Such an augmented representation is shown in Table 2.

The second step involves segmenting the episode. As discussed in Section 2, a segmentation condition is a relation that must hold between adjacent events of the segment. SPARC/G segments the episode into strings of maximal length that satisfy the segmentation condition, and then evaluates the potential usefulness of the segmentation. For example, the segmentation is not considered potentially useful if the segmented episode has nearly the same number of events as the original episode, or if the whole episode satisfies the segmentation condition.

The next transformation step involves making the order of the events explicit in the events. If the lookback parameter is one or more, the episode is transformed by augmenting each event with previous events falling within the lookback parameter window. Table 3 is the result of such a transformation derived with null segmentation condition and a lookback of one, then augmented with difference attributes. Now, the episode goes through model specific transformations explained in the next section.

3.3   Model-Dependent Rule Generation

This section explains how each description model is used in searching for a qualitative prediction rule.

Table 3 Transformed VL$_1$ events.

Event	txtr1	orient1	size1	shaded1	txtr0	orient0	size0	shaded0	dtxtr01	dorient01	dsize01	dshaded01
1	blank	45	small	false	striped	90	big	true	1	45	1	1
2	striped	90	big	true	blank	135	small	false	1	45	1	1
3	blank	135	small	false	solid	180	big	true	1	45	1	1
4	solid	180	big	true	blank	225	small	false	1	45	1	1
5	blank	225	small	false	striped	270	big	true	1	45	1	1
6	striped	270	big	true	blank	315	small	false	1	45	1	1
7	blank	315	small	false	solid	0	big	true	1	45	1	1
8	solid	0	big	true	blank	45	small	false	1	45	1	1
9	blank	45	small	false	striped	90	big	true	1	45	1	1
10	striped	90	big	true	blank	135	small	false	1	45	1	1
11	blank	135	small	false	solid	180	big	true	1	45	1	1

3.3.1   Rule generation of the decomposition model

The decomposition model describes an episode by a sequence of production rules. It accepts as input a set of positive events with, optionally, a set of negative events. Some attributes are designated as "left-hand-side" attributes. A decomposition seeks to explain current events in terms of the values of "left-hand-side" attributes. A decomposition-model-based description for the events in Table 3 would be

[shaded1 = true] → [txtr0 = blank][shaded0 = false]
[shaded1 = false] → [txtr0 = solid v striped][shaded0 = true]

This description **decomposes** events on attribute shaded1. It breaks the description of the episode into two if–then rules. The → can be interpreted as an implication. The decomposition algorithm assumes that both the left-hand and right-hand parts of the if–then rules must be single VL_1 complexes, and that the left-hand sides must be logically disjoint.

The decomposition algorithm starts by performing a trial decomposition on each possible left-hand-side attribute. A trial decomposition for a left-hand-side attribute is formed by creating a complex for each value of the attribute occurring in the episode. The complex is formed by merging (set union) the references of corresponding selectors of all events following the left-hand-side attribute. For example, using the events of Table 3, trial decompositions could be performed on txtr1, orient1, size1 and shaded1, but for simplicity Figure 2 represents a decomposition in terms of txtr1 and shaded1. The general idea is to form trial decompositions, choose the best decomposition, and break the problem into subproblems, one for each if–then rule in the selected decomposition. The algorithm can then be applied recursively until a consistent description has been developed.

Figure 2 shows the raw trial decompositions. These are very-low-generality descriptions. They must be processed further before a decision can be made as to which decomposition is best and should be further investigated. Three processing steps are applied to the trial decompositions.

The first processing step involves linear and cyclic interval attributes. These attributes often have many values, and raw trial decompositions based on them may be uninteresting and implausible. An attempt is made to apply the "close interval" inductive inference rule on the left-hand side of the trial decomposition (Michalski, 1983). The algorithm operates by computing distances between adjacent if–then rules, and looking for sudden jumps in the distance measure. Where a jump occurs (a local maximum), the algorithm tries to split the domain into cases.

The distance computation is a weighted multiple-valued Hamming distance. The weights are determined by taking user-specified plausibilities for

Decomposition on txtr1:

[txtr1 = solid] ⟶ [txtr0=blank][orient0=45 v 225][size0=small][shaded0=false]
[dtxtr01=1][dorient01=45][dsize01=1][dshaded01=1]

[txtr1 = blank] ⟶ [txtr0=solid v striped][orient0=0 v 90 v 180 v 270][size0=big][shaded0=true]
[dtxtr01=1][dorient01=45][dsize01=1][dshaded01=1]

[txtr1 = striped] ⟶ [txtr0=blank][orient=45 v 135 v 315][size0=small][shaded0=false]
[dtxtr01=1][dorient01=45][dsize=1][dshaded01=1]

Decomposition on shaded1:

[shaded1=true] ⟶ [txtr0=blank][orient0=45 v 135 v 225 v 315][size0=small][shaded0=false]
[dtxtr01=1][dorient=45][dsize01=1][dshaded01=1]

[shaded1=false] ⟶ [txtr0=striped v solid][orient0=0 v 90 v 180 v 270][size0=big][shaded0=true]
[dtxtr01=1][dorient01=45][dsize01=1][dshaded01=1]

Figure 2 Trial decompositions.

Decomposition on txtr1:

[txtr1 = solid] ⟶ [txtr0=blank][orient0=45..225][size0=small][shaded0=false]
[dtxtr01=1][dorientC1=45][dsize01=1][dshaded01=1]

[txtr1 = blank] ⟶ [txtr0=solid v striped][orient0=0..270][size0=big][shaded0=true]
[dtxtr01=1][dorient01=45][dsize01=1][dshaded01=1]

[txtr1 = striped] ⟶ [txtr0=blank][orient=45..315][size0=small][shaded0=false]
[dtxtr01=1][dorient01=45][dsize=1][dshaded01=1]

Decomposition on shaded1:

[shaded1=true] ⟶ [txtr0=blank][orientC=45..315][size0=small][shaded0=false]
[dtxtr01=1][dorient=45][dsize01=1][dshaded01=1]

[shaded1=false] ⟶ [txtr0=striped v solid][orient0=0..270][size0=big][shaded0=true]
[dtxtr01=1][dorient01=45][dsize01=1][dshaded01=1]

Figure 3 Generalized trial decompositions.

each attribute and relaxing these weights according to the discriminating power of each attribute (taken singly). For instance, if right-hand-side attribute is irrelevant in some if–then rules, i.e., its reference contains all possible values, then its weight is reduced to zero. The distances between adjacent if–then rules are computed and local maxima are located. If there is one maximum then the interval is split there, and two if–then rules are created. If there are two maxima then there are three intervals, and each creates one if–then rule. If there are more than two maxima then the smaller maxima are suppressed. Similar techniques are used for cyclic interval domains.

Once the cases have been determined, each trial decomposition is processed by applying the domain type specific rules of generalization to the selectors on the right-hand sides of the if–then rules. The "close interval" inference rule is applied to linear and cyclic attributes. Special domain types are defined for difference attributes (attributes derived by subtracting two other attributes). The rules of generalization for difference attributes attempt to find intervals about the zero point of the domain. Thus [dvalue01 $= -3$ v 1 v 2] would be generalized to [dvalue01 $= -3.. + 3$]. One-sided intervals away from zero are also created: [dvalue01 $= 3$ v 4 v 6] would be generalized to [dvalue01 > 0]. These generalizations are only performed if the reference contains more than one value. Corresponding to the trial decompositions of Figure 2 we get the generalized trial decompositions shown in Figure 3. The notation [size0 $= *$] is used when an attribute can take on any value from its domain.

The third processing step examines the different if–then rules and attempts to make the right-hand sides of the rules disjoint by removing selectors whose references are overlapping among them. Figure 4 shows the results of this step.

Decomposition on txtr1:

[txtr1 = solid] $\longrightarrow$ Any Event
[txtr1 = blank] $\longrightarrow$ Any Event
[txtr1 = striped] $\longrightarrow$ Any Event

Decomposition on shaded1:

[shaded1 = true] $\longrightarrow$ [txtr0 = blank][shaded0 = false]
[shaded1 = false] $\longrightarrow$ [txtr0 = solid v striped][shaded0 = true]

Figure 4   Trial decompositions with overlapping selectors removed.

The selection of the best decomposition uses a set of cost functions that measure characteristics of each trial decomposition. The cost functions are as follows.

(1) Count the number of negative examples that are incorrectly covered by this decomposition.

(2) Count the number of cases (if–then rules) in this decomposition.

(3) Return the user-specified plausibility for the attribute being decomposed on.

(4) Count the number of null cases for this decomposition

(5) Count the number of "simple" selectors in this decomposition. A simple selector can be written with a single value or interval in the reference (e.g. [value01 > 4] is a simple selector). After applying the generalization rules (as in Figure 3) all selectors except those with nominal attributes are simple.

The cost functions are applied in an ordered fashion using the lexicographic sort algorithm developed by Michalski (1980). The trial decomposition with the lowest cost is selected. The lowest cost solution is the decomposition on shaded1 shown in Figure 4. It states that if the figure is shaded then the texture of the next figure is blank and its shade is not shaded. And if the figure is not shaded then the texture of the next figure is solid or striped and is shaded.

Once the best trial decomposition has been selected, it is checked to see if it is consistent with the events (covers no negative events). If so, the decomposition algorithm terminates. If it is not then the problem is decomposed into separate subproblems, one for each if–then rule in the selected decomposition. Then the algorithm is repeated to solve these subproblems. (The subproblems are solved simultaneously, not independently.)

The strengths of the decomposition algorithm are as follows.

(1) Speed—good decompositions are located quickly.

(2) Transparency—decomposition descriptions are easy to interpret.

(3) Generality—the algorithm can discover a large class of symbolic relations between the current event and past events within a given lookback.

3.3.2   *Rule generation using the periodic model*

The periodic model is used to test if events in the episode display a periodic behaviour. It is assumed that the parameter defining the number of phases is provided to the algorithm. In searching for a periodic description, the system may try different values of this parameter. Each phase is treated in a manner similar to the treatment of the different if–then cases in the trial decomposition algorithm described earlier. First, the events in each phase are combined to form a single complex (by forming the union of references of corresponding selectors). For the episode in Figure 1, using a phase of two, the results are

Phase1:   [txtr0 = blank][orient0 = 45 v 135 v 225 v 315]
           [size0 = small][shaded0 = false]
Phase2:   [txtr0 = solid v striped][orient0 = 0 v 90 v 180 v 270]
           [size0 = big][shaded0 = true]

Note that in order to simplify descriptions, no difference attributes or attributes describing previous events are included in these derived events. First, overlapping complexes are dropped. Complexes that do not cover examples of other phases or negative examples are then generalized further:

Phase1:   [txtr0 = blank][orient0 = 45..315]
           [size0 = small][shaded0 = false]
Phase2:   [txtr0 = solid v striped][orient0 = 0..270]
           [size0 = big][shaded0 = true]

If these generalized complexes still do not cover negative examples, selectors with overlapping references (overlapping with selectors in other phases) are removed:

Phase1:   [txtr0 = blank][size0 = small][shaded0 = false].
Phase2:   [txtr0 = solid v striped][size0 = big][shaded0 = true]

If these complexes are still consistent, they are returned as the final description.

Both the periodic and the decomposition algorithms go through the above postprocessing steps until the description becomes inconsistent, at which time the algorithm backs up and returns the version of the description before it was overgeneralized to become inconsistent. In some cases, the star generation process of the Aq algorithm is invoked to attempt to extend the description against negative examples and examples of other phases.

For each phase from the above, a new episode is assembled. This episode is considered a full-fledged episode so that the periodic algorithm is invoked recursively until either the newly assembled episode is trivial, such as having length of one, or the description returned from the next call to the model is implausible. For the example, the episode for the second phase is again periodic:

Phase21:   [txtr0 = striped]
Phase22:   [txtr0 = solid]

Here the second phase of the top level is described by an embedded periodic rule of two phases, Phase21 and Phase22. The full recursive periodic description is

$$\text{Period}([\text{txtr0} = \text{blank}][\text{size0} = \text{small}][\text{shaded0} = \text{false}],$$
$$[\text{size0} = \text{big}][\text{shaded0} = \text{true}]$$
$$[\text{Period}([\text{txtr0} = \text{solid}], [\text{txtr0} = \text{striped}])])$$

This rule states that the episode has two phases: the events in the first phase have "blank" texture, "small" size and shaded; the events in the second phase have "solid" or "striped" texture, "big" size and not-shaded, also the textures alternate from striped to solid.

3.3.3   Rule generation using the DNF model

The DNF (disjunctive normal form) model employs the Aq algorithm (Michalski, 1969, 1971), which was originally developed in the context of switching theory and subsequently used for inductive inference (Michalski, 1972, 1973). The algorithm accepts as input a set of positive events and a set of negative events, and produces an optimized cover of the positive events against the negative events. Such a cover is a description that is satisfied by all of the positive events, but by none of the negative events. The process of developing a cover involves partially computing the complement of the set of negative events and intelligently selecting complexes which cover positive events. The final cover may be a single complex or a disjunction of complexes. Aq seeks to develop covers that satisfy predefined criteria, such as minimizing the number of complexes in the cover, the total cost of attributes, etc.

The algorithm proceeds in best-first fashion by the method of disjoint stars. A positive event **e1** is determined, and a star is built about **e1**. A **star** is the set of all maximally general complexes that cover **e1** and do not cover any negative event. The best complex in the star, **lq**, is chosen and included in the goal description. All events covered by **lq** are removed from further consideration. The above process is then repeated. However, the newly selected **e1** must not be covered by any element of *any previous star*. In this manner the algorithm builds disjoint, well-separated stars. It has been shown that the number of such stars is a lower bound on the minimum number of complexes in any cover (Michalski, 1969). The process repeats until all events are covered by at least one **lq** complex. Disjunctions of the selected complexes forms the goal discription. Some clean-up operations are required in the case where some positive events were covered by some star, but by no **lq**.

A simplified description of the process of building a star about an event **e1** is given as follows: each negative event is complemented, and then multiplied out, with the proviso that each resulting complex must cover **e1**. After each event is multiplied out, the set of intermediate products (so-called partial stars) is trimmed according to a user-specified preference criterion, and only the *MAXSTAR* best elements are retained. The final star has at most *MAXSTAR* elements in it.

Note that all of the steps mentioned (complementation, multiplication, etc.) are performed on attributes which can take on a set of values. This is a multiple-valued covering process.

The strengths of the algorithm include the following.

(1) Quasi-optimality—the algorithm efficiently generates covers that are optimal or near-optimal.

(2) Flexibility of cover optimality and type—the user can specify the cover optimality criterion that reflects the specific aspects of the problem. The criterion determines which **lq** is chosen from each star and which partial stars are retained during the star-building process. The algorithm can also be told the type of the cover sought. The cover can be disjoint (complexes are disjoint), intersecting (complexes are overlapping) or ordered (complexes are linearly ordered).

(3) Optimality estimate—if no trimming is performed, the algorithm provides an estimate of the maximum difference between the number of complexes in the solution and in the minimum solution.

The DNF model is used to discover properties that describe the collection of all positive/negative events. Sequential information, if any, exists in the form of attributes that characterize the relationship between events. The Aq algorithm is given the set of all positive events and negative events augmented with the derived attributes. The algorithm then attempts to find descriptions that describe all positive events, but none of the negative events. With orientation defined as a cyclic attribute so that zero degree is considered to be 45 degrees "larger" than 315 degrees, a difference attribute **dorient01** can be defined. Given appropriated negative events (not shown in Figure 1), a description

$$[dorient01 = 45]$$

is discovered as the description that perfectly characterizes the positive events.

3.4 Description Evaluation and Selection

This phase examines rules developed by the above induction algorithms in order to filter out redundant information in the generated rules. For example, the following are the rules given in Figure 4:

[shaded1 = dark] → [txtr0 = blank][shaded0 = false]
[shaded1 = clear] → [txtr0 = solid v striped][shaded0 = true]

Note that [txtr0 = blank] is equivalent to [shaded0 = false], and [txtr0 = solid v striped] is to [shaded0 = true]. This redundancy was caused because the induction algorithms were not aware of the structural relationships between attributes. This redundancy is removed by the following procedure:

for each rule in the rulebase **do**
  for each complex in the rule **do**
    for selectors A and B in the complex, and both A and B are based on some attribute **do**
      if they are equivalent **then** keep the syntactically simpler one
      else if $A \subset B$ **then** drop A
        else if $B \subset A$ **then** drop B

If A and B are based on two different attributes then A and B cannot be redundant. For example, shaded0 and dshaded01 cannot be redundant, since shaded0 is based on txtr0 while dshaded01 is based on both shaded0 and shaded1.

When an episode is segmented, some additional operations may be required. For example, given the episode

$$S = \langle 3, 4, 4, 5, 5, 5, 6, 6, 6, 6, 7, 7 \rangle,$$

one would not want to create a segment for the sevens. Such a segment would indicate that there is a string of sevens of length 2. If the induction algorithms received such an event, they would not be able to discover that the length of a string always increases by 1. So the segmentation process must leave the end of the episode unsegmented. Each description produced by the induction algorithm must be checked to verify that it is consistent with the tail end of the episode.

Finally the plausibility of the descriptions is assessed. First of all, the rule must be consistent; that is, it should not predict incorrectly events within the episode. Another criterion for plausibility is that the rule should be conceptually simple. This is approximated in the program by measuring syntactic complexity of the rule, such as the number of values in a reference, the number of selectors in each complex, the number of complexes in the rule and so on.

4 APPLICATIONS

This section presents results from applying the SPARC/G program (written in Berkeley PASCAL, running under Unix 4.2 BSD on a Sun-2/120 workstation) to a few example problems. Possible improvements and extensions to the program are also suggested.

Example 1: Discover Safe Passage through Channels

Suppose that two oceans Ocean$_1$ and Ocean$_2$ are connected by a network of channels, and the passageways are full of mines. The mines are regularly activated or deactivated by the enemy through remote control. The enemy signals the safe passageway to its ships by left and right beacons located before and after the junctions. The colour and frequency of the beacon are governed by a secret code indicating the safe passage. The ally observes the enemy ships passing from Ocean$_1$ to Ocean$_2$, and would like to discover the code so that its ships can also pass through the channels safely. SPARC/G was given the following descriptors:

(1) LeftColor (colour of the left beacon): {green, red, blue};

(2) RightColor (colour of the right beacon): {green, red, blue};

(3) LeftFrequency (frequency of the left beacon): {low, medium, high};

(4) RightFrequency (frequency of the right beacon): {low, medium, high}.

A map of the channel is given in Figure 5. The routes not taken by the enemy are considered unsafe, and are marked as an arrow with a bar across it. To discover the rule that characterizes the safe passage, it is hypothesized that all relevant information for the secret code is provided by the attributes of the beacons before and after each junction. The input episode is given in Table 4.

Table 4   Input events for Example 1.

Event	LeftColor	RightColor	LeftFrequency	RightFrequency	Route
1	red	green	medium	medium	taken
2	green	blue	high	low	not-taken
3	green	blue	low	high	taken
4	red	green	high	high	not-taken
5	blue	red	medium	medium	taken
6	red	blue	medium	high	not-taken
7	red	green	medium	low	not-taken
8	green	red	low	medium	taken
9	blue	red	medium	high	not-taken
10	red	red	high	low	taken
11	green	blue	medium	low	not-taken
12	green	blue	high	low	not-taken
13	blue	green	low	medium	taken
14	blue	green	low	high	not-taken
15	blue	red	low	medium	taken

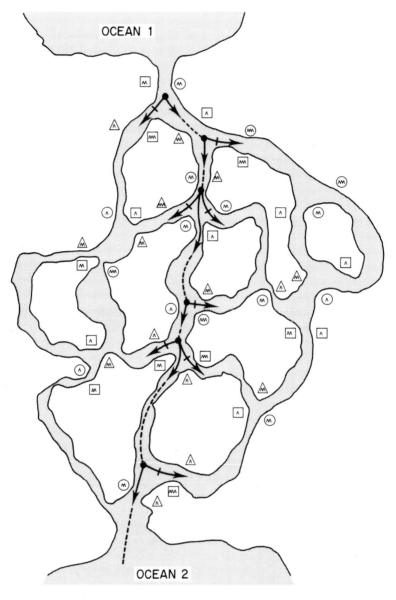

Figure 5   Mined channels.

The program discovered the following safe-passage rule using the decomposition rule model:

Rule 1: decomposition model, lookback: 1, nphases: 0
[LeftColor-before = red] → [RightFrequency-after > RightFrequency-before]
[LeftColor-before = green] → [RightFrequency-after < RightFrequency-before]
[LeftColor-before = blue] → [RightFrequency-after = RightFrequency-before]

The computation time was approximately one second on a Sun-2/120. The rules can be paraphrased as follows. The passage is safe if

- the colour of the left beacon before a junction is red, and the frequency of the next beacon on the right is lower than that of previous beacon on the right; or

- the colour of the left beacon before a junction is green, and the frequency of the next beacon on the right is higher than that of previous beacon on the right; or

- the colour of the left beacon before the junction is blue, and the frequency of the next beacon on the right is the same as that of previous beacon on the right.

In the paraphrase, the "implication" is interpreted as "and". This is allowed because the left-hand sides of the implication in decomposition rules are disjoint and complete with respect to the domain of the attribute. The program discovered the rules that are exactly the ones used to generate the example of safe passage. This is a very satisfactory result.

Example 2: Learning Preconditions in a Blocks World

In many planning systems, operations are often expressed as precondition–postcondition pairs. Preconditions specify the conditions that must be satisfied before an operation, while postconditions generally state the changes caused by the operation. For example, the operation **put-on(block1, block2)**, which puts block1 on top of block2 in blocks world, has the following preconditions and postconditions:

Preconditions: there must be no other object on top of block2, and the top of block2 must be flat;
Postconditions: block1 is on-top-of block2; block1 is "deleted" from its previous position.

This example shows how a system can acquire the rules by learning from examples. In this example, the world consists of four objects: two cubes, a cylinder and a pyramid. The following variables are defined for SPARC/G:

(1) top-of-cube1: its value is the name of the object that is on top of cube1;

(2) top-of-cube2: its value is the name of the object that is on top of cube 2;

(3) top-of-cylinder: its value is the name of the object that is on top of the cylinder;

(4) top-of-pyramid: its value is the name of the object that is on top of the pyramid;

(5) put: the action of putting an object on top of another; for example [put = cylinder-on-cube1], specifies the action of putting the cylinder on top of cube1;

(6) put-on-cube1: a binary variable that states the legitimacy of putting an arbitrary object on top of cube1.

The positive events given to SPARC/G are arbitrary legitimate actions and statuses permitted by the blocks world. The negative events are, on the other hand, illegitimate actions and status. Here is one example given to the program:

[top-of-cube1 = cube2][top-of-cube2 = clear]
[top-of-cylinder = clear][put = cylinder-on-cube2][put-on-cube1 = no]

This example states that if cube2 is on top of cube1, and the tops of the cube2 and cylinder are clear, then one may put the cylinder on top of cube2 (put = cylinder-on-cube2) but may not put anything on cube1 (put-on-cube1 = no). The input episode is shown in Table 5.

Table 5   Input events for Example 2.

Event	top-of-cube1	top-of-cube2	top-of-cylinder	put	put-on-cube-1
1	clear	clear	clear	cube2-on-cube1	yes
2	clear	clear	clear	cylinder-on-cube1	yes
3	clear	clear	clear	pyramid-on-cube1	yes
4	clear	clear	clear	cube2-on-pyramid	no
5	clear	clear	clear	cube1-on-cylinder	yes
6	cube2	clear	clear	cylinder-on-cube2	no
7	cube2	clear	clear	cube2-on-cube1	no
8	pyramid	clear	clear	cylinder-on-cube1	no
9	cylinder	clear	clear	pyramid-on-cube1	no

SPARC/G discovered the following rule using the DNF model with a lookback of 0 in 2.2 seconds:

$$[\text{top-of-cube1} = \text{clear}] \vee [\text{put-on-cube1} = \text{no}]$$

which can be reexpressed as

$$[\text{put-on-cube1} = \text{yes}] \rightarrow [\text{top-of-cube1} = \text{clear}]$$

which in effect says that if you want to put something on top of cube1 then the top of it must be clear. This is obviously correct. On the other hand, this example shows one of the limitations of SPARC/G: the currently used description language allows only one-argument functions or predicates. A desirable extension of the program would be to allow in its description language predicates and functions of two or more arguments.

Example 3: Learning a Symbolic Description of Motion

Motion is one of the most basic notions that governs our understanding of the physical world. How does motion of an object affect the state of the world and what type of motions are possible given the state of the world? The answer depends on discovering relations governing motion. We need not know Newtonian mechanics to understand the physical interactions of motion. The first step toward such discovery is to hypothesize causal connections between descriptions of the world. Since motion occurs in time, a sequential pattern recognition program like SPARC/G can play an important role. This example illustrates how the program can discover the causal relationships between the state of a spring and motion of an object. The program was given the following descriptors as perceptual vocabulary:

(1) Spring (state of the spring): {compressed, relaxed, stretched};

(2) Pos (the position of the block with respect to the position of the spring at rest): {left, center, right};

(3) Move (direction of the movement of the block): {left, still, right};

(4) Accel (the block slows down, accelerates, or moves with constant speed): $\{-1, +1, 0\}$.

Initially, the spring is stretched and the spring oscillates back and forth as shown in Figure 6. The corresponding input episode is shown in Table 6.

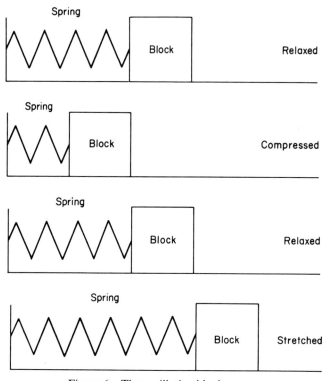

Figure 6   The oscillating block.

SPARC/G discovered the following decomposition rule with lookback of 1 in 1.1 seconds:

> Rule 1: decomposition model, lookback: 1, nphases: 0
> [Spring1 = stretched] → [Move0 = left]
> [Spring1 = relaxed] → [Move0 = still]
> [Spring1 = compressed] → [Move0 = right]

The rule can be paraphrased as follows:

(1) if the spring is stretched then the block is going to move to the left;

(2) if the spring is relaxed then the block is coming to a halt;

(3) if the spring is compressed then the block is going to move to the right;

SPARC/G was able to predict the movement of the block from the state of the spring. Even though this rule may fail (for example, if the spring is stretched too much then it may break), it seems to be a good first approximation of our intuitive notion of spring motion.

Table 6   Input events for Example 3.

Event number	Spring	Pos.	Move	Accel.
1	stretched	right	still	−1
2	relaxed	center	left	0
3	compressed	left	still	+1
4	relaxed	center	right	0
5	stretched	right	still	−1
6	relaxed	center	left	0
7	compressed	left	still	+1
8	relaxed	center	right	0
9	stretched	right	still	−1
10	relaxed	center	left	0
11	compressed	left	still	+1
12	relaxed	center	right	0
13	stretched	right	still	−1
14	relaxed	center	left	0
15	compressed	left	still	+1
16	relaxed	center	right	0
17	stretched	right	still	−1
18	relaxed	center	left	0
19	compressed	left	still	+1
20	relaxed	center	right	0
21	stretched	right	still	−1
22	relaxed	center	left	0
23	compressed	left	still	+1
24	relaxed	center	right	0
25	stretched	right	still	−1
26	relaxed	center	left	0
27	compressed	left	still	+1
28	relaxed	center	right	0
29	stretched	right	still	−1
30	relaxed	center	left	0
31	compressed	left	still	+1
32	relaxed	center	right	0
33	stretched	right	still	−1
34	relaxed	center	left	0
35	compressed	left	still	+1
36	relaxed	center	right	0

Physicists can explain the episode from first principles, but most human beings are not physicists. It seems that we typically derive qualitative relations existing in the world by doing inductive inferences from our observations, such as those performed by SPARC/G. Thus it appears that the program can be used to capture some important aspects underlying our processes of acquiring models of the physical world.

Example 4: Learning a Sequence of Actions

The operation of most planning or problem-solving systems is usually based upon a predefined set of rules. These rules represent the direct injection of knowledge from human users to the system. In this example, we show how SPARC/G can be used to acquire these rules by learning from training episodes.

Suppose we wish to teach a robot to operate a simplified cassette recorder by giving examples. Several legitimate actions are defined for the robot, such as to put a cassette into the recorder, eject the cassette, play, stop, etc. The robot is allowed to play with the cassette recorder, and a tutor labels each of the robot's actions as being either correct or incorrect. Whenever the robot effects an incorrect action, it is assumed that the robot will retract the incorrect action before making any further attempt. The robot must figure out the right sequence of actions all by itself. It is assumed that the rules to be learned are in the form

$$\text{ACTIONi} \rightarrow \text{ACTIONj or ACTIONk}$$

Such a rule states that after ACTIONi is executed, the next legitimate action can only be either ACTIONj or ACTIONk.

In this example, four legitimate actions on the recorder are defined:

(1) Put: putting the cassette into the recorder;

(2) Play: begin playing the cassette;

(3) Stop: stop playing the cassette;

(4) Eject: taking the cassette out of the recorder.

The legitimate sequence of actions is as follows:

(1) after putting the cassette into the recorder (Put), one may either eject the cassette (Eject) or start playing (Play);

(2) after begin playing the cassette (Play), the only legitimate action is Stop;

(3) after Stop, one may either Eject or Play;

(4) after Eject, the only legitimate action is Put.

A variable Action, among some other irrelevant variables, is defined in this example. The variable Action can take on either one of the four values: put, play, stop or eject.

Part of the episode given to SPARC/G is shown in Table 7.

Table 7   Input episode for Example 4.

Event number	Action	Legal?
1	put	yes
2	put	no
3	stop	no
4	play	yes
5	put	no
6	stop	yes
7	eject	yes
8	play	no
9	put	yes
10	eject	yes
11	put	yes
12	eject	yes

SPARC/G discovered the legal sequences of actions using the decompositional model with a lookback of 1 in 2.5 seconds. The rules produced take the form of implications:

Rule 1: decomposition model, lookback: 1, nphases: 0
$[\text{action1} = \text{eject}] \rightarrow [\text{action0} = \text{put}]$
$[\text{action1} = \text{stop}] \rightarrow [\text{action0} = \text{play v eject}]$
$[\text{action1} = \text{play}] \rightarrow [\text{action0} = \text{stop}]$
$[\text{action1} = \text{put}] \rightarrow [\text{action0} = \text{play v eject}]$

The rules can be paraphrased as follows:

Following Eject, the next action must be a Put;

Following Stop, the next action must be either a Play or an Eject;

Following Play, the next action must be a Stop;

Following Put, the next action must be either a Play or an Eject.

Thus these rules exactly characterize the legal actions.

Example 5: ELEUSIS: A Game of Scientific Discovery

This example shows the program's capability to discover rules in the card game Eleusis that models the process of scientific discovery (Gardner, 1977).† The game is played between a dealer and several players. Given a

---

† *The New Eleusis* is available from Robert Abbott at Box 1175, General Post Office, New York, NY 10001, USA.

sequence of cards that represent an instantiation of a qualitative prediction rule invented by the dealer (e.g. alternating colour of cards), the players are supposed to guess the secret rule invented by the dealer. In order to make the game more interesting, the dealer is penalized for inventing rules too difficult for any one to discover, or rules so simple that everyone can discover them. For the purpose of this example, it is assumed that SPARC/G poses as a player trying to figure out the rule governing the card sequence. The following is a simple Eleusis example designed to show the versatility of SPARC/G. A specialized version of the program, SPARC/E, has shown expert level performance in playing the game, and has beaten its human counterparts on many occasions.

The card sequence is given as a main line and a side line. The cards (read from left to right) in the main line represent positive instances that conform to the dealer's secret rule, and the cards in the sidelines represent negative instances that defy the rule:

Main line	JC	AD	QH	10S	QD	9H	QC	7H
Side line	KC	5S				4S		10D

The above layout of cards shows a card sequence of alternating faces, with Jack, Queen and King as face cards. The layout indicates that it is legitimate to play an Ace of diamonds (AD) following a Jack of clubs (JC), but not a King of clubs (KC), etc.

When given the above sequence, SPARC/G discovered the dealer's secret rule in three ways:

Rule 1: decomposition model, lookback: 1, nphases: 0
[face(card1) = false] → [face(card0) = true] v
[face(card1) = true] → [face(card0) = false]

Rule 2: periodic model, lookback: 1, nphases: 1
period([face(card0) <> face(card1)])

Rule 3: periodic model, lookback: 1, nphases:2
period([face(card0) = true], [face(card0) = false])

The rules can be paraphrased as follows.

Rule 1 If the previous card is a face card, then the next card must be a non-face card. If the previous card is a non-face card, then the next card must be a face card. This rule was discovered using the decomposition model with a lookback of one. (4 seconds)

Rule 2 Adjacent cards in the card sequence have different face values. This rule was discovered using the periodic model with a phase of one. (1 second)

Table 8   Results from other ELEUSIS game sessions.

Secret rule	Rule discovered	Execution time (s)	Source of the rule
• If previous card is red then play a faced card; If previous card is black then play a nonfaced card.	Rule 1: lookback: 1 nphases: 0 Decomposition [color(card1) = red] → [face(card0) = true] v [color(card1) = black] → [face(card0) = false]	2.9	Tom Channic
• If previous card is odd then play a card of different colour; If previous card is even then play a card of same colour.	Rule 1: lookback: 1 nphases: 0 Decomposition [parity(card1) = odd] → [color(card0) <> color(card1)] v [parity(card1) = even] → [color(card0) <> color(card1)]	1.6	Donald Michie
• Play any card that is either red and odd, or black and even.	Rule 1: lookback: 0 nphases: 0 DNF [color(card0) = red][parity(card0) = odd] v [color(card0) = black][parity(card0) = even]	1.2	Patrick Winston
If previous card is odd then play a black card; If previous card is even then play a red card.	rule 1: lookback: 1 nphases: 0 Decomposition [parity(card1) = odd] → [color(card0) <> color(card1)] v [parity(card1) = even] → [color(card0) <> color(card1)]	1.5	Gardner (1977)

Rule 3 The sequence is composed of two interleaving sequences of cards, where one sequence are all face cards, and the other sequence all non-face cards. This rule was discovered using the periodic model with a phase of two. (1 second)

Table 8 shows the result of several other game sessions.

5 SUMMARY AND RESEARCH DIRECTIONS

The methodology presented is applicable to a wide range of qualitative prediction problems. The major strengths of the methodology lie in its generality and the use of several description models and corresponding sequence transformations. These models and transformations guide the search through an immense space of plausible qualitative prediction rules. The representation space of DNF and Decomp Model is $2^{A \times (lb+1) \times v \times D}$, and $2^{A \times (lb+1) \times v \times p^R}$ for periodic model, where A is the number of attributes, lb is the lookback parameter, v is the size of the domain of an attribute, D is the maximum number of disjunctive terms, p is the number of phases in periodic model, and R is depth of recursion in periodic model.

The methodology assumes that the information contained in the events, plus the information that can be inferred from the events using the program's background knowledge, is sufficient to predict a plausible continuation of a process. One way to improve the capability of the system is to enhance the background knowledge and the program's ability to utilize this knowledge. The current implementation utilizes mainly the information contained in the events, and to a lesser extent those contained in the background knowledge.

Background knowledge consists primarily of description models and associated sequence transformations, domains and types of variables, and various domain-specific constructive induction rules that generate new variables from the old ones. It does not, however, have capabilities for testing the consistency of generalized selectors in the complexes for utilizing various interdomain constraints, or for performing a chain of deductions to see if the episode is explained by the rules of inference in the background knowledge (Dejong, 1986).

The search strategy invokes two processes simultaneously:

(1) a specialization of description models by instantiating the models with the given parameters to generate restricted rule forms;

(2) a transformation of the original episode into a new form, more amenable for rule discovery.

The algorithms presented here work best when negative events are available, but satisfactory performance can be obtained without negative events. Processes that contain noise or error are currently not handled by the program.

The generality of the program has been demonstrated by a series of examples from different domains. Among desirable paths for future research are improving the efficiency of the search process, extending the representation to more powerful description language such as the annotated predicate calculus (Michalski, 1983) so that multiple-argument descriptions are allowed, and developing the capability for incremental learning.

ACKNOWLEDGEMENTS

The authors are grateful to Peter Haddawy, Carl Kadie, Igor Mozetic, Gail Thornburg and Carl Uhrik for their comments on the earlier draft of this paper. This research was supported in part by the National Science Foundation under grant NSF DCR 84-06801, the Office of Naval Research under grant N00014-82-K-0186 and the Defense Advanced Research Projects Agency under grant N00014-K-85-0878.

REFERENCES

Box, G. E. P. and Jenkins, G. M. (1976). *Time-Series Analysis: Forecasting and Control*, Revised edn. San Francisco: Holden-Day.

Chilausky, R., Jacobsen, B. and Michalski, R. S. (1976). An application of variable valued logic to inductive learning of plant disease diagnostic rules. *Proc. 6th Ann. Symp. on Multiple Valued Logic, Logan, Utah, 1976.*

DeJong, G. (1986). An approach to learning from observations. *Machine Learning: An Artificial Intelligence Approach*, Vol. II. (ed. R. S. Michalski, J. G. Carbonell and T. Mitchell). Los Altos, California: Morgan Kaufmann.

De Kleer, J. and Brown, J. S. (1984). A qualitative physics based on confluences. *Artificial Intelligence* **24**, 7–83.

Dietterich, T. G. (1980). The methodology of knowledge layers for inducing description of sequentially ordered events. M.S. thesis, Department of Computer Science, University of Illinois, Urbana.

Dietterich, T. G. and Michalski, R. S. (1979). Learning and generalization of characteristic descriptions: evaluation criteria and comparative review of selected methods. *Proc. 6th Int. Joint Conf. on Artificial Intelligence, Tokyo, August 1979*, pp. 223–231.

Dietterich, T. G. and Michalski, R. S. (1985). Discovering patterns in sequences of events. *Artificial Intelligence* **25**, 187–232.

Forbus, K. (1984). Qualitative process theory. Ph.D. thesis, MIT.

Gardner, M. (1977). On playing the New Eleusis, the game that simulates the search for truth. *Scientific American* **237** (October), 18–25.

Hedrick, C. L. (1974). A computer program to learn production systems using a semantic net. Ph.D. thesis, Department of Computer Science, Carnegie-Mellon University, Pittsburgh.

Hunt, E. B. (1966). *Experiments in Induction*. New York: Academic Press.

Larson, J. (1976). A multi-step formation of variable logic hypotheses. *Proc. 6th Int. Symp. on Multiple-Valued Logic, Logan, Utah, 1976.*

Larson, J. (1977). Inductive inference in the variable valued predicate logic system VL21: Methodology and computer implementation. Rep. 869, Dept Computer Sci. Univ. Illinois, Urbana.

Larson, J. and Michalski, R. S. (1977). Inductive inference of VL decision rules. *SIGART Newsletter* (June), 38–44.

Michalski, R. S. (1969). Algorithm Aq for the quasi-minimal solution of the covering problem. *Archiwum Automatyki i Telemechaniki*, No. 4, Polish Academy of Sciences. (In Polish.)

Michalski, R. S. (1972). A variable-valued logic system as applied to picture description and recognition. *Proc. IFIP Working Conf. on Graphic Languages, Vancouver.*

Michalski, R. S. (1973). Discovering classification rules using variable-valued logic system VL1. *Advance Papers of 3rd Int. Joint Conf. on Artificial Intelligence, Stanford University*, pp. 162–172.

Michalski, R. S. (1974). Variable-valued logic: System VL1. *1974 Int. Symp. on Multiple-Valued Logic, West Virginia University, Morgantown, West Virginia, 29–31 May.*

Michalski, R. S. (1977). Variable-valued logic and its application to pattern recognition and machine learning. *Computer Science and Multiple-Valued Logic* (ed. D. C. Rine), pp. 506–534. Amsterdam: North-Holland.

Michalski, R. S. (1980). Pattern recognition as knowledge-guided inductive inference, IEEE Transactions on Pattern Analysis and Machine Intelligence, Vol. PAMI-2, No. 4, pp. 349–61, July 1980.

Michalski, R. S. (1983). A theory and methodology of inductive learning. *Machine Learning: An Artificial Intelligence Approach* (ed. R. S. Michalski, J. Carbonell and T. Mitchell), pp. 83–134. Palo Alto, California: TIOGA Publishing Co.

Michalski, R. S., Chen, K. and Ko, H. (1985). SPARC/E(V.2): A Eleusis rule generator and player. Rep. Dept Computer Sci., Univ. Illinois, Urbana.

Mitchell, T. M., Richard, M. K. and Kedar-Cabelli, S. T. (1985). Explanation-based generalization: A unifying view. Rutgers Computer Sci. Dept Tech. Rep. ML-TR-2.

Schwenzer, G. M. and Mitchell, T. M. (1977). Computer-assisted structure elucidation using automatically acquired carbon-13 NMR rules. *ACS Symp. Ser.* 54: *Computer-Assisted Structure Elucidation* (ed. D. H. Smith).

Soloway, E. and Riseman, E. M. (1977). Knowledge-directed learning. *Proc. Workshop on Pattern Directed Inference Systems. SIGART Newsletter* (June), 49–55.

Waterman, D. A. (1975). Serial pattern acquisition: A production system approach. Working Paper 286, Dept Psychology, Carnegie-Mellon Univ. Pittsburgh.

6.   Decision support systems and PROLOG

FRANK KRIWACZEK

Abstract.   After a brief introduction to the concept of a decision support system, this chapter discusses some of the ways that PROLOG can be used to implement such systems successfully.

1   INTRODUCTION

Decision support systems (DSS) are interactive computerized systems, used by decision makers, in person, to assist in the solution of semi-structured problems. Semi-structured decisions (Keen and Scott Morton, 1978) can only be automated to a limited extent, as they require subjective assessments and judgement in combination with statistical analysis and model building.

A DSS would normally have access to the analytic power, models and databases held in the machine. But the key element is the decision maker whom the system is designed to assist. Consequently, the system should incorporate a human-oriented user interface, it should display its information in a format and terminology which is familiar to the user and should avoid exposing the user to information overload (Freyenfeld, 1984).

In order to lay a formal foundation to the subject, Boncek *et al.* (1981) have proposed a three-component generic description of DSS comprising a language system, a knowledge system and a problem-processing system (Figure 1).

The language system (LS) incorporates all linguistic facilities made available to the decision maker by the DSS. It encompasses both languages for retrieval of data and languages for directing computation, using one or more of the models. The LS does not include the interface between the models and the database.

The knowledge system (KS) is the body of knowledge possessed by the DSS. Much of it will consist of databases of facts organized in a systematic manner. A variety of types of application specific knowledge have been identified (Holsapple, 1983), including

empirical or environmental (i.e. about the state of the application environment in which the decision maker operates);

CURRENT ISSUES IN EXPERT SYSTEMS
ISBN 0-12-714030-1

Decision   support   system

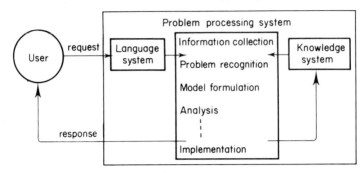

Figure 1

modelling (i.e. methods for performing relevant computations);
derived (i.e. from existing knowledge through the use of models);
meta (i.e. knowledge about knowledge);
linguistic (e.g. application-specific vocabulary and grammar rules);
assimilative (i.e. how new knowledge can be added to the KS); and
presentation (i.e. how responses are displayed to the user).

The problem-processing system (PPS) acts as the interfacing mechanism between the KS and the LS. Since the main role of a DSS is to produce information in response to a user query (expressed in LS syntax), based upon domain knowledge (expressed in KS syntax), the PPS is seen to play a crucial role in the DSS. It should be capable of information collection both from the user (via the LS) and the KS, and may also have problem-recognition and analysis capabilities. A PPS may either have models embedded within it or may generate models from appropriate knowledge stored in the KS.

Mechanical theorem proving methods can be extremely relevant to information collection (e.g. natural-language processing), problem recognition and model formulation. PROLOG and its descendents will play an increasingly important role both in the building of PPS and the specification of modelling knowledge.

For the purposes of looking in more detail at the part that Logic Programming can play in DSS, it will be simpler to adopt Sprague's (1980) model of DSS that categorizes performance characteristics into three parts: dialogue handling (the user-DSS interface); database and database management capability; and modelling and analytic capability (Figure 2).

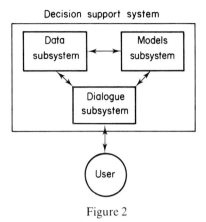

Figure 2

2   THE DATA SUBSYSTEM

Horn clause logic databases subsume relational databases. Variable-free assertions such as

smith works_in finance_dept

correspond to tuples of a relation. General rules serve a variety of purposes (Kowalski, 1985):

data can be described both explicitly and implicitly, e.g.
main_library takes herald_tribune
main_library takes X if
   X is_newspaper and
   X is_published_in London

rules generalize user views, e.g.
X is_first_class_student if
   X is_student and
   X received_aggregate_mark Y and
   Y greater than 70

rules implement integrity constraints, e.g.
X is_grandparent_of Y if
   X is_parent_of Z and
   Z is_parent_of Y

rules implement heirarchies, e.g.

>   X is entitled to pay rise if
>   X is manual worker
>   X is manual worker if
>   X is painter
>   X is manual worker if
>   X is bricklayer

rules implement programs.

Although Horn clause logic is an expressive database language, the direct use of PROLOG to query data kept in core poses questions of efficiency. Methods of *query optimization* have been investigated (Grishman, 1978; Reiter, 1978; Warren, 1981), in order to improve response times to submitted queries. Optimization usually includes standardization, simplification and transformation. Metarules may be employed to guide the choice among the various query transformation rules.

Of course, in large organizations the relevant data may be too large to fit into core, in which case techniques for external file management will be required. Vassilou *et al.* (1983) describe a range of strategies for coupling PROLOG systems with database management systems (DBMS). The options seem to be as follows:

to build a DBMS in PROLOG:

to *loosely couple* the PROLOG system with an existing DBMS (where data is extracted from the existing data and stored as a "snapshot" in the PROLOG workspace prior to solving a query); or

to *tightly couple* the PROLOG system with an existing DBMS (where the external database appears to the PROLOG system as an extension of the workspace).

Work on loosely coupled systems, in which PROLOG does all its work before the database query, is based on the idea of *query compilation*, in which stereotypical user queries are transformed in advance into a conjunction of straight database queries and model calls (Chang, 1978; Fishman and Naqvi, 1982; Henschen and Naqvi, 1982; Chen and Henschen, 1985). On the other hand, the tightly coupled system DADM (Kellogg, 1982), interleaves deduction with partial search in the DBMS.

3   THE MODEL SUBSYSTEM

Models can often be expressed in rule-based form. Such models are then homogenous with data, it is easier to trace their operation, and to explain and to modify them. In some cases a rule is the most natural way of representing a model. Consider the following model (Westfall and Boyd, 1961), which was used by a large Chicago-based department store chain to narrow down its site choices:

> X is possible site if
>> Y is annual achievable sales at X and
>> Y is between $3 million and $5 million and
>> X is located in centre Z and
>> Z is a one stop shopping centre and
>> X is in area U and
>> U is a secondary area and
>> U has population growth potential and
>> U has consumer income growth potential and
>> V is the distance from X to Chicago and
>> V is less than 200 miles
>> X is leasable and
>> U has population W and
>> W is greater than 100000

This rule is interesting because the various conditions can be solved in differing ways. Conditions 1, 7 and 8 might call marketing, demographic and econometric models, conditions 2, 10 and 13 would call arithmetical primitives, conditions 3, 5, 9 and 12 would be database lookups, conditions 4 and 6 would access rules defining "one stop shopping centre" and "secondary area", and condition 11 might result in a query to a (human) expert in real estate.

Many of the well-known models of operations research can be expressed in rule-based form. For example, the critical-path-analysis algorithm can be written in PROLOG (Kriwaczek, 1984). The rules include the following:

> A has earliest_start_time 0 if
>> A is_a begin_activity
> A has earliest_start_time S if
>> not (A is_a begin_activity) and
>> L isall (F:P precedes A and
>>   P has_earliest_finish_time F) and
>> L has_maximum_value S

> A has earliest_finish_time F if
>> A has earliest_start_time S and
>> A has_duration D and
>> F is S + D

Efficiency can be improved by compiling the PROLOG, employing machines that are microcoded in PROLOG, implementing appropriate primitives in machine code and calling on routines written in other languages, such as C or FORTRAN. In the latter two cases the model calls would be in the form of what Boncek *et al.* (1981) term *virtual relations*.

4   THE DIALOGUE SUBSYSTEM

Conventional dialogue methods such as menus, command languages, forms and interactive graphics can all be implemented in PROLOG. In addition, a spreadsheet interface, LogiCalc, has been developed in PROLOG (Kriwaczek, 1986). This tool can behave like a conventional spreadsheet, but has an enhanced functionality. It can deal with non-numeric functions, can access a knowledge base and can carry out goal-seeking. Relations can be declared between cells of the spreadsheet, various values entered in certain cells, and the system set to "complete the picture". The user can then comment on the resulting pattern, "freezing" some values and "forbidding" others. In this way the spreadsheet can be used as a man–machine interface for cooperative search for solutions to problems (e.g. interactive scheduling). Finally, cells can contain structured objects such as lists, graphs, diagrams, text or even complete spreadsheets—viewed through windows onto the cells.

One of the areas in which PROLOG has been most conspicuously successful is that of natural-language processing (Colmerauer, 1982; Pereira and Warren, 1981; McCord, 1987). Grammars for natural and artificial languages can be expressed easily as logic programs, and parsing can be accomplished by direct execution of these programs. Furthermore, because of PROLOG's strong connection with logic, the meaning of natural-language utterances can be represented with the help of PROLOG.

Consequently, PROLOG is very well suited as a tool for building front ends to databases. Such front ends normally work by parsing the natural-language query and in the process building up a semantic representation of the query in logic. In some simple cases this logical representation can be transformed into PROLOG by minimally tidying it up (for example by removing redundant brackets). The resulting PROLOG query can then be executed and the answer obtained. Sometimes there needs to be a set of rules to bridge the gap between the semantic representation of a query and the appropriate database and model queries. For example, the query *What are the critical paths?* might be translated into

$$(\text{SETOF X Y} : (\text{path Y})(\text{critical Y}))(\text{write}(X))$$

literally: *print the set of all paths that are critical.* If this were executed directly by PROLOG then the paths through the network would be generated one-by-one, and each one tested for criticality. This would be hopelessly inefficient for a sizeable network. However, if there is a critical path algorithm in the model subsystem, with the relation *critical_path*, then we need a rule that scans the semantic representation of natural language queries and replaces any pair ((path X)(critical X)) by (critical_path X). The PROLOG query would then become

$$(SETOF \ X \ Y : (critical\_path \ Y))(write \ (X))$$

which would have the correct effect.

Expert systems written in PROLOG, such as APES (Hammond and Sergot, 1983), have two very useful features that are most relevant to DSS. The first feature, Query-the-User (Sergot, 1983), generates prompts to the user automatically whenever matters of fact are required that are not found in the database, whenever decisions that could be mechanized but are more easily or efficiently handled by the human user are required, and whenever matters of judgement or "political" decisions are concerned.

The second feature is the provision of explanations regarding the system's reasoning. The user can ask why he is being queried by the system for a piece of information, and can ask how the system arrived at a particular answer. Clearly, a decision maker, who is likely to have to justify his own choice of actions, will find the provision of such explanations reassuring.

5 DSS DESIGN

Keen, one of the originators of the DSS concept, has stated "The *Support System* is meaningful only in situations where the *final* system must emerge through an adaptive process of design and usage" (Keen 1980). In a case study he found that

the actual use of DSS differed from the intended use;

usage is personalized;

DSS evolve;

functions provided are not generally elaborate—complex systems evolve from simple components; and

major benefits cited by users include flexibility, improved communication, insight and learning.

Because

users cannot provide functional specifications—either through lack of knowledge or because there is an intrinsic lack of procedures,

users do not know what they want,

users' concepts of task or decision situation are often sharpened by DSS,
   and there is a consequent unpredictability of usage, and
users require personalized usage,
it is necessary for DSS to emerge through an *adaptive process of design and
usage*. Of course, the system can never be final. It needs to change frequently
to track changes in the user, problem and environment.

The solution proposed was *Iterative Design* (Sprague and Carlson, 1982):
  (i) identify an important subproblem;
  (ii) develop a small but usable system to assist the decision maker;
  (iii) refine, expand and modify the system in cycles; and
  (iv) evaluate the system constantly.

PROLOG is ideally suited to such a methodology. Rules are extremely
modular and need not have any side effects, allowing *piecewise programming*. Rules can have great clarity, and can be easy to understand and to
modify. Rules can be run directly on the machine—there need be no delay
between introducing or modifying a rule and testing the consequences.
Lastly, it is relatively easy to make logic programs more elaborate and
sophisticated, either by uniformly adding parameters to a relation to hold
extra information, or by adding extra clauses to handle new situations.

6   CONCLUSION

We have argued that the methods of logic programming and the language
PROLOG are appropriate to all parts of a DSS. There is an elegance and
economy in adopting a single language. Furthermore, PROLOG is also
clearly well suited as a medium for implementing intelligent features such as
problem recognition and user modelling. Finally, we have seen that the
recommended method of DSS creation is completely in line with the normal
methods of developing logic programs.

REFERENCES

Boncek, R. H., Holsapple, C. W. and Whinston, A. B. (1981). *Foundations of
Decision Support Systems*. New York: Academic Press.
Chang, C. L. (1978). DEDUCE 2: Further investigations of deduction in relational
databases. *Logic and Databases* (ed. H. Gallaire and J. Minker), pp. 201–236.
New York: Plenum Press.
Chen, M. C. and Henschen, L. J. (1985). On the use and internal structure of
logic-based decision support systems. *Decision Support Systems* **1**, no. 3.
Colmerauer, A. (1982). An interesting subset of natural language. *Logic Program-
ming* (ed. K. L. Clark and S.-A. Tärnlund), pp. 45–66. New York: Academic
Press.

Fishman, D. and Naqvi, S. (1982). An intelligent database system: AIDS. *Proc. Workshop on Logical Bases for Data Bases, 1982*. Section 22.

Freyenfeld, W. A. (1984). *Decision Support Systems: An Executive Overview of Interactive Computer-Assisted Decision Making in the UK*. Manchester: NCC Publications.

Grishman, R. (1978). The simplification of retrieval requests generated by question-answering systems. *Proc. 4th VLDB Conf., 1978*, pp. 400–406.

Hammond, P. and Sergot, M. J. (1983). A PROLOG shell for logic based expert systems. *Proc. Conf. on Expert Systems*, pp. 95–104. Cambridge: British Computer Society.

Henschen, L. J. and Naqvi, S. A. (1984). On compiling queries in recursive first-order databases. *J. ACM* **31** (1), 47–85.

Holsapple, C. W. (1983). The knowledge system for a generalized problem processor. Krannert Inst. Pap., Purdue University, West Lafayette, Indiana.

Keen, P. G. W. (1980). Adaptive Design for DSS. *Database* **12**, nos. 1, 2.

Keen, P. G. W. and Scott Morton, M. S. (1978). *Decision Support Systems: An Organizational Perspective*. Reading, Mass.: Addison-Wesley.

Kellogg, C. (1982). Knowledge management: A practical amalgam of knowledge and data base technology. *Proc. 3rd Nat. Conf. on Artificial Intelligence, 1982*.

Kowalski, R. A. (1985). Logic programming and its applications. Seminar notes, PLS Programming Logic Systems, Milford, Connecticut.

Kriwaczek, F. R. (1984). A critical path analysis program. *micro-PROLOG: Programming in Logic* (ed. K. L. Clark and F. G. McCabe), pp. 277–293. Englewood Cliffs, N.J.: Prentice-Hall.

Kriwaczek, F. R. (1987). LogiCalc—A PROLOG Spreadsheet. *Machine Intelligence*, Vol. 11 (ed. D. Michie, J. Hayes-Michie and J. Richards). Oxford: Oxford University Press.

McCord, M. C. (1987). Natural language processing and Prolog. *Knowledge Systems and Prolog: A Logical Approach to Expert Systems and Natural Language Processing* (ed. A. Walker, M. C. McCord, J. Sowa and W. Wilson), pp. 291–402. Reading Mass.: Addison-Wesley.

Pereira, F. C. N. and Warren, D. H. D. (1981). Definite clause grammars for language analysis—a survey of the formalism and a comparison with augmented transition networks. *Artificial Intelligence*, **13**, 231–279.

Reiter, R. (1978). Deductive question-answering on relational data bases. *Logic and Databases* (ed. H. Gallaire and J. Minker), pp. 149–177. New York: Plenum Press.

Sergot, M. J. (1983). A query-the-user facility for logic programs. *Integrated Interactive Computer Systems* (ed. P. Delgano and E. Sandwell), pp. 27–41. Amsterdam: North-Holland. Also published in *New Horizons in Educatonal Computing* (ed. M. Yazdani), pp. 145–163. Chichester: Ellis Horwood.

Sprague, R. H. (1980). A framework for the development of DSS. *MIS Quarterly* **4** (4), 1–26.

Sprague, R. H. and Carlson, E. D. (1982). *Building Effective Decision Support Systems*. Englewood Cliffs, N.J: Prentice-Hall.

Vassilou, Y., Clifford, J. and Jarke, M. (1983). How does an expert system get its data? NYU Working Paper, New York.

Warren, D. H. D. (1981). Efficient processing of interactive relational data base queries expressed in logic. *Proc. 7th VLDB Conf., 1981*, pp. 272–281. Cannes.

Westfall, R. and Boyd, H. W. (1961). *Cases in Marketing Management*. Homewood, Ill.: Irwin.

7. Command languages and logic-based front-ends

PETER HAMMOND

Abstract. The command language is one of the most commonly employed control methods in implementing an interface to a software system. We discuss the benefits of expressing a command language as a set of Horn clauses in the description of a logic-based front-end. The features of such an approach are illustrated with respect to the augmented PROLOG software **apes**, which possesses a command driven front-end implemented in the manner advocated in this chapter.

1 INTRODUCTION

Many software systems possess front-end programs with command-driven control whereby the user issues commands that are interpreted for immediate execution (or possibly execution following the correction of errors of syntax or semantics). The cycle of command input, interpretation and execution continues indefinitely and is organized by some underlying supervisory program. Somewhere within the front-end there is a description of the correct syntax (and possibly the correct semantics) of the available commands—it might be separately identifiable or it might be inextricably embedded within the implementation of the commands.

The paper describes the use of Horn clauses to explicitly describe the correct syntax of the command language and the many uses to which this command-language grammar can be put, including

on-line documentation for correct command forms;

the prompting of the user for command components;

the detection, notification and explanation of incorrect command forms;

alternative definition of commands, including foreign-language translation.

CURRENT ISSUES IN EXPERT SYSTEMS
ISBN 0-12-714030-1

The major benefits of the proposed approach are

the explicit and declarative definition of the command language, and

the separation of the command language grammar from both the description of the interaction with the user and the implementation of the commands,

offering the builder of such logic-based front ends improved intelligibility and modularity, greater elegance and easier modification. The improved error detection, notification and recovery that results is of direct benefit to the user of the front-end.

1.1 Command-Language Grammars and Man–Machine Interfaces

The first experiments with the ideas presented here were carried out in 1982/3 before PROLOG systems supported multiple, independent windows and menu-based interfaces. Without such facilities, these early implementations appeared to potential users to be inelegant and unwieldy, and so further development was shelved until 1984. Unfortunately, the term command-language grammer was employed to refer to the Horn-clause description of a command language before it was realized that it had a much more general and far-reaching interpretation in the field of MMI. Moran (1981) proposed a command-language grammar as a

representational framework for describing the user interface aspects of interactive computer systems, and

a top-down design process in which the conceptual model of the system is first specified and then a Command Language is created to communicate with it.

The material presented in this chapter is far less ambitious and is restricted to the description of the syntax of the command language as a logic program and its use along with facilities supplied by the augmented PROLOG system **apes** in running the associated command-driven front-end.

The use of the command-language grammar to drive the interaction between the user and the logic-based front-end requires the support of Query-the-User, the declarative model introduced by Sergot (1983) for interactive logic programming. The robustness of this interaction (in particular, the protection of the underlying software from spurious user input) is effected by separate descriptions of valid user responses. It is within these validity constraints that the builder of the front-end can provide semantic checks on the command components selected by the user. Typically, though, these restrictions are not formally defined (for example, in the way that Moss

(1981) has combined syntax and semantics in the description of programming languages).

The set of interactive logic programming tools, **apes** (Augmented PROLOG for Expert Systems) (Hammond and Sergot, 1983, 1985), provides all the features for building the logic-based front-ends described here. Indeed, the **apes** system now has a standard front-end built precisely in the manner advocated in this paper. Thus, in addition to proposing **apes** as a set of tools for building command driven front-ends, we also illustrate the ideas with respect to the existing **apes** front-end that **apes** itself can be said to run in the same way as it runs queries to application programs or logic knowledge bases.

1.2 Query-the-User: A Brief Summary

In the Query-the-User model of declarative input/output for logic programming, the user is viewed as an extension to any logic-program/logic-knowledge base from which deductions are to be made and so takes an active role in the evaluation of queries. Whenever necessary, the user supplies information that is missing or possibly not deducible given the current state of the program. In the simplest implementation of Query-the-User, the user is **always** asked **immediately** to provide missing "clauses" that correspond to any subgoal which arises during the evaluation process and for which there is no definition. Other, more interesting, variants of this simple interactive control strategy can be implemented.

The two PROLOG clauses below constitute an interactive program of sorts:

```
aspirin suppresses pain
_person should-take _drug if
        _drug suppresses _symptom and      (IP1)
        print(Does _person complain of _symptom ?) and
        read(_answer) and
        _answer = yes
```

Variables are denoted by strings preceded by an underscore and the second clause includes references to the input/output primitives **read** and **print**. All PROLOG implementations provide such primitives, so it should not be difficult to imagine the interaction that would result from the evaluation of a query such as

confirm(Peter should-take aspirin)

where following the question about Peter's pain and the user's reply, the query evaluates to success if the user answers **yes** and to failure otherwise.

In addition to the obscuring presence of the **read** and **print** primitives, these clauses have a limited mode of use. Consider the interaction that would result from an evaluation of the query

find(_person such that _person should-take aspirin)

where the user would be asked

Does _person complain of pain ?

which is not the intended or expected request of, say,

Who complains of pain?.

Of course, it is possible to repair (IP1) to cope with other input/output patterns for queries associated with the definition of " _person should-take _drug" by defining separate clauses to cope with each query pattern. Such reparations, though, usually reduce the intelligibility and subsequent modifiability of the programs even further.

If the underlying logic programming system that handles the query evaluation is augmented with Query-the-User, then the original clauses can be re-expressed as follows:

aspirin suppresses pain
_person should-take _drug if
            _drug suppresses _symptom and
            _person complains-of _symptom
complains-of interactive

The assertion **complains-of interactive** indicates that any information involving the relation **complains-of** is to be obtained by querying the user. The actual implementation of Query-the-User and the manner in which the user is questioned and responds need not concern us for the moment. The important points are that the declarative nature of the program is restored and that the programmer is spared the explicit use of input/output primitives. The posing of the question (defined separately) and the retrieving of the user's answers are all handled by the Query-the-User extensions. This revised form of the program is more likely to express the intended meaning of the program as well as cope with the complete set of associated input/output patterns.

In the next section we explore the application of the Query-the-User model to interaction arising during the control of software systems using sequences of commands. There are many such software systems, notable examples being operating systems, PROLOG programming environments and software supporting numerical or statistical analysis. It is the common feature of their control by the issuing of commands that is to be the main focus of interest. We intend to demonstrate that there are benefits to the implementor of such command-driven front-ends similar to those available to the constructor of knowledge-based applications if the Query-the-User model is combined with that of an explicit command-language grammar.

2   A COMMAND-LANGUAGE GRAMMAR FOR THE apes SYSTEM

The augmented PROLOG system **apes**, a set of tools for building interactive logic programming applications and for expert and knowledge-based systems applications, has at its heart an implementation of Query-the-User. **apes** also possesses a command-language front-end whereby a programmer defines, lists, deletes, edits and queries logic programs in the development of some larger knowledge base. Besides these program-modification and some program-debugging tools, there are also facilities for manipulating files and even the front-end itself, also controlled by a simple command language. We shall motivate the use of the command-language grammar approach to the **apes** front-end by illustrating some of the shortcomings of one of its earlier implementations.

2.1   The User's View of the Command Language

In order to demonstrate the benefits that accrue from an explicit definition of a command language, we consider the reimplementation of a single command (used to delete clauses from a logic knowledge base) in terms of a command-language grammar. The initial definition is a slightly modified version of the implementation of the **delete** command used in an early version of the **apes** software.

One of the objectives in **apes** is to provide the user with a set of commands to manipulate programs during their development. The command language is intended to be more "friendly" than would otherwise be necessary for direct use of the underlying PROLOG system. Thus, for example, instead of directly issuing PROLOG commands such as

        ? ((ADDCL ((should-take _person _drug)
                        (suppresses _drug _symptom)
                        (complains-of _person _symptom)
                        (NOT may-harm _drug _person)) 2))

to add a new clause in a particular position (here, as the second clause) amongst those clauses defining **should-take**, or

?((DELCL should-take 3))

to remove a particular clause (here, the third) for **should-take**, the user is allowed to issue commands such as

add (_person should-take _drug if _drug suppresses _symptom and
_person complains-of _symptom and not _drug may-harm _person) 2

and

delete should-take 3

respectively.

The front-end in **apes** comprises an extra layer of PROLOG software that reduces the demands on the user's knowledge of the underlying PROLOG implementation. Of course, the "depth" of this extra layer varies and depends very much on the disparity between the system's and the user's versions of the same command as well as the appropriateness of correspondence of any built-in functions in the underlying PROLOG system. As is depicted in Figure 1, in the case of the **delete** command, this extra software layer is fairly shallow; for the **add** command, however, considerably more software is required to translate the command form and translate the "sentence" syntax employed by the user in defining a clause to that acceptable by the underlying PROLOG system.

There is a hidden link (as far as the user is concerned) between the commands issued and those actually executed. An ever-running supervisory program reacts to the user's input, and where necessary prompts for completion of a command before execution can take place. In the version of PROLOG corresponding to **apes** version 1, the supervisory program simply reacts to the first two terms that the user enters. If these two terms do not

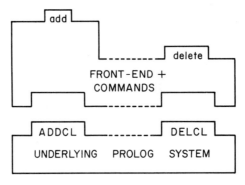

Figure 1

correspond to the invocation of some program, file or environment-manipulation tool, then the user is presented with a suitable error message. Thus, to begin with, there is an implicit assumption about the structure of available commands, since their definition must correspond in some way to an executable program call. Although the user may issue the command

⟨command name⟩ ⟨argument1⟩ ⟨argument2⟩,

for example **delete should-take 2**, only the first two terms are used to invoke the implementation of the command, the third argument (or remaining arguments) being absorbed by explicit calls to input primitives in the code associated with the command. There is then a potentially confusing mismatch between the user's and the system's view of the command structure.

2.2   Implementation of a Command Directly in PROLOG

The discussion above of command execution and the invocation of the PROLOG code corresponding to the command should become clearer following an inspection of the implementation of the **delete** command below:

```
delete( relation) if
        constant( relation) and
        delete*( relation)

delete( relation) if
        not constant( relation) and
        print( relation not recognized)    ERROR NOTIFICATION
```

As has already been pointed out, the supervisory program handles input for the command name itself and the single argument that the supervisory program assumes that the command invocation needs. The clauses for **delete** react to the relation name and constitute a filter with an error notification, should that be necessary. Consider the clauses for **delete***:

```
delete*( relation) if
        defined( relation) and
        read( index) and              INPUT PRIMITIVE
        delete**( relation _index)

delete( relation) if
        not defined( relation) and
        print( relation is undefined)    ERROR NOTIFICATION
```

delete* is used to check that there are indeed clauses for **relation**, that it is worth reading and accepting the user's description of the index of the clause to be deleted. Once again, the alternative clause for **delete*** is used simply to provide the appropriate error notification. The completion of the definition of **delete** is as follows:

    delete**(rel _index) if
              INTEGER(index) and
              trydelete(relation _index)

    delete**(rel _index) if
              not INTEGER(index) and
              print(index is not an integer)　　　**ERROR NOTIFICATION**

    trydelete(rel _index) if
              CLAUSE(rel _index) and
              DELCL(rel _index)

    trydelete(relation _index) if
              not CLAUSE(relation _index) and
              print(There is no clause _index for _relation)
                                ERROR NOTIFICATION

The clauses for **trydelete** check that there is indeed a clause of the cited index for the named relation before executing the built-in PROLOG **DELCL** primitive and removing the relevant clause. Once more, a suitable error message is provided should the clause in question not exist.

Note that capitalized relation names generally refer to built-in system functions.

This relatively short extract of PROLOG code contains many implicit assumptions about the behaviour of the command-driven nature of the front-end, and in particular has embedded a number of important and, as we intend to illustrate, potentially separable features. To begin with, we have already identified the places where the user is required to provide the various components of the command before its execution. Secondly, there is the explicit inclusion of error notification in three places (marked in the clauses above) subject to the included type checking on putative command components. It is worth noting also that this implementation of **delete** offers the user no error recovery, that is, no ability to keep track of those correctly formed components of a command while an incorrect one can be re-entered—it is to be hoped by editing the incorrect one or by reselecting and not by requiring its complete retyping. Of course, it is not difficult to amend the clauses so that they do offer some sensible scheme of error recovery. However, it would be very much ad hoc and, as with the repaired version of (IP 1) earlier, would only reduce the intelligibility and modifiability of the program.

Later, we shall deal with the question of robustness: error detection, notification and recovery. For the moment, though, we concentrate simply on the interactive process of entering command components.

2.3   Redefining the Command Within a Command-Language Grammar

Suppose the underlying supervisory program is altered so that it makes no assumptions about the command-language structure and also does not directly call the input primitives. It still comprises an ever-running program, but now it simply attempts to construct a correct command according to the definition

$(\_command-name|\_arguments)$ is-chosen-command if
        $\_command-name$ is-chosen-command-name and   **(CLG1)**
       $\_arguments$ are-chosen-arguments-for command-name

is-chosen-command-name front-interactive

where $(a|b)$ denotes a list whose first element is a and whose remainder is b. In other words, the supervisory program, in a sort of self-conscious manner, executes the query

      find($\_command$ such that $\_command$ is-chosen-command).

If, for the moment, we can assume that we have something like Query-the-User available, then the user would initially be prompted to supply a command name, since the relation name **is-chosen-command-name** has been declared interactive. The exact form of such a request to the user is unimportant for the moment. The description of a correct **delete** command can be completed very easily:

$(\_relation\ \_index)$ are-chosen-arguments-for delete if
        $\_relation$ is-chosen-relation-name-for-deletion and   **(CLG 2)**
       $\_index$ is-chosen-index-for-deletion-of $\_relation$

is-chosen-relation-name-for-deletion front-interactive
is-chosen-index-for-deletion-of front-interactive

where spaces are used to separate elements of a list, so (a b) denotes a list with two elements a and b.

The subsequent dialogue, also handled by our Query-the-User subsystem, would include requests for the name of the relation for which a clause is to be removed and the index of the actual clause to be deleted—on each occasion, the user is prompted for a command component. We shall show later how this prompting can be extremely subtle, without the user being aware of it, or how it can be very prescriptive and involve the presentation to the user of menus of command names, relation names and indices of (or even the actual) clauses. The principle is the same in each case.

It is this extract, (CLG 1) and (CLG 2), of the command language grammar and its completion that determine the command syntax and the relevant command components matching individual command names. Other parts of the command-language grammar might include the following descriptions:

> (clause position) are-arguments-for add if
>   clause is-chosen-clause and
>   position is-chosen position-of clause
> is-chosen-clause front-interactive
> is-chosen-position-of front-interactive
>
> (relation) are-arguments-for list if
>   relation is-chosen-relation-for-listing
>
> is-chosen-relation-for-listing front-interactive
> (conditions) are-arguments-for confirm if
>   conditions is-chosen-conjunctive-query and
>
> is-chosen-conjunctive-query front-interactive

where the commands **add**, **list** and **confirm** are used for adding a new clause, listing programs and posing confirmatory queries respectively.

3 THE COMMAND-LANGUAGE GRAMMAR IN PROGRAM DEVELOPMENT

Now that the basic idea of a command-language grammar has been introduced, it is worthwhile discussing its relationship with the different kinds of users of interactive logic based systems and its role in the software tools they employ.

Some end-users of expert systems and deductive databases eventually become interested in implementing similar application-oriented systems themselves. Furthermore, once these converted and other existing logic programmers have experimented with the programming tools provided by PROLOG and augmented PROLOG systems, there is often a desire to construct general-purpose logic-based tools tailored to specific application domains, such as the **apes** expert-system tools. In other words, there is a natural transition for the end-user to become a programmer and for a programmer to become a tool-builder.

It is therefore advantageous if, at each stage of such transitions, the software tools used have some commonality of approach and similar features so as to encourage users to exploit their earlier experience and newly acquired expertise. If programmers are to be encouraged to build declarative application-oriented logic programs then so should tool-builders, and in particular they should be provided with as many declarative programming tools as possible.

3.1   Interactive Logic Programs, Their Development and Their Users

It is straightforward to make a distinction between the different kinds of users of interactive logic programming systems and development tools, even though these separate classes of user may coincide in one individual during the development of a particular system or application.

3.2   The USER

The name USER refers to the end-user of an application-oriented logic program supported by some convenient environment that enables the USER to solve problems by posing suitable queries that are evaluated by some underlying logic programming theorem-prover, typically an augmented PROLOG system such as **apes**, or maybe even a raw PROLOG system. During the evaluation process, it is assumed that some variant of the Query-the-User model is available to involve the user in the problem-solving process, should that be necessary. As far as the USER is concerned, the system contains a knowledge base and a query-posing front-end—often supplemented by a component that allows inspection of the logic knowledge base and an explanation of its use in the solution of a problem.

3.3   The PROGRAMMER

The PROGRAMMER's role is to design and implement the logic knowledge base that aids the USER's problem-solving activity. The PROGRAMMER requires tools for the construction of logic programs as well as for their debugging and editing. The PROGRAMMER's interaction with the supplied tools is assumed to involve a command language through which programs are manipulated until a satisfactory problem-solving performance is obtained.

Figure 2 summarizes the roles of the USER and the PROGRAMMER:

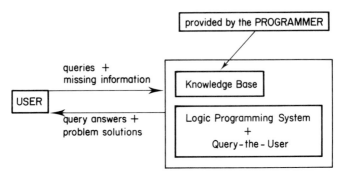

Figure 2

3.4 The TOOL-BUILDER

The PROGRAMMER's program modification tools are implemented by a TOOL-BUILDER, as is the command driven front-end that provides the PROGRAMMER with access to the tools. The relationship between the PROGRAMMER and USER is obviously similar to that between the TOOL-BUILDER and the PROGRAMMER, since one is a provider of the other's software tools.

During the development of the knowledge base, the PROGRAMMER separately defines programs that control the precise nature of the interaction with the USER: which (and how) questions are posed, the offering of possible/acceptable answers, the descriptions of menus etc. from which answers can be constructed, as well as the vetting of the USER's answers so as to protect the query-evaluation process from spurious input. Every expert-systems shell/toolkit provides facilities for making such declarations for controlling interaction—the **apes** system is no exception.

The focus of interest here is the interaction that the PROGRAMMER has with the program-modification tools provided by the TOOL-BUILDER. The PROGRAMMER constructs commands, possibly by complete input from a keyboard or possibly by selecting command components from menus, and if the commands are correctly formed, they are executed. Obviously, an important part of the program development process enacted by the PROGRAMMER is a simulation of the USER's interaction with the developing knowledge base. Thus the posing of queries is an essential component of the PROGRAMMER's debugging and testing activity.

Simply speaking, the USER interacts with the knowledge base and the underlying logic programming system (usually PROLOG) via Query-the-User. In using an analogous model, it is proposed that the PROGRAMMER should interact via some variant of Query-the-User with a command lan-

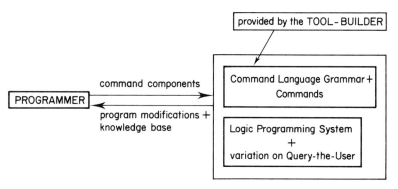

Figure 3

guage grammar, the implementation of the commands and the underlying logic programming system. Hence Figure 3, with a similar structure to Figure 2, summarizes the model in mind:

Just as with the description of a knowledge base, the command-language grammar contains two components: one covers the definition of the command language syntax, and the other describes the nature of the interaction with the PROGRAMMER when commands are being constructed.

4   SOME FEATURES OF THE COMMAND-LANGUAGE-GRAMMAR APPROACH

There are many advantages to the command-language-grammar approach in defining command-driven front-cnds. Here we discuss in detail some particular features. Once again, the discussion is illustrated with respect to the **apes** command-driven front-end.

4.1   Extending a Command Description

The definition of the arguments for the **add** command defined earlier would cause the user to be prompted for the entire clause to be added to the existing logic program. Suppose that we wish to separate the entering of the head or conclusion of a clause from its body or set of conditions. We may even want to go a step further and allow the user to enter the relation name corresponding to the head separately from its associated arguments. To do this, we would simply remove the assertion.

is-chosen-clause front-interactive

and replace it by something like

(_relation _arguments if|_conditions) is-chosen-clause if
           _relation is-relation-to-be-defined and
           _arguments are arguments-for-clause-defining _relation and
           _conditions are-conditions-for-clause-defining (_relation _args)

is-relation-to-be-defined front-interactive
are-arguments-for-clause-defining front-interactive
are-conditions-for-clause-defining front-interactive

With this revised definition, we could, for example, offer the user a menu of relation names from which to select, saving some effort in typing and reducing the likelihood of erroneous typing. The method by which such menu declarations are made is covered later.

The command structure can be extended in various ways. In the example illustrated, the alteration was to the level of detail at which the system interacted with the user. Alternatively, the command structure itself might need extending with extra parameters to increase the power or flexibility of the associated commands.

4.2   Collecting Commands in Terms of a Common Task

It makes sense to gather together commands related by particular tasks to be performed. A task-oriented front-end is likely to be closer to the user's own model of how to use the available tools to solve the current problem. For example, in **apes**, commands for querying programs are separated from those for editing and further separated from commands for manipulating the programming environment. This division of command types can be captured by a very simple extension to the command-language grammar:

(_task|_command) is-top-level-command if
           _task is-chosen-task and
           _command is-chosen-command-for _task.

It is worthwhile extending the definition of **is-chosen-command** with the extra parameter describing the task, since it can be used to preselect a subset of commands (those associated with the task) to offer the user. Lower-level clauses and the top-level invocation of the grammer will obviously need to be amended accordingly.

An example of a simple task-orientation, at the topmost level, is the current front-end to **apes** (Figure 4), where commands have been grouped according to similarity of function and a menu (horizontal, in this case) of tasks is offered for selection. if, for example, the PROGRAMMER decides

```
┌─ apes  options ─────────────────────────────────────────────────┐
│ │query│ listing  browse  file  editor  window  dos  command  quit  dialogue │
└─────────────────────────────────────────────────────────────────┘
┌─ command ───────────────────────────────────────────────────────┐
│                                                                  │
│                                                                  │
│                                                                  │
│                                                                  │
│                                                                  │
│                                                                  │
│                                                                  │
└─────────────────────────────────────────────────────────────────┘
```

Figure 4

to perform some operation on a file (which is somewhere resident on diskette) a subset of relevant commands can be offered for selection (Figure 5).

Should the PROGRAMMER be ready to test a query against the knowledge base, selecting **query** for the command task and then, say, selecting **find** for the command name, results in a request for the user to supply the full query description in a free input mode (Figure 6). The actual prompt that is used here to request the query is determined separately by the meta-level assertion

front-template(is-chosen-query (_query) (_query) (The output
        pattern and the conditions in the form: "~M~J" ⟨output pattern⟩
        : ⟨conditions⟩))

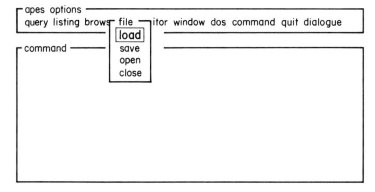

Figure 5

```
┌─ apes options ──────────────────────────────────────────────────┐
│ ┌─────┐                                                          │
│ │query│ listing browse file editor window dos command quit dialogue │
│ └─────┘                                                          │
└──────────────────────────────────────────────────────────────────┘
┌─ command ────────────────────────────────────────────────────────┐
│                                                                   │
│ ┌─ Provide the following ──────────────────────────────────────┐  │
│ │ The output pattern and the conditions in the form :          │  │
│ │ < output pattern >  :  < conditions >                        │  │
│ │                                                              │  │
│ └─ Enter your answer here  ( < RETURN > for options ) ─────────┘  │
│                                                                   │
│                                                                   │
│                                                                   │
└───────────────────────────────────────────────────────────────────┘
```

Figure 6

where the general format

front-question(⟨clg-relation⟩ ⟨args⟩ ⟨vars⟩ ⟨question template⟩)

means that ⟨question template⟩ is the prompt when the user is asked about the unbound variables ⟨vars⟩ in the subgoal ⟨**clg-relation**⟩ ⟨**args**⟩.

4.3   Construction of Commands from Components

In the new **apes** front-end, command components are usually requested one at a time. There are two forms of component entry, by free input or by menu selection. This limitation to two modes is of course solely due to the paucity of interactive facilities in the **apes** software and is not restricted by the use of a command-language grammar. Alternative interactive strategies, including delays in prompting and form-filling, are currently under development for **apes**.

Where it is likely to reduce tedious keyboard entry and mistyping, menus are used to offer the PROGRAMMER command components. Menu descriptions are defined in meta-level rules in which atomic relationships, for example **relation is-chosen-relation-name-for-deletion**, are associated with a menu along with parameters that describe the type of menu and where it should appear on the computer screen. An example of such menu declaration by the TOOL-BUILDER is

in-menu(is-chosen-relation-name-for-deletion (relation) _menu
⟨screen-parameters⟩) if isall(_menu _r (_r defined-in-knowledge-base).

The interpretation of **in-menu(_clg-relation _args _vars _menu _pars)** is that _**vars** is the list of unbound variables in the list of arguments _**args** for the command language grammar relation **clg-relation** and that the PRO-GRAMMER will be offered the list **menu** as a menu to select from. ⟨**screen-parameters**⟩ are simply the type and coordinates for the location of the menu.

The condition in the menu describing the rule above generates the entries of the menu, namely those relation names for which there is an entry in the PROGRAMMER's evolving knowledge base. It is straightforward to arrange that an assertion defining **defined-in-knowledge-base** appears whenever a clause defining a new relation is added to the knowledge base. Thus menu entries can be computed dynamically at run-time if necessary.

These separate menu descriptions add to the modularity and hence to the modifiability of the front-end. Notice, further, that the same rule-based language that is available to the PROGRAMMER is also available to the TOOL-BUILDER; such homogeneity aids the transition from PRO-GRAMMER to TOOL-BUILDER.

4.4   Error Detection, Notification and Recovery

When the PROGRAMMER is offered menus from which to select command components, there is no need to check that the selected answers are acceptable since any such checks can be used in the generation of the menu entries. If the PROGRAMMER is allowed complete freedom to enter an answer directly from a keyboard, then, in order to protect the underlying software from spurious input, it is essential that checks are made before the command is completed and finally executed.

These constraints on acceptable input are defined once again by separate meta-level descriptions. In terms of the direct implementation in PROLOG of the command

delete ⟨relation⟩ ⟨index⟩

illustrated earlier, these input constraints correspond to the various tests included in the implementation of the command—for example, the checks that ⟨index⟩ is an integer and that there is a clause for ⟨relation⟩ with the cited index. The following are examples of declarations of validity constraints on PROGRAMMER input:

(_index is-chosen-index-name-for-deletion-of _relation) **implies**
        (_index is-integer and clause-in-kb(_relation _index _clause))

(_args are-arguments-for-clause-defining _relation) **implies**
        (_args is-a-list)

where clause-in-kb(_relation _index _clause) holds if the knowledge base currently contains a clause for the relation of the cited index. The general form of the validity constraint is

⟨atomic relationship⟩ implies ⟨conjunction of conditions⟩.

The second of the example constraint descriptions above is very much a syntactic restriction for the command language, whereas the first one is much closer to a semantic check, since it makes implicit reference to the effect the command has when it is executed, in the sense that a clause that does not exist cannot be removed.

Should the PROGRAMMER return an answer for a command component that does not satisfy the validity check then the validity constraint itself can be used as both a notification of the incorrect reply and a description of an acceptable one in some suitable display window. Because the front-end is working in a mode where individual command components are entered separately, those command components that have been entered before the error occurred are still available for completion of the command once the PROGRAMMER re-enters an acceptable version of the incorrect component. In this way, the error notification and recovery is very much improved.

4.5   Explanation of Errors

So far the front-end we have described expects the PROGRAMMER to enter separately each command component that is associated with an interactive command-language relation. There will be some PROGRAM-MERs who wish to have more direct control over the issuing of commands and who might for instance want to enter complete commands without any prompting and without any checks being made on the individual command components as they are entered. This is straightforward to arrange, and the **apes** standard front-end, for example, does allow such control. However, it is still important that the underlying software is protected from erroneous input.

The interactive nature of the command-language grammar does not interfere with its declarative reading, because the clauses defining it are devoid of any calls to input/output primitives and instead all associated interaction is supported by Query-the-User. Hence the grammar can be used to check correct command forms as well as to generate them (as has been the case hitherto). Indeed, both the grammar and the validity constraints can be used to check that the entered command is executable. Furthermore, the command-language grammar can itself be used as on-line documentation to remind the PROGRAMMER of the correct command syntax.

When the grammar was used to generate commands, the syntax of the constructed command could be guaranteed to be correct. Now, however, the PROGRAMMER may introduce errors of syntax. These can, of course, be identified easily by an application of the rules in the command-language grammar. The question remains, though, of how best to notify the user of the syntax error. In early implementations of the command-language-grammar version of the **apes** front-end it was thought that **apes'** own facilities for explaining the behaviour of logic programs might be suitable. However, in the case of explanations of failure (a syntactically malformed command corresponds essentially to a failure to conform to the grammar rules), the **apes** explanations were most unsuitable. The major drawback was the completeness of the explanation, since all possible options for successful evaluation must be shown to fail. So, to find the failure, it is necessary to inspect all relevant rules successively, as well as any lower level rules associated with failed conditions in the higher level ones. What is needed is some way of taking a "peek" into the grammar to find some likely "deep" failures—for example, by identifying that **12** is not a list or that **(a b)** is not an interger. Some experimentation has been carried out with such explanations of failure (Wolstenholme, 1986), but no entirely satisfactory solution has yet been found.

4.6 Alternative Descriptions of Commands

One interesting extension to the command-language-grammar description as it has been described so far enables a PROGRAMMER to customize the command language. In particular, it would enable a foreign translation of the front-end to be made without major alterations to the command-language grammar. It also allows the PROGRAMMER to replace the implementation of individual commands with some more desirable feature, assuming, of course, that the supplied implementation of the commands is documented sufficiently well so as to enable the PROGRAMMER to make such alterations. The definition we make now for a command makes use of both internal and external formats, for use by the system and the PROGRAMMER respectively:

(_internal-command-name| _arguments) is-chosen-command if
  _external-command-name is-chosen-command-name and
  _external-command-name translates-to _internal-command-name
 and
  _arguments are-chosen-arguments-for _internal-command-name

is-chosen-command-name front interactive

delete translates-to "?DELETE?"
list translates-to "?LIST?"
add translates-to "?ADD?"
etc.

The definitions for command arguments need to be altered accordingly. For example,

>   (_relation _index) are-chosen-arguments-for "?DELETE?" if
>   _relation is-chosen-relation-name for deletion and
>   _index is-chosen-index-for-deletion-of _relation

>   is-chosen-relation-name-for-deletion front-interactive
>   is-chosen-index-for-deletion-of front-interactive.

The actual words used, **list**, **delete**, **add**, etc., can be whatever the TOOL-BUILDER or for that matter the PROGRAMMER decides to make them. Similarly, other natural-language components of the command language can be translated to alternative forms. This includes, of course, the meta-level descriptions of question templates/prompts, menus and validity constraints. The **apes** front-end, for example, has been translated in this fashion into Dutch, Greek, Italian and Spanish.

Each internal command name is related to some PROLOG code corresponding to an implementation of the effect that the full command should have in program (or other) manipulation. In theory, at least, it is possible for the PROGRAMMER to remove the existing implementation of a command and replace it by some more desirable (but presumably similar) feature. The separate layers now contained within the front-end are shown in Figure 7.

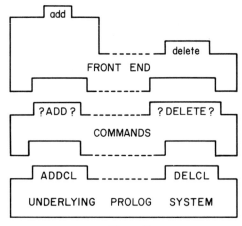

Figure 7

4.7   Variation on Query-the-User

The implementation of Query-the-User that **apes** employs to help USERs solve queries about application programs is not entirely suited to handling the interaction arising in the use of command-language-driven front-ends. In particular, the explicit storage of a USER's answers, which is essential for expert-system applications, is unsuitable for command-driven software. The PROGRAMMER needs to be prompted on each cycle of the supervisor program that generates (or checks) correct commands.

One option is to remove remembered command components before each command generation (check). The other is not to remember any information about individual command components whatsoever. The latter approach has a minor implication for the programming style employed by the TOOL-BUILDER in the description of the command language—in the sense that parameters or arguments that are to be entered by the PROGRAMMER must be passed as explicit parameters to wherever they are needed in lower-level definitions in the grammar. This is essentially the only difference between the two implementations of Query-the-User in the **apes** system.

There are other uses to which this variation on Query-the-User can be put. Already, it has been used in implementing games-playing programs and database-query systems. For whichever kind of logic-based system it is used, there will be benefits in terms of the improved intelligibility and the separation of the associated interaction from the description of the application.

5   CONCLUSIONS

The combination of an explicit command-language grammar and Query-the-User has many advantages over conventional, direct implementations of logic-based front-ends in PROLOG. The major benefits have been summarized in Section 1 and have been discussed in detail throughout the chapter. This approach to building command-driven front-ends has been illustrated in terms of the standard front-end to the **apes** system for two reasons. First, because **apes** itself is implemented in precisely this fashion. Secondly, it is the use of **apes** or similar tools that is advocated in the implementation of such front-ends. Obviously, other command-driven front-ends can be implemented in this way with benefits to the clarity of the implementation, not to mention increased flexibility and greater modifiability.

The disadvantages of the approach are generally caused by inadequacies in the interactive tools provided by **apes** or the inefficiency of the underlying PROLOG system. Extensions to the existing **apes** tools and also to Query-the-User are under investigation, and a variety of PROLOG interpreters and compilers are being used in order to improve efficiency and test other interactive environments inherent in the host systems.

ACKNOWLEDGEMENTS

The implementation of the software described here and the contents of the paper have benefited greatly from discussions with Bob Kowalski, Marek Sergot and David Wolstenholme. This work was carried out while the author was supported on an Advanced Research Fellowship awarded by the British Science and Engineering Research Council.

REFERENCES

Hammond, P. and Sergot, M. J. (1983). A PROLOG shell for logic based expert systems. *Proc. BCS Conf. Expert Systems, Cambridge*.

Hammond, P. and Sergot, M. J. (1985). *apes System Documentation*. Richmond, Surrey, England. Logic Based Systems.

Moran, T. P. (1981). The Command Language Grammar: a representation for the user interface of interactive computer systems. *Int. J. Man–Machine Stud* 15, 3–50.

Moss, C. D. S. (1981). The formal description of programming languages using Predicate Logic. Ph.D. thesis, Imperial College, London.

Sergot, M. J. (1983). A Query-the-User facility for logic programs. *Integrated Interactive Computer Systems* (ed. P. Degano and E. Sandwell). Amsterdam: North-Holland.

Wolstenholme, D. E. (1986). Unpublished Seminar, Logic Programming Group, Department of Computing, Imperial College, London.

8. Knowledge-engineering workstations

NORIHISA SUZUKI

Abstract. Knowledge engineering requires high-performance workstations for advanced research and low-cost workstations to disseminate research results. These workstations need very high-level languages such as LISP, SMALLTALK or PROLOG to run on them. The paper first gives a brief overview on workstations and object-oriented languages for expert system development. Then we present a set of techniques we used for the design of a bytecode emulating, microprogrammable 32-bit microprocessor for SMALLTALK-80. Some of the architectural features are compared with other existing SMALLTALK implementations. The logic design and microprogramming has been completed; the layout design was carried out by a semiconductor manufacturer. Experiments showed that SMALLTALK-80 can run on our system three to five times faster than SMALLTALK-80 on DORADO, an ECL-based workstation developed at Xerox PARC. In a third part, we present a methodology for specifying and verifying hardware systems using Concurrent PROLOG. The methodology is illustrated through the specification of the DORADO memory system.

1 WORKSTATIONS FOR EXPERT-SYSTEM DEVELOPMENT

In order to improve the quality of expert-system development, LISP-based workstations are beginning to be used by knowledge engineers. On the other hand, the Japanese Fifth Generation Computer Project has adopted PROLOG as the official language. Creation of a PROLOG-based workstation is the major goal of the first phase of the project. Another new language for expert systems is SMALLTALK-80, and workstations for SMALLTALK-80 are available widely. One of the reasons why workstations are useful for expert systems is their versatile user interface. Ideally, expert systems work automatically, but they often require human interaction in order to guide them through the inference steps. In this section we shall review characteristics of workstations.

1.1 Definition of a Workstation

A workstation is a high-performance personal computer with the following characteristics.

CURRENT ISSUES IN EXPERT SYSTEMS
ISBN 0-12-714030-1

It has a high-performance display called a *bitmap display*. The resolution of the display is 1000 pixels × 1000 pixels or higher. In a bitmap display the colour and intensity of each pixel can be changed independently by software. The image on the display is created as a bit pattern in the memory, called a *bitmap*. Furthermore, the bitmap display has to be refreshed very quickly for fast drawing. There are low-level operations to modify the bitmap in the memory called *raster operations*. These changes in the bitmap are immediately reflected in the display.

Another feature of a workstation is a screen interaction device. It enables the programmer to point to any place in the screen. Furthermore, the move from one point to another point of display must be instantaneous. The most widely used devices are the mouse, the touch screen and the tablet. The mouse is the most widely accepted among them because it is an accurate device, and it remains pointing to the same location, even if the programmer leaves his hand off the mouse.

Workstations also have large hard disks to store system programs as well as application programs. The capacity of the hard disk is increasing rapidly, and it is now common to have a 100 megabyte disk.

Workstations do not exist alone. In an organization there may be hundreds of workstations, and information in the form of electronic mail or programs must be exchanged in order for programmers to cooperate with each other. Some of the work must be uploaded to mainframe computers, and the results must be downloaded. For these purposes we require very-high-bandwidth communication links among workstations, and the local area network is the only solution at present.

So far the input and output devices that distinguish workstations from mainframes or minis have been listed. However, we need most of all a powerful computation unit. There are two distinct approaches in designing the computation unit. One approach is to make it out of random logic—usually out of TTL or ECL MSI circuits. More and more gate arrays are used for these purposes, but essentially the design is similar. Workstations built using these kinds of circuits are usually microprogrammable, and especially suited for language-directed workstations, such as LISP machines, PRO-LOG machines or SMALLTALK machines. In these workstations most of the systems are written in one language, so the efficiency of the execution of these languages is critical. Commercial products in this category are the Symbolics 3600, Xerox 1100, and Mitsubishi PSI.

Another approach for designing the computation unit for workstations is to use commercially available standard microprocessors. Processors built using random logic were much faster than processors built using standard microprocessors until the early 1980s. However, the advance of VLSI circuit production techniques made CMOS microprocessors very fast. 32-bit microprocessors are becoming available, and they are comparable in speed with random-logic processors. Examples of this new breed of high-performance 32-bit microprocessors are the 68020, 80386 and ROMP.

1.2 History of Workstations

The first workstation was built at the Xerox Palo Alto Research Center (PARC) in 1973; it was named Alto. Xerox PARC was set up to do research in office automation. The scientists at the center conceived that in the office of the future each worker will have a workstation, with all the workstations connected by a local area network. These workstations have flexibile displays on which documents can be composed and then transmitted or printed.

Alto was a dynamically microprogrammable processor, which had no standard instruction set. Various different instruction sets are realized on one machine by loading a different microcode for each language system.

The first successful local area network was built at Xerox PARC; it was called the experimental Ethernet, with a very high bandwidth at that time, 3 MHz. It had a bitmap display with 600 by 800 pixels. Alto also had a mouse as the pointing device. More than 1000 Altos were produced, but they never became commercially available.

Innovative software was produced for Alto, utilizing rich input and output devices. Various programming languages have been invented and implemented on Alto: SMALLTALK-80, INTERLISP-D, and MESA. These languages are compiled into their own instruction sets called *bytecodes.* Microcode emulators to execute these bytecodes are loaded onto Alto. SMALLTALK-80 is an object-oriented language, which has various innovative user-friendly interfaces such as window systems. INTERLISP-D is a LISP system originally developed for DEC10. MESA is a modular system description language, which has influenced MODULA 2. Not only have a number of programming languages been implemented, but also a number of new application programs have been created. One of these application systems is a Bravo text editor. This is a WYSIWYG editor, in which one can write text with various fonts and sizes at different locations. Then exactly what one sees on the screen can be printed using a laserprinter.

One of the first commercial workstations was the Xerox Star workstation. This has all the characteristics of Alto, but is not programmable.

At about the same time, two workstations that used the current fastest commercial microprocessor, MC68000, became available: the Apollo and SUN workstations. Since they used standard microprocessors, the price was low and they became very popular. Also, in the same year Symbolics 3600 and Xerox 1100 were produced as LISP machines.

1.3 Trends in Workstations

The market of workstations is expanding rapidly into many areas such as program development, office use, engineering and education. As the market expands it has the room to accept different kinds of workstations. There are now three categories. One comprises language-directed workstations. They are expensive and almost all the software is written in one high-level language. Then there are general-purpose workstations, which are medium price. The architecture of the processor is similar to that of general-purpose computers, so that existing software can be run. The third category is at the high-power end of mass-produced personal computers. These are inexpensive. However, because microprocessors are becoming faster, and memory chips are becoming denser, one can buy very powerful computers at a reasonable price.

Most of the language-directed workstations now support one of the very high-level languages: LISP, PROLOG or SMALLTALK-80. They are built using MSI bit-slice chips or gate arrays, and are usually microprogrammable. The reason why such an architecture was selected is that these workstations do not have to run programs written in common programming languages such as FORTRAN written for old computers. They have hardware support to execute very high-level languages efficiently. A large microstore enables very frequently executed routines such as garbage collector to be written in microprograms for high-speed execution. Therefore they are expensive, and the largest use of such computers is in artificial intelligence. There are now several commercial products. Symbolics 3600, Xerox 1100, LMI Lambda, Texas Instrument Explorer and FACOM Alpha are major LISP machines. There is one PROLOG machine, the Mitsubishi PSI, which is the personal inference machine built for ICOT. The Xerox 1100 is a SMALLTALK-80 machine; the Tektronix 4404 is also a SMALLTALK machine, but it can be classified as a general-purpose workstation, since it uses MC68000.

Even though we have classified language-directed workstations as of high performance, general-purpose workstations, which are built using commercially available microprocessors, are becoming very powerful. Because of rapid progress in VLSI technology, microprocessors are becoming much faster, and with the introduction of 32-bit microprocessors and efficient software, general-purpose workstations may become equal to or surpass language-directed workstations in performance. Currently general-purpose workstations are mostly built using MC68020, and have UNIX as the basic operating systems. Many of them have window systems and can be bought at medium price. Some of them are SUN workstations and Apollo Domain workstations.

On the other end of the market spectrum, there are inexpensive PCs (personal computers) built by large computer manufacturers such as IBM and NEC. They are inexpensive because they are mass-produced, and are built using inexpensive parts. However, their computing power is becoming very powerful also, and is now almost equivalent to that of general-purpose workstations. Up until quite recently, system software for the PCs has generally been very poor, because they are inexpensive. However, the trend is that powerful system software is becoming available for PCs.

2   OBJECT-ORIENTED LANGUAGES FOR EXPERT SYSTEMS

Most expert systems are written using LISP, rule-based languages or logic programming languages. Typical rule-based languages are production systems such as OPS5. The most well-known logic programming language is PROLOG. However, a new trend in languages for writing expert systems is to use object-oriented languages; they are more natural for representing individuals. For example, expressing cooperating robots, one wants to represent each robot as one data item in the program, and they are executed concurrently. The new programming paradigms for representing such situations are objects and concurrency. Objects were first widely introduced in SMALLTALK-80, but new languages for expert systems such as FLAVORS, LOOPS and KEE have objects.

Furthermore, the Japanese Fifth Generation Computer Project has been trying to incorporate objects and concurrency into their language, ESP, which is based on PROLOG and objects, and MANDALA, which is based on Concurrent PROLOG. However, the basis of MANDALA has recently become Guarded Horn Clause, a new logic programming language with concurrency.

A number of new languages that embody object-oriented programming are emerging. Among them SMALLTALK-80 is the most well known. SMALLTALK-80 is the first major language and system with object orientation. It is also the first language designed for a workstation.

One of the founding members of Xerox PARC was Alan Kay. He foresaw the importance of computers used by an individual to manage his information. For this purpose he conceived the idea of a personal computer the size of a book that can be easily held by hand and carried to school. It may contain all the information necessary for a student; documents can be created and stored in the computer. The idea was called Dynabook.

With this aim in mind, the first personal computer, called Alto, was built in 1973. Alan Kay and his group aimed to build a software system for their personal computer. For this purpose they designed the language called SMALLTALK, which exploited the new hardware features. SMALLTALK is not only a programming language, but also an entire software system to run on these personal computers. It has since been developed in cycles. First, the language was designed, then application programs were written, and feedback was obtained by these application programs to aid the new language design.

SMALLTALK-80 is the main reimplementation of the language that has been released as a product. Therefore many features have been cleaned up. Its parameter passing mechanism is call by value. It therefore requires some mechanism to pass unevaluated programs as parameters. For this purpose the language has a construct called block.

(a) Concepts of SMALLTALK-80.   The basic concepts of SMALLTALK-80 are object, message, class, instance and method.

Objects are data structures with internal values and a collection of operations that can directly access and change these internal values. Internal values can only be manipulated through these operations.

Classes are the specifications of objects: the description of the internal states and the operations of the objects. Classes are also objects; therefore messages can be sent to classes. Messages sent to objects are understood by the classes of these classes. They are called metaclasses. Classes have a hierarchy. Each class has a father called a superclass; except the class Object, which does not have any superclass. Information in the superclass is accessed by the subclasses.

Instances are objects created from classes to obey the class specification.

Methods are operations that belong to objects. When a message is sent to an object, a method that has the same message selector and belongs to the object is activated.

(b) Object.   An object is created by sending a message new to a class. A typical message for creating an object is

$$f \leftarrow \text{Ship new.}$$

After the completion of this statement, f denotes an object, which is an instance of a class *Ship*. In this expression one should note that the argument comes before the operator. In ordinary language like PASCAL we would write

$$f \leftarrow \text{new(Ship).}$$

(c) Message.   Messages correspond to function calls in ordinary programming languages. There are several kinds of messages. A unary message is of the form

$$\text{Ship new}$$

where *Ship* is the receiver and *new* is the message and also the message selector. A binary message is of the form

$$1 + 3$$

where *1* is the receiver and *+3* is the message. The message selector is + and *3* is the parameter. A keyword message is

window open: 5

where *window* is the receiver and *open: 5* is the message sent to the object. The message selector is "open:" and the parameter is *5*.

(d) Expression.   An expression is the basic unit of evaluation. It denotes an object as a value. It is either a variable, a block, or a message send.

(e) Syntax.   The syntax of a message send is

$$\langle \text{message send} \rangle :: = \langle \text{expression} \rangle \langle \text{message} \rangle$$
$$\langle \text{message} \rangle :: = \langle \text{unary selector} \rangle$$
$$\langle \text{message} \rangle :: = \langle \text{binary selector} \rangle \langle \text{expression} \rangle$$
$$\langle \text{message} \rangle :: = \{\langle \text{keyword} \rangle \langle \text{expression} \rangle\}+$$

Here *unary selector* is a simple identifier that is made up of alphabet followed by alphanumeric characters. Binary selector consists of one or two delimiters: $+, -, *, /, \backslash, <, >, =$. Keyword is a simple identifier followed by a colon. Thus *move:*, *now:*, and *pair:* are keywords. A keyword selector is created by concentrating all the keywords.

(f) Parsing rule.   Expressions have to be parsed according to the following rule. Selectors have priorities. Unary selector has the highest priority, binary selector has the second highest priority, and keyword selector has the lowest priority. Selectors of the same priority are grouped from left to right. Keyword selectors are treated together as one construct. For example, an expression

Point with: Zero new add1 + 5 * 6 y: 7 − 8 / 9

is parsed as

Point with: ((((Zero new) add1) + 5) * 6) y: ((7 − 8) / 9).

(g) Message.   A Message is a request to perform a method of the receiver. Arguments are assigned to the parameter. When a message *with: 5 y: 6* is sent to an object, a method is searched using a selector of the message. The selector for a unary expression is the message itself, for a binary expression

it is the special characters, and for a keyword expression it is the string obtained by concatenating keywords. Therefore, in the case of a message *with: 5 y: 6*, the selector is *with: y :*.

(h) Block.   An example of a block is [a ← a * a. a ← a * a]. The block specifies delay of the execution of the statements in the square brackets. These statements are executed when a message value is sent to an expression that denotes a block. It is executed in the environment where the block is defined, whether the block is passed as a parameter to a message and evaluated further down the execution stack, or whether it is returned as a value of a method, and therefore executed further up in the stack. In SMALLTALK-80 all the control structures, including the most primitive control structures such as conditional expressions and conditional loops, are expressed using blocks.

Some examples of blocks are

$$x ← [3 + y].$$
$$y ← 1.$$
z ← x value. "z has 4 since y has 1"
$$y ← 3.$$
u ← x value. "u has 6 since y has 3"

Another example is an implementation of a control structure using a block:

$$3 \text{ timesRepeat: } [a ← a * a].$$

Here *timesRepeat:* is a method defined in the class Integer to repeat the number of times specified by the receiver. After the execution of the block, the value of a is eight times more than before the expression is evaluated.

A conditional expression (*if-then-else expression*) is written as follows:

$$x \backslash\backslash 2 = 1 \text{ ifTrue: } [\text{ odd } ← \text{ true }]$$
$$\text{ifFalse: } [\text{odd} ← \text{ false }].$$

The following is a conditional loop (*while* statement) represented by two blocks:

$$i ← 1.$$
$$[i < 10] \text{ whileTrue: } [\text{ sum } ← \text{ sum } + i. \ i ← i + 1]$$

which computes the sum of the first nine integers.

(i) Block with parameters.   Sometimes it is necessary to pass parameters to a block, so there is a special block that accept parameters. They are used, for example, to implement a *for* loop:

$$1 \text{ to: } 10 \text{ do: } [: i \,|\, a \text{ at: } i \text{ put: } 0]$$

is equivalent to a *for* loop in Smalltalk-80, and it assigns 0 to the first ten elements of an array a. In the block with parameters, the vertical bar separates the parameters and statements. To the left of the vertical bar are parameters, which are preceded by colons. To the right of the vertical bar are statements.

(j) Class. A class is an object that specifies a collection of objects that have the same characteristics. These objects are called *instances* of the class. The class specification consists of

(1) name,
(2) superclass,
(3) pool dictionaries,
(4) class variables,
(5) class methods,
(6) instance variables,
(7) instance methods.

(k) Class hierarchy. There are a number of classes, but each class is not independent. One of the most common and useful relationships is specialization. A class is similar to another class, but differs from it in several respects. Then the most general class is called a superclass, and the specialization of it is called a subclass. There are two kinds of hierarchies. One that allows only one superclass is called single inheritance, and one that allows more than one superclass is called multiple inheritance. SMALLTALK-80 implements single inheritance.

(l) Inheritance. The superclass is a generalization, and all the subclasses share the common features of the superclass. In the single-inheritance hierarchy the more general class is called a superclass of the more special class. All the internal states (instance variables) and all the methods (instance methods) of the superclass can be used by the subclass.

Therefore when we define a new class, all we have to specify are the new instance variables, and new instance methods that are not defined in the superclass. In this way we can share the definitions among subclasses and eliminate the effort of programming. We call this method of programming, differential programming.

New instance methods may have the same name as methods in the superclasses. When this occurs, it is said that the methods are *overridden*.

(m) Class variables and class methods. Class variables and class methods are specified in the class definition. Class variables are global variables that can be accessed by all the instances of the class. Class methods are methods specified in the metaclass.

(n) Method: example.   This example is a program that checks the parity of the data. The method *odd* is defined as an instance method of the class SmallInteger:

> odd "message pattern"
> | parity | "temporary variable"
>   self \\ 2 = ifTrue: [parity ← false]
>   ifFalse: [parity ← true].
> ↑ parity

(o) Method search.   When a message is sent to an object, the method has to be sought that will execute the message. The algorithm to search for the method is to first look at the class of the receiver. If the method with the message selector exists, then it is invoked. Otherwise, the superclass is searched for the method. This process is repeated until a class that does not have a superclass is reached. Then it will be an error.

(p) Pseudovariables.   Pseudovariables are variables that cannot be assigned to. In particular, *self* and *super* are important pseudovariables. They are the way of referring to the receiver of a message from the method body.

Self refers to the receiver. Suppose the class Number is a superclass of the class Integer and the class Float. The class Number is an abstract superclass in that an instance of it must not be created. For example, the definition of $<=$ in the class Number is

> $<=$ a
>   ↑ (self $>$ a) not.

Then the operator $>$ can be defined in both subclasses as

> $>$ a
> $<$primitive: #$>$

When $<=$ x is sent to an instance of Integer, it searches and obtains the method in Number.

Self and super both denote the receiver, but the method search starts from the class of the receiver when a message is sent to self, whereas the method search starts from the superclass of the class in which the method is defined when a message is sent to super.

A typical use of super is an initialization program. It is a method that initializes instance variables. Since it usually knows the instance variables declared in the class, the initialization of instance variables declared in the superclass ought to be done by the initialization programs in the superclass.

This use of super is often called *after demon*. The following is an example of initialization:

> init
> > "Initialization of instance variables."
> > ↑ super init "after demon"

3   DESIGN OF A MICROPROCESSOR FOR SMALLTALK-80

This is a reflection of the design of a 32-bit microprocessor, Sword32. The project was to design a microprocessor for an object oriented language, SMALLTALK-80, that will be 10 to 20 times faster than the SMALLTALK-80 system running on MC68000.

Not only is our design novel but also our design methodology. We designed the entire microprocessor hierarchically in the ordinary programming language C. We did not use a special language for logic design; the description is converted to an input to a switch-level transistor logic simulator, and then to a layout design. The reason we prefer ordinary programming languages over special hardware-description languages is that the libraries of tools for the ordinary programming languages are far richer than those for the special logic description languages.

Many people prefer special-purpose logic design languages for hardware design. However, we have shown that we can describe hardware systems at a very high level and use the description for simulation and microprocessor production with ordinary programming languages.

3.1   A Microprocessor for Object-Oriented Languages

Since the spring of 1982 we have been studying whether a late-bound object-oriented language like SMALLTALK-80 should be used as a principal programming language for our research in computer-system software, VLSI design and computer-assisted instruction. We concluded that a SMALLTALK-80 system has a number of attractive features, including the fact that a large collection of useful software to support programming environment can be obtained for free, but the current implementation is inefficient and furthermore runs on a very limited range of computers. Alternatives are UNIX and LISP, but the versions of source programs available at universities lack the sophisticated display-oriented programming systems.

Therefore we decided to invest our research efforts in improving the performance of SMALLTALK-80 systems, and devised new techniques for compiling and creating run-time systems for such a late-bound, object-oriented language (Suzuki and Terada, 1984). We came up with a number of new techniques that make SMALLTALK-80 much faster, and created two SMALLTALK systems to try out our ideas on a standard microprocessor MC68000 (Suzuki *et al.*, 1984). The attempt was quite satisfactory, and the performances of our systems were in line with other implementations (Deutsch and Schiffman, 1984; Wirfs-Brock, 1983; Unger, 1984). However, we thought that we could create a system faster by an order of magnitude if we built a special-purpose microprocessor with powerful features designed to execute SMALLTALK. Therefore we started to design a microprocessor tuned to execute SMALLTALK bytecodes particularly efficiently in the summer of 1983.

While we could have written our SMALLTALK system in microcode of Perq or Symbolics 3600, building our own VLSI microprocessor allows us to explore several new architectural ideas that should result in a system that is significantly faster than one implemented on Perq or Symbolics 3600. Furthermore, as one of our research goals is to design and build our own computer systems, particularly ones based on VLSI microprocessors, such an undertaking seems appropriate.

Nevertheless, because this is the first microprocessor we have designed, we have kept our aspirations modest. We have eliminated many features that might have improved the speed or flexibility, but at the cost of increased architectural and layout complexity. However, as we wrote the microcode for SMALLTALK-80 (Suzuki, 1983), we discovered that it may run significantly faster than all the other implementations, even those on sophisticated bytecode emulation computers built using ECL (Deutsch, 1983). We also have kept our software aspirations modest. We made the instruction set of Sword32 completely compatible with the SMALLTALK-80 Virtual Machine, except that Sword32 uses 32-bit object pointers with slightly different encodings of small integers. This is because we did not want to spend our efforts in creating a special system in order for SMALLTALK to run on Sword32. Furthermore, since we have no control over the future systems, we decided to conform to the standard format, so that we need to keep creating versions of the Virtual Image ourselves.

We completed the first architectural design of the microprocessor in the autumn of 1983, and have designed an ALU in NMOS technology. This was a 16-bit microprocessor, which we called Sword (Suzuki *et al.*, 1983). We first designed a 16-bit microprocessor, since we intended to run the SMALLTALK-80 Virtual Image as is. We did not have enough experience to know the limitations of the 16-bit system and to know how to rewrite it for a 32-bit computer. However, after we created the first virtual machine on a SUN workstation, we knew immediately that the size of the object memory was too small to implement any serious application program. So we redesigned the virtual machine to have 32-bit object pointers, and have implemented it on a SUN workstation (Suzuki *et al.*, 1984). From this experience and from the fact that we were able to have access to fast CMOS technology, we decided to redesign the whole system to have 32-bit data paths. This is the Sword32 microprocessor, which we shall describe in this chapter.

3.2 Comparison with Other Systems

We compare architectural features of several distinct implementations of Smalltalk-80 (Table 1).

The systems compared in this table are Dolphin, sold by Xerox, the SUN workstation system (Deutsch and Schiffman, 1984), the SOAR microprocessor emulator of UC Berkeley running on SUN (Unger *et al.*, 1984) and Sword32.

The Dolphin system is a microcoded emulator of the SMALLTALK-80 Virtual Machine implemented in a way very close to the book. SUN implementation is the fastest-running system besides Dorado implementation; it dynamically compiles bytecodes into native codes. Throughout the rest of this chapter we mean Deutsch and Schiffman's implementation if we mention SUN implementation without any qualification. SOAR is a reduced-instruction-set microprocessor tailored for SMALLTALK. All the

Table 1   Comparison of SMALLTALK systems.

	Dolphin	SUN	SOAR	Sword32
Implementation	Microcode emulator	Dynamic compiler	Static compiler	Microcode emulator
Object Pointer	16 bit	24 bit	28 bit	32 bit
Object Table	Yes	Yes	No	Yes
Garbage Collector	Reference counting	Transaction	Generation	Transaction
Instruction	Bytecode	Native code	Native Code	Bytecode
Method Search	Method cache	Inline cache	Inline cache	Method cache
Context Allocation	Heap	Stack	Stack	Stack
Primitives	Microcode + BCPL	Assembler	C (?)	Microcode + C
Multiprocessor	No	No	No	Yes

object codes are native codes. Sword32 is a microcoded emulator of the SMALLTALK-80 Virtual Machine just like Dolphin, but the implementation techniques are close to those of SUN.

Object pointers are unique identifiers of objects. In Dolphin an object pointer is an index of an object table, whose entry contains the real address of the object, the reference count and several flags. The object pointer of the Sword32 is the absolute address of the object-table entry. The object pointer of SOAR is the absolute address of the object, so it does not have an object table. We do not know the details of SUN implementation.

Dolphin employs reference-counting garbage collection. Since this was a major performance bottleneck, the SUN implementation uses Deutsch–Bobrow transaction garbage collection (Deutsch and Bobrow, 1976). We also use transaction garbage collection in Sword32. SOAR uses a generation scavenger, which is a variant of a copying garbage collector.

Both Dolphin and Sword32 directly execute SMALLTALK-80 bytecodes, which are very-high-level instruction sets for stack machines. Therefore, the decompilation can be done easily, and the system software does not have to be rewritten in order to run on Sword32. The programs of SUN run MC68000 native code, but the compilation is done dynamically, so that it still retains compatibility with the system software. SOAR uses its own instruction set, so that system software has to be rewritten. SMALLTALK-80 is a late-bound language. The link between a message and a method is determined at run-time every time a message is sent. In order to speed up the linking, various implementations use some kind of cache. Dolphin uses a method cache, which is a global hash table where the keys are the class of the receiver and the message selector, and the values are the method and the primitive index. The table size is usually from 256 to 2048 entries, but the hit rate is quite high, 95% (Conroy, 1983). SUN implementation uses an in-line cache. After each *message send* instruction, the class and the address of the object code for the method are stored. If the receiver's class is the same as the class stored in line, the direct subroutine call is done. SOAR uses the same technique. Sword32 uses the method cache; in order to speed up the linking, we store the absolute address of the instruction, which is the address of the first bytecode of the method if the method is implemented by SMALLTALK-80 code, and the microcode address if the method is implemented by a primitive, the absolute address of the method, and the number of temporaries other than the parameters.

Contexts are the objects that store information necessary for method activation; they are usually called stack frames in other programming languages. In Dolphin contexts are the first class objects; they are allocated and deallocated for all the method activations and returns, and even reference-counted. This inefficiency has been eliminated in SUN implementation by allocating contexts on the stack as long as the contexts are not retained. SOAR and Sword32 use the same technique.

We provide a hook to create a high-performance multiprocessor system in which each processor has its own cache and caches are connected to a common memory bus and share a main memory. A microinstruction is provided that can implement a test-and-set instruction for such a system.

3.3   Overview of the System Design

Most of our architectural features are derived from our knowledge of the inefficiencies of Dolphin system. The bottlenecks are reference-counting garbage collection, method search and the context allocation in the heap.

3.3.1   Reference counting

In order to create a personal computer system that provides real-time response, we have to use a real-time garbage-collector. Therefore the Dolphin implementation employs a reference-counting garbage collector. However, this consumes a substantial amount of computation time. According to our calculation 80% of the time spent for pushes and pops is spent for reference counting.

There are two algorithms for real-time garbage collection that lead to successful implementations of SMALLTALK-80 (Deutsch and Schiffman, 1984; Unger, 1984). We implemented Deutsch–Bobrow transaction-based garbage collection with a satisfactory result in our MC68000 implementation (Suzuki *et al.*, 1984). Therefore we use this algorithm for Sword32.

There is no special hardware support for transaction garbage collector, except that most of the program is written in microcode.

3.3.2   Object representations

References to objects are made through object pointers just like in Dolphin implementation. Object pointers are absolute addresses of object-table entries, in which the absolute addresses of the objects and reference counts are stored (Figure 1).

Both Dolphin and SUN implementations use object pointers in order to simplify compaction. Furthermore, there is a method called *become:*, which swaps objects that are pointed by two object pointers. This is difficult to implement without the object table. SmallIntegers are encoded in object pointers; if the least significant bit is zero, the rest of 31 bits denote SmallIntegers. We chose this form because ordinary arithmetic on SmallIntegers can be performed by an ALU designed to work for unsigned

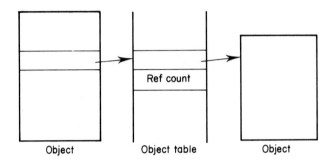

Figure 1   Object pointers are absolute addresses of entries in the object table.

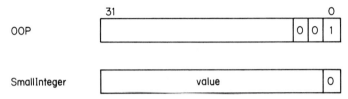

Figure 2   The formats of object pointers.

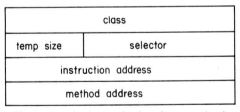

Figure 3   Each entry in the method cache occupies four words.

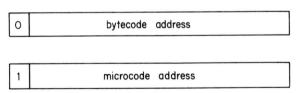

Figure 4   Format of an instruction address.

integers. Therefore the least significant three bits of object pointers are zero, zero and one, if they are indexes to an object table (Figure 2).

In order to accommodate special encodings of object pointers and perform type checks, we have unique memory operations. Memory operations of Sword32 are fetch, store, fetch byte and store byte. Fetch and store read and write aligned four bytes, and fetch byte and store byte read write any byte in the memory. For fetch and store the memory operation is started if the least significant bit in MAR is one, and the memory address put out from the chip has zero as the least significant bit. If the bit is zero, no operation is performed, but the least significant bit of the address of the next micro-instruction is *or*ed with one. So fetch and store operations always cause conditional branches.

3.3.3   Method lookup

In order to speed up the message linking, most SMALLTALK-80 implementations use cache. Dolphin implementation uses a method cache, each entry of which consists of selector, class, method and primitive index. By a proper choice of a hash function, the hit rate can be quite high, as much as 95%, but still the time to compare two entries, selector and class, and then to decode the locations of bytecodes is substantial. Deutsch and Schiffman's implementation used an in-line cache; after each *send* instruction the class and the address of the instruction of the method last called from the particular message send is stored. The link is fast, but it rewrites and expands codes. This method is also used for SOAR. We use a global method cache, but we store information that enables faster method activation; they are the absolute address of the method, the address of the instruction, and the number of temporaries other than the arguments. The format of an entry of the method cache is shown in Figure 3.

The address of the instruction is encoded in such a way that if the most significant bit is zero, it is the absolute address of the bytecode, and if the bit is one, the least significant 12 bits are microcode address of the primitive (Figure 4).

The number of temporaries other than the arguments is the number of NILs that have to be pushed on the stack.

3.3.4   Stack organization

Since procedures are invoked very frequently in SMALLTALK-80, hardware support for procedure calls is important. Sword32 has a large (128 words) on-chip stack and 32 general-purpose registers. We would use these registers to cache the top part of the contexts.

There are four stack pointers, FP, CP, TP and SP; the data are accessed from the parts pointed by these pointers. In the SMALLTALK-80 emulator, FP is a context base pointer, TP is the work pointer to retrieve local variables in the active context, and SP is the top of the stack pointer. FP itself is organized as an eight-level stack. The current frame pointer is pointed by CP. The first 16 words of the general-purpose registers can also be used as two eight-level stacks, whose pointer is also CP. These two stacks can be accessed through CP, if we access the lowest address register in each stack. Thus if the value of CP is 5 and if we fetch register 0, we actually obtain the value of register 5. If we fetch register 8, we actually register 13. We can still access other registers at random. If we fetch register 2, we really fetch register 2.

The stack organization for emulating SMALLTALK-80 is shown in Figure 5. At most 8 contexts can be stored in the stack. FP points to the beginning of each context. Two 8-word stacks store the bytecode instruction counter and the method address. Each context occupies a stack region bounded by two consecutive FPs.

The stack is organized this way so that there is no need for copying arguments from the sender to the method as is done in Dolphin. The receiver and the arguments are pushed in the evaluation stack of the active context, and the message is invoked. The several topmost locations defined by each bytecode become the bottom part of the newly activated context.

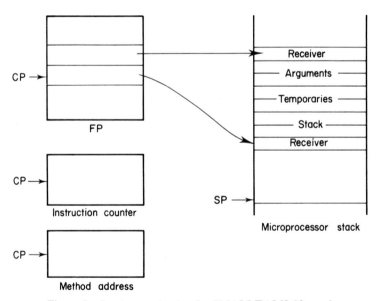

Figure 5   Stack organization for SMALLTALK-80 emulator.

3.4 Microarchitecture

Our guiding principle throughout architectural design was to keep the microprocessor simple. We would supply just enough hardware, so that most of the complex jobs could be done efficiently with microcode. We encountered a number of occasions where if we added some hardware features, a particular microprogram or a particular bytecode would run faster. However, in most cases we found that either a different microcoding for the same job would give us the same speed-up, or that the part that was speeded up was executed relatively infrequently so that the hardware addition would not result in a significant overall performance improvement. Furthermore, adding hardware often has a negative effect on the overall speed of the machine, because the basic machine cycle has to be slowed down to accommodate the addition. Therefore we were very careful whenever we were tempted to add new hardware features.

Probably the most successful practice was that we started to write micro-code within a week after the project was started. The first version of the microcode was written within two weeks. This helped immensely in tuning the machine; many features were found to be unnecessary, and many new features were added to improve the performance. Another successful practice was that we wrote a microassembler very early with only a couple of days effort. This was probably made possible because we used LISP. The microassembler discovered many programming errors that tried to assign several different values to microinstruction fields. This resulted in micro-programs that were more packed than logically possible. Without the error detection the machine would have been designed under the false assumption that efficient codings can be done under the architecture.

Some of the big surprises were that we thought, at the beginning, that we needed special hardware for handling small objects such as integers that are encoded in the pointer fields. However, after writing the microcode, we realized that we did not need any special hardware for treating encoded integers. All we are using are masking, shift and standard arithmetic hardware. Another piece of hardware that we dropped is a barrel shifter. A barrel shifter may be useful in SMALLTALK-80 execution in three ways: decoding the bytecode, decoding the data and executing shift bytecode. However, in all cases, microprograms without a barrel shifter perform just as well as or better than microprograms with a barrel shifter.

On the other hand, we decided to include special hardware for bytecode dispatch. We first tried to use the general dispatch mechanism for the bytecode dispatch, but that uses one field of a microinstruction, and needs one instruction before the next bytecode is executed, since the general dispatching requires one instruction delay. This additional hardware reduced the length of most microprograms by 1 or 2.

By continuously tuning the architecture, we came up with a quite efficient bytecode emulator for SMALLTALK. We describe the design strategies of the components in the following.

3.4.1 Bytecode fetching

Efficient bytecode fetch machinery is important, but we did not support any sophisticated instruction fetch unit such as the one found in Dorado (Lampson *et al.*, 1981a,b). What we are providing are hardware for fast bytecode dispatching, automatic fetching of bytecode, process switch and dynamic switching of bytecode dispatch tables.

As explained previously, there is no delay between the microinstruction to signal the end of a bytecode execution and the first instruction of the next bytecode; if the microinstruction is a branch to zero, the next instruction executed is the first instruction of the next bytecode. Furthermore, this does not use a microinstruction field. There is a 32-bit instruction buffer; if the bytecode read is the least significant byte of the buffer, the buffer is filled automatically by issuing a fetch. It is the responsibility of the microprogrammer to make sure that the bytecode fetch does not occur while a memory operation is in progress.

The process-switch requirements of internal or external reasons are reported by setting a ProcessSwitch flag by a microinstruction. Then at the bytecode dispatch time, if this flag is set, the control transfers to a fixed microprogram address to perform the process switch and may continue to execute from the original process.

Another valuable mechanism is the two sets of bytecode dispatch tables, and the fast dynamic switching of microcode dispatch tables. We cache the topmost context in the internal stack. It is, however, costly to maintain the topmost context, which is called an active context, always in the stack at each bytecode dispatch. So, at the beginning of each bytecode execution the active context may be on the stack or in the heap. Since most of the bytecodes and primitives behave very differently according to whether the active context is on the stack or in the heap, the interpreter has to know which state the machine is in at the beginning of each bytecode. However, we would not like to have to check by microcode the state of the contexts at the beginning of each bytecode; instead, we have two sets of microcode according to the state of the active context, and switch among them, thus speeding up most of the bytecodes by two cycles.

3.4.2 I/O

Unlike Alto (Thacker *et al.*, 1981) or Dorado (Lampson *et al.*, 1981a,b), we assume that there will be another microprocessor (MC68000) to perform most of the I/O work, such as disk I/O, raster operations and keyboard I/O.

The input and output mechanisms of Sword32 resemble those of the SMALLTALK-80 Virtual Machine. There is one input queue implemented as a cyclic buffer in the main memory. When some input events such as keyboard depress and mouse movement occur, they are detected by MC68000. The input is decoded and the input data are added to the queue, and MC68000 notifies Sword32 by asserting PWR. Sword32 increments the input semaphore, asserts PWRAck, and resumes the bytecode emulation.

3.4.3 Microsequencing

Microprogrammable microprocessors often use a microsequencer to eliminate address fields in microcodes. In Sword32 we decided to use NEXT field, because a large portion of the microprograms are shared, and there are a number of placement constraints, so that without NEXT field explicit branch instructions would be very frequent.

3.4.4 Pipeline organization

The pipeline organization of instruction decoding and execution depends on how we organize the data-path structures. We considered two approaches to pipeline organization. One approach is to organize like Dorado (Lampson *et al.*, 1981a,b), where the basic machine operation is to read an accumulator and a data word from the register file, perform an operation, and store the result back into the register file. This organization requires three-stage pipeline and a by-pass circuit in order to attain maximum speed: a stage to read a microcode, a stage to read two registers and put data into ALU, and a stage to get the result from ALU and write it into a register. Since the write-register cycle of an instruction is overlapped with the read-register cycle of the next instruction, it must be possible to read and write different locations in the register file in one cycle. Another organization is used in Alto (Thacker *et al.*, 1981), in which the pipeline has two stages: one stage that reads an instruction, and another stage that either reads one word from the register file, performs an operation and stores the result in special latches, or else gets a data word from the latches and stores it into the register file.

The Dorado approach is suitable if the time taken to read and write the register file is short compared with the ALU operation time. In particular, this approach requires reading from a register file in the first half of the cycle and writing to the register file in the second half of the cycle; the time to read and then write the register file should be approximately equal to the time to perform the ALU operation. On the other hand, the Alto approach is suitable if the register-file read and write times are longer than the ALU operation time. Since in MOS VLSI circuits register files are implemented using (in our case, static) memory arrays, and read and write times are relatively large compared with the ALU operation time, we adopted the Alto approach for pipeline organization.

3.4.5 Data paths

Figure 6 shows the logical organization of data paths, latches and registers in the Sword32 microprocessor.

The data paths in Sword32 are 32 bits wide. Even though the standard SMALLTALK-80 Virtual Image is built on 16-bit data-path computers, we adopted 32-bit data paths, because the large object space is inevitable if SMALLTALK is going to be used for serious applications. The actual layout of the data paths is more orderly (Figure 7).

3.4.5.1 Register file. The largest overall performance gain comes from having many internal registers. They are used for various purposes—stack, context cache, or cache or the real addresses of frequently accessed objects. If we organized these registers into separate groups, the number of busses and the number of ports to the busses would be very large. Therefore we put as many registers as possible into one large register file, so that the number of separate ports and wires in the entire chip is small.

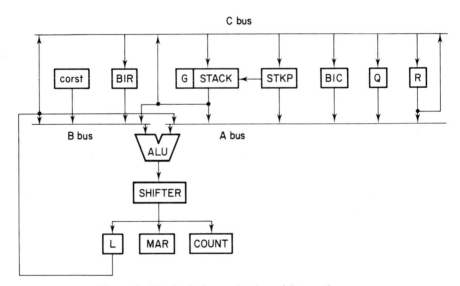

Figure 6 The logical organization of data paths.

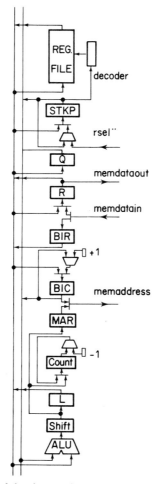

Figure 7   The diagram of the data paths, which correlates closely with the physical layout.

The register file is 160 words of 32 bits each. The first 128 words are used as a stack that can be accessed through the stack pointers. The other 32 words are general-purpose registers. The first 16 words can be used as general-purpose registers or two stacks of 8 words each. They are accessed either through the RSEL field of a microinstruction or through a stack pointer CP.

3.4.5.2   Stack-pointer manipulation.   The four stack pointers can be manipulated in two ways. First, each stack pointer can be a bus source. Therefore in one cycle a stack pointer can be read onto the bus and subjected to an ALU operation; then, in the next cycle, it can be written back to the stack-pointer register. However, most of the stack-pointer operations increment or decrement a stack pointer by some small constants. So, there is a second mechanism for altering a stack pointer in which a special adder is used to add or subtract small amounts from a stack pointer in one cycle; one can read from or write to the stack using the value of a stack pointer at the beginning of the cycle. In the same cycle one can modify that stack pointer.

3.4.5.3 Temporary registers. L, R and Q are temporary registers to store the intermediate results. Q can be shifted left or right by one bit to be used for multiplication and division. In SMALLTALK-80 emulator R contains the top of the stack and SP points to the second from the top of the stack.

3.4.5.4 External memory interface registers. The micromachine interfaces with the memory system through MAR and the temporary register R. When writing to memory, R must be loaded at least a cycle before the store operation starts. MAR is loaded by a fetch instruction, and the data comes into R at least two cycles later. If a reference is made to R a cycle after the fetch operation, the instruction is held until the data transfer is completed.

3.4.5.5 Shifters. As was explained earlier, we did not include a barrel shifter. Instead we have a byte swapper and a one-bit shifter. Both shifters operate on the result of the ALU before the data is loaded to L, Count or MAR. The byte swapper transposes the 8-bit halves of the least significant 16-bit result of the ALU.

3.4.6 Control System

Microprograms are executed continuously at a rate of one microinstruction per machine cycle. There are six different ways to choose the next microinstruction.

MPC is the program counter of the microinstruction. This value is set at the end of the microcode read stage from several sources. The sources of MPC are the NEXT field of the previous instruction, 1024 when a wake-up request signal is detected, 1025 if a process switch is waiting, the RETURN register when it is returning from a microsubroutine, the INTRETURN register when it is returning from interrupt processing, the logical disjunction of the NEXT field and Abus if dispatching, and BIR when it dispatches to a new bytecode.

The order for granting the sources is the following: 1024 has the highest priority, all of the 1025, RETURN, INTRETURN, dispatch and IR are mutually exclusive and have the middle priority, and the NEXT field has the lowest priority.

3.5 Performance

The performance of Sword32 is measured using the standard benchmark (McCall, 1983). We compiled several benchmarks by the existing compiler to produce bytecodes. Then we wrote microprograms for these bytecodes and measured the time to compute benchmarks. Since we are calculating the performance estimates by hand simulation, it is only feasible to compute for some small sample programs. SMALLTALK-80 benchmarks consist of microbenchmarks and macrobenchmarks. Microbenchmarks consist of small programs that test several specific bytecodes. The microbenchmark whose performance correlates best with the performance of the overall system performance as well as the performance of macrobenchmarks is the method activation and return benchmark.

The source program for method activation and return is

recur: n
   n = 0 ifTrue: [↑ self].
   self recur: n − 1.
   self recur: n − 1

This method is called with 14 as the argument; thus *recur:* is called 32767 times. It is compiled into the following sequence of bytecodes. The number on the right is the number of microinstructions to implement the bytecodes.

pushTemp: 0	3
pushConstant: 0	2
send: =	3
jumpFalse: 10	3 or 6
returnSelf	4
pushSelf	2
pushTemp: 0	3
pushConstant: 1	2
send: −	4
send: recur:	21
pop	1
pushSelf	2
pushTemp: 0	3
pushConstant: 1	2
send: −	4
send: recur:	21
returnTop	4

When the argument is 0, it takes 15 cycles to complete the execution, and when the argument is not 0, it takes 83 cycles. Since the number of times *recur*: is sent with 0 is one more than the number of times *recur*: is sent with nonzero argument, it takes 49 cycles on average. If we can accomplish the initial plan and can fabricate the microprocessor with 125 ns cycle time, the average execution time is 6.125 μs. This translates to 17 bytecodes per 12.25 μs, or 1.4 million bytecodes per second. This is 5.03 times faster than Dorado SMALLTALK, and 23% faster than SOAR on this test.

3.6   Conclusion

We have designed a general-purpose bytecode-emulating microprocessor. We completed the logic design and the microprogramming; the layout design has been carried out by Hitachi Corporation.

We did not even consider an architecture that would have required substantial rewriting of any part of the source program of the standard SMALLTALK-80 Virtual Image. This is because we would like to run SMALLTALK-80 as soon as the chip is fabricated. This requirement virtually rules out a register-oriented architecture. Even though we have kept our architectural aspirations modest, the SMALLTALK-80 emulation microcode we wrote for Sword32 would be 25% faster than the SOAR SMALLTALK, and would probably be many times faster than Dorado SMALLTALK.

There are many features that we might include in a future version of the microprocessor. These features include: multiple-stage pipelines, an internal cache for instruction and data, and tag support hardware.

This work was carried out jointly and with funding from Hitachi Corporation. Hitachi Corporation is planning to produce a commercial version of this chip under the brand name AI32.

4   SPECIFICATION AND VERIFICATION OF A COMPLEX COMPUTER USING CONCURRENT PROLOG

4.1   Introduction

We shall be putting very complex computer systems into chips that are only available in today's very-large-scale mainframe computer systems. In such VLSI chips, sophisticated control structures like pipelines and concurrency that are useful in obtaining high performance will be used extensively. Even in conventional computers, where debugging is easier, taking out all the bugs is a major problem. It was reported that a very complex memory system contained 50 bugs when the first breadboard model was created (Clark *et al.*, 1981). Therefore a very important issue in VLSI chip design is to take out all the bugs before the mask is produced, so that we do not have to repeat the expensive process of mask design. An important step in creating a correct design is to generate functional specifications in a very-high-level language and to debug these specifications against many test data. We developed a VLSI specification language called SAKURA based on a highly typed algorithmic language MESA (Mitchell *et al.*, 1979). A detailed description of SAKURA was reported previously (Suzuki and Burstall, 1981). In this chapter we shall take a very different approach to functional specification and verification; we use a higher-level language, Concurrent PROLOG. We specify a complex memory system of a high-performance personal computer, the Dorado (Lampson and Pier, 1981). We shall describe techniques to specify hardware in Concurrent PROLOG and discuss the comparison of these two experiences.

I had an opportunity to write microcode for an undebugged Dorado, which is a complex pipeline computer (Lampson *et al.*, 1981a,b). When we encountered the most difficult bug, it took two of us three days to create a test case so that the bug was isolated and regenerated repetitively. The bug only appeared under the following circumstances: the instruction pipeline was first full, then it was emptied by a jump, and at the same time an interrupt occurred. We first noticed this bug only after running the most complex software system written for the computer; all the other programs, including a compiler, an editor and a loader, could run successfully. This experience told us that it is extremely important to have a very large library of software to test new computers in order to make them reliable if we are to use conventional design and debug methodologies. Transistor-level logic simulation is much too slow for complete debugging of VLSI circuit design. Therefore the only practical approach to creating complex, reliable VLSI chips is to create a breadboard model using TTL circuits and to run the software on it. When we are convinced that the breadboard model works reliably, we can create a chip by directly converting TTL circuits to corresponding MOS circuits.

This approach has been working so far but it limits the scope of VLSI chips in four ways.

(1) It is a slow and expensive process, since we have to build a TTL prototype.
(2) We cannot exploit all the potentialities of MOS circuits; path transistors will not be used. Therefore the resulting chips can be large and inefficient.
(3) Since prototypes are much larger than the chips and cannot be easily replicated, this approach does not work for multiprocessors.

(4) If we are to build computers with new architectures, this approach may often not be very effective, since we do not have a large library of programs.

The alternative approach that we are taking is to use functional simulators. We specify the functionality of the computer in a high-level language; then test programs are run on this functional specification. Since functional specifications are written at an abstract level, they usually run much faster than the transistor-level logic simulators. Thus we may be able to create VLSI chips without building breadboard prototypes.

Once the top-level protocols are rigorously defined, there are a number of ways to create masks that satisfy these protocols reliably. We are confident that design automation tools are becoming quite adequate for such tasks. Electric and timing characteristics of building blocks such as adders, shifters and registers can be precisely obtained by advanced circuit-simulation programs on supercomputers. The logical behaviour of the entire chip can be rapidly obtained by the logic simulators.

Therefore a major issue in creating complex VLSI chips is to give the top-level protocol specifications in a very-high-level language and verify that the protocol specifications actually satisfy what we want.

We designed a VLSI modelling language called SAKURA and specified a complex VLSI multiprocessor system (Suzuki and Burstall, 1981). SAK-URA is a derivative of a strongly typed algorithmic language, MESA (Mitchell et al., 1979). We added several features that we felt are useful for hardware specification. There have been few real attempts to use a strongly typed language for hardware specification. Many errors, such as misconnections and underspecification, were found at compile-time; we were very satisfied with the use of a strongly typed language.

After the entire specification was written and was successfully compiled, we ran it with several test programs. We discovered a number of bugs in the specification, but most of them were introduced when the formal specification was created from the natural-language prose specification.

Another lesson we learned from this exercise was that randomly created test data are not very useful. It is much more effective if we know the implementation, and select test data carefully so that critical logic can be tested often.

It is also very important to be able to observe internal states, since the input and output sequences do not often reveal errors. For example, a cache is considered incorrect if it contains two copies of the same main memory block. However, from the outside it is merely a somewhat inefficient cache.

On the other hand, as long as we rely on simulation, the hardware is just as good as the test data. This is the severe limitation of this methodology. Most of the widely used computers have hardware bugs; they occur sufficiently rarely that people are no longer bothered by the bugs. However, if we want to become perfect, the only technique theoretically known to take out all the bugs is verification. People think that this might be a good idea, and many efforts are spent to make verification practical; so far, very few systems really work.

We shall explore a methodology between the functional simulation and the formal verification. We specify hardware just as in the formal verification. We give input and output assertions in predicate calculus. Then, instead of showing that output assertions will be satisfied by hardware for all the inputs that satisfy input assertions, we only show that this relation holds for some selected inputs. We actually run the triple—input assertion, hardware specification and output assertion—against test data. The advantage of this method over the functional simulation is that the output data are automatically checked for correctness. The advantage over the formal verification is that they can be executed so that we do not have to worry about inefficiencies of theorem provers.

We chose PROLOG as the language to write input and output assertions as well as hardware specifications. PROLOG is the natural choice for writing executable assertions, since it is based on logic and much research has been done to create efficient and convenient PROLOG programming systems. We actually used Concurrent PROLOG (Shapiro, 1983), a derivative of PROLOG developed by Ehud Shapiro; this language has multiprocessing primitives, so it is suited for description of hardware. Hardware specification is also written in Concurrent PROLOG, so that input and output assertions can be executed together with the hardware specification. Even though PROLOG is used widely for automatic-programming research, we believe that our way of using PROLOG is new. What we were doing is to execute requirement specifications, which are input and output assertions, together with implementation specifications, which are hardware specifications, on test data to check consistency. Because of the characteristics of PROLOG, assertions can be executed directly. We chose the Dorado memory system as the target of specification (Clark *et al.*, 1981). We selected it because the details of the implementation are published, it has a very complex memory system, and is implemented and widely used.

4.2 Brief Introduction to Concurrent PROLOG

Concurrent PROLOG is a superset of PROLOG with multiprocessing features. These new features are as follows.

4.2.1   Parallel and

Written as

$$P :- A \, / \! / \, B.$$

A and B are executed concurrently; if both succeed then P succeeds.

4.2.2   Communication

Communication among processes is accomplished by parameters. If two processes want to communicate, they have the same variables as the parameters. The direction of the information flow is one way. The receiver of the information has read-only variables; they are distinguished by putting ? as a suffix, as in

$$A(X) \, / \! / \, B(X?).$$

In this case the data is only passed from A to B. More than two processes can be the writers and readers. Writers have to write the same data; otherwise, the computation fails. The information is broadcast to all the receivers. Actual data are passed by queries. When B tries to know the information passed from A, it unifies some patterns against the input parameter X; if the unification is successful, B knows that the matched data is what was actually sent. If nothing is sent, B is suspended. Therefore processes are suspended when unification occurs with bound variables and unbound read-only variables. It is also possible to say

$$wait(X)$$

on a read-only variable X. The process will be suspended until X becomes bound.

4.2.3   Commit operator

The backtracking and parallel computation may cause quite undeterminable behaviours. During the computation of a predicate, several backtracks may take place; therefore the values of parameters may change several times before they settle for the final values. Since the communication is done through parameters, other processes may obtain intermediate values, which may be quite different from the final values of the parameters. If this is allowed, the relative speed of the processes determine the result of computation: an undesirable characteristic for a concurrent language. In Concurrent PROLOG the control of backtracking is done by commit operators. The body of the predicate is separated into two parts by a commit operator "|", and any effects that happened before the commit operator will not appear to the outside through parameters. However, backtracking is free to occur before the commit operator without causing any effects to other processes. Once the commit operator is executed, the execution is deterministic; backtracking is not allowed.

4.3   Specification Methodology

Methods used to describe highly concurrent circuits are described. In this description we take the stand that the hardware is described hierarchically. At each level the building components are called circuits, which are connected together by wires.

4.3.1   Circuits

Each circuit is represented by a predicate. Circuits communicate among themselves through wires. The wires are represented by the parameters of the predicates. Circuits have to receive an infinite chain of signals and produce an infinite chain of results signals. These infinite chains are represented by sequences.

Consider a circuit for generating error correction codes. It is described by the following predicate ECGen:

$$ECGen([In \mid InTail], [Out \mid OutTail]) :-$$
$$generate(In, Out), ECGen(InTail?, OutTail).$$
$$ECGen([], []).$$

ECGen receives a sequence of signals, the head of which is In, and produces a sequence of signals, the head of which is Out. Out is produced from In by the predicate generate, and the succeeding signals are accepted by recursively calling ECGen. The fact that InTail is a read-only variable to this second call means that the call is held until some input comes in.

4.3.2   Representing semantics of hardware by timed-event history

We now have circuits and wires to represent the physical structure of hardware. If we were to provide a sequence of data at the input, we would obtain a sequence of data at the output.

This is not enough for hardware simulation. We need to represent timings. We need to capture the facts that data are coming at certain clock times and that there are delays at each circuit, and some synchronization may take place because of these timings.

We first introduce a clock so that all the components operate at the same time. We describe how to implement a clock later. Then we can write a predicate describing a circuit's behaviour at a certain time. We also attach a time to each datum in the input stream denoting the arrival of the datum. We also attach time to the data in the output stream.

In this way we can describe the behaviour of a circuit by a timed input stream and a timed output stream. These are, however, not sufficient in most cases, because what is important is the internal behaviour of circuits for a given input; that is, the data flow view of the circuits. Each datum in the sequence may go through different subcomponents, or different events. We keep track of what events each datum went through at what time.

Instead of looking at the circuit as producing results, we look at a timed input sequence and an output sequence, each datum of which has a history of subcomponents it went through.

Then the description of ECGen becomes as follows:

```
ECGen([],[],X).
ECGen(I,O,[Clock | NextClock]) :-
    wait(Clock),
    ECGenTail(I,O,[Clock|NextClock]).
ECGenTail([[In,InTime,InHistory]|InTail],
    [[Out,OutTime,OutHistory]|OutTail],[Clock|NextClock]) :-
    InTime>=Clock |
        generate(In,Out),
        OutTime is InTime+2,
        append(InHistory,[[ecGen,InTime,OutTime]],OutHistory),
        ECGen(InTail?,OutTail,NextClock).
ECGenTail(I,O,[Clock|NextClock]) :-
    ECGen(I?,O,NextClock).
```

The first statement of ECGen is the terminal condition. The second statement asks the clock to advance to the next tick, and waits until the Clock holds the real time. Then it computes the error-correcting code in ECGenTail when the right time comes. The first statement of ECGenTail shows that it takes a sequence of triples and produces a sequence of triples. The first element of the triple is the datum, the second is the arrival time of the datum and the third is the history of events of this datum. In the body, first it checks whether the system time has come to the input time. If not, nothing is done, because the checking is done before the commit operator. If the time has come, it computes the output data, the output time, and creates the output history and proceeds to accept the next datum by recursively calling ECGen. If the time has not come, it merely fails, and the second statement of ECGenTail is executed. It advances to the next time.

4.3.3   Parallel circuits

Circuits essentially operate in parallel; in order to represent these parallelisms we use the concurrency of Concurrent PROLOG. Signals can be transmitted to concurrently running processes quite easily by supplying a sequence to all the processes that are connected. The output must, however, be merged to form a single output sequence. Consider for example a memory system consisting of two parts, one of which stores the lower half of the address space while the other stores the upper half. When one wants to access data, the fetch command with an address is sent to both modules and the data come out from the one that holds it. This can be specified as

```
System :-
    Processor(X) //
    Memory(0, 999, X?, Out1) //
    Memory(1000, 1999, X?, Out2) //
    Merge(Out1?, Out2?, Out).
```

The Memory is specified as

```
Memory(Low, High, [Address | InTail], [[hit, Data]|OutTail]) :-
    Low<=Address, Address<=High |
        getResult(Address, Data),
        Memory(Low, High, InTail?, OutTail).
Memory(Low, High, [Address | InTail], [[miss, 0] | OutTail]) :-
    Memory(Low, High, Intail?, OutTail).
Merge([[hit, Data1]|In1], [[miss, Data2]|In2], [Data1|Out]).
Merge([[miss, Data1]|In1], [[hit, Data2]|In2], [Data2|Out]).
```

4.3.4   Clock

Since the hardware system reports all the events by the time when they occur, it is essential to have a clock. Once the clock is working and all the circuits can obtain the time, there will not be any scheduling problem, since each circuit looks at the time and is invoked at the right time.

The requirement for the clock is that it produce times continuously. In our system we would like a clock to be producing an infinite sequence of numbers: $[0, 1, 2, \ldots]$. This may be a problem, since if the clock has too high a priority, it is taking up all the time producing a continuous sequence of numbers, so that other processes cannot proceed.

The solution to this problem shows a unique use of Concurrent PROLOG. Even though, the communication is one-way because of the read-only variables, one can actually transmit values back and forth. This is done by sending a skeleton in the form of a list structure with an unbound variable as

a component from the sender to the receiver: then the receiver puts a value
inside the skeleton. Using this technique, we make the clock to be the
receiver of the skeleton. Other circuits need to look at the clock in order to
tell the time. Whenever this happens, they send skeletons to the clock. The
clock is suspended waiting for some request, and as soon as it receives a
request it sends back the time. This is explained by the following example:

> System :-
>   Clock(X?) //
>   Processor(. . . , X) //
>   Memory(. . . , X) //
>   IO(. . . , X).

Now the clock is defined as

> Clock(Time) :-
>   ClockNext(0, Time).
> ClockNext(S, [S | Tail]):-
>   U is S+1,
>   ClockNext(U, Tail?).

Each circuit has the following form:

> Memory(. . . , [Time | T]) :- . . . .

Then the suspended ClockNext is invoked and fills in the time at the head of
the list.

These are all the methodologies we used to describe the Dorado memory
system.

4.4   Description of the Dorado Memory System

The Dorado is a high-performance personal computer designed and built at
the Xerox Palo Alto Research Center (Lampson *et al.*, 1981a,b). Even
though the Dorado is a personal computer, it uses the most sophisticated
hardware technologies and mechanisms available only in today's large
mainframe computers, such as ECL (emitter-coupled logic) and cache
memory. Unlike most other cache memory systems, the Dorado cache
retains written data as long as the cache block is not flushed out. Cache keys
are virtual addresses, so the virtual address to real address translation takes
place only when there is a cache miss.

The memory system is made up of pipeline stages and resources. Pipeline
stages provide control and are organized into two pipelines: the cache
pipeline and the storage pipeline. The cache pipeline consists of ADDRESS
and HITDATA stages and the storage pipeline consists of MAP,

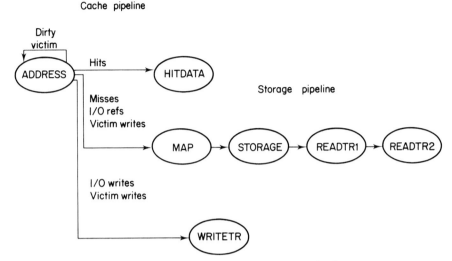

Figure 8   Organization of cache and storage pipelines.

WRITETR, STORAGE, READTR1, and READTR2 stages. The organization of these stages is shown in Figure 8.

Resources provide the data paths and memories. The major resources mentioned in this section are CacheA, CacheD, StoreReg, FetchReg, MapRAM, WriteReg, StoreRAM, and ReadReg.

4.4.1   Cache pipeline

Every memory reference is handled by the ADDRESS stage. This stage checks whether the virtual address is in the cache; if it is, and the reference is a Fetch or Store, ADDRESS starts HITDATA. ADDRESS starts MAP, if a reference misses or is an I/O reference.

The cache address is passed from ADDRESS; the HITDATA stage fetches a word from CacheD storage into FetchReg register if the reference is a Fetch, and stores a word into CacheD from StoreReg register if the reference is a Store.

4.4.2   Storage pipeline

The MAP stage translates a virtual address into a real address by looking it up in a hardware table called the MapRAM, and then starts the STORAGE stage. MAP takes 8 cycles to complete, but starts the STORAGE stage at the fifth cycle.

The STORAGE stage is started by MAP; it controls the StorageRAM. STORAGE receives 16 words from WRITETR through WriteReg and sends 16 words to READTR1 and READTR2 through ReadReg.

The WRITETR stage transports a block into WriteReg, either from CacheD or from an input device; it shares WriteReg with STORAGE. It is started by ADDRESS on every write, and synchronizes with STORAGE. The WRITETR takes at least 11 cycles; the next-to-last cycle waits until the third cycle of STORAGE is started.

The read operation takes more than 8 cycles because it does error correction and data transport from ReadReg to cache. Therefore it is split into two stages. On a read, READTR1 shifts words out of ReadReg and through the error corrector, READTR2 reports faults and completes cache read operations either by delivering the requested word into FetchReg (for a Fetch), or by storing the contents of StoreReg into the newly-loaded block in the cache (for a Store).

4.4.3   Concurrency control

Since the memory system is pipelined, it is possible that more than one control stage is active. Special mechanisms are implemented to prevent multiple accesses to a single resource.

There are three mechanisms to prevent conflicts.

(1) The memory system rejects requests by asserting Hold, if the memory system cannot accept a new request.
(2) A reference waits in ADDRESS until its immediate resource requirements are met.
(3) All the remaining conflicts are dealt with in a single state of MAP.

The third stage of MAP, denoted as MAP.3 is the only stage to implement interlocks. The conditions that MAP.3 waits are as follows.

WRITETR activated by the same reference to pass the fifth stage.
If the previous reference is a clean miss and this reference is a clean miss, MAP.3 waits two cycles.
When loading and unloading of CacheD occur, conflicts must be avoided.
MAP.3 waits until WRITETR for dirty-victim-write reference is started.

4.5   Specification of the Dorado Memory System

We specified the Dorado memory system described in Section 4.4 in Concurrent PROLOG using the techniques of Section 4.3. The whole specification is given in the Appendix. In this listing we only treated Fetches and Stores; other types of references can be accommodated very easily. We made some simplifications: the cache memory is fully associative and the size of a block of cache is one word. We have not treated the faults; in order to treat faults completely, the intermediate results in the pipeline have to be written in the register called history. Since the description of the management of the history register is completely missing from the report (Clark *et al.*, 1981), we decided not to treat these cases.

The top-level predicate corresponding to the entire memory system is called Memory. The description closely parallels the organization of the Dorado memory system control structure shown in Figure 8:

> memory(InStream, OutStream) :-
> clock(S?) //
> addressHead(InStream, X1, S) //
> hitDataHead(X1?, O1, S) //
> mapHead(X1?, X2, 0, S) //
> writeTrHead(X1?, X2?, X5, S) //
> storageHead(X2?, X5?, X3, S) //
> readTr1Head(X3?, X4, S) //
> readTr2Head(X4?, O2, S) //
> merge2(01?, O2?, OutStream).

The predicate clock is the same clock described in Section 4.3.4, and produces an infinite sequence of numbers, [0, 1, 2, . . .]. The predicate merge2 merges the two sequences O1 and O2 to produce the behaviour of the system against the input sequence: O1 is the cache hit sequence and O2 is the cache miss sequence. The other seven predicates correspond to the pipeline stages.

The behaviour of the Dorado memory system is described in Clark *et al.* (1981) by giving several examples, showing how data go through pipeline stages. We checked each case by giving an input sequence and an environment so that the desired effects would occur. The output sequence was checked against the diagrams given in the report.

An interesting case is a dirtymiss because it is quite complicated. A dirtymiss occurs when a fetch or store misses cache, and the cache is full. Then an empty space has to be made in the cache before a block can be brought in from the main memory. Therefore a victim, the block to be emptied, is determined; the victim has been written by the processor since it was brought in from the main memory, so the contents of the cache block are different from the corresponding location in the main memory. Thus a memory reference actually creates two data streams. From the description of the dirtymiss, it seems that the data stream of writing back the dirty victim should proceed before the data stream of reading in the target block. However, that sequence of steps has the unfortunate consequence that the data to be transferred to the processor comes out late. So, in the actual implementation, the data stream to bring in the block from the main memory proceeds first.

We tested this case by supplying the input sequence

$$[[fetch, 15, \_, 0]].$$

The environment has been set up so that this will cause a cache miss, and the victim is dirty. Then the output is

[[address, 0, 0],
 [map, 1, 8],
 [storage, 6, 13],
 [readtr1, 13, 20],
 [readtr2, 20, 27]],
[[address, 1, 8],
 [map, 9, 16],
 [writetr, 2, 17],
 [storage, 14, 21],
 [readtr1, 21, 28],
 [readtr2, 28, 35]].

This has the same behaviour as the one described in the Dorado report; thus we have verified the specification for this particular case.

4.6 Conclusion

A functional description of a complex memory system of a high-perform-ance personal computer has been written in Concurrent PROLOG. The input and output assertions were also written in Concurrent PROLOG, so that the consistency between implementation specifications, functional specifications, requirement specifications, and input and output assertions can be checked by running the program with some data.

Since we have shown that we can write functional specifications using a general-purpose language, it is not necessary to create a special-purpose functional simulation language. It is very important and useful to write requirement specifications, when we are to create rigorous reliable func-tional specifications. One can find out logical flaws in writing requirement specifications. What is more important is that we can easily check the consistency between two specifications by executing them so that bugs are discovered at the early stages of the design.

Using Concurrent PROLOG for functional specifications is new. We have found several advantages of Concurrent PROLOG for such purposes. First of all, it is very easy to write and debug Concurrent PROLOG programs. It is like writing LISP, but one can use pattern-matching and backtracking. We wrote the Dorado specification in a week; it took us about a month to describe a memory system of similar complexity in SAKURA. The majority of the time was spent in debugging when we used SAKURA, because we had to rely on the MESA debugger, which does not have a good debugging facility for concurrent programs. In the future, a crucial factor in the cost of VLSI chip development will be the amount of time taken for design. The use of Concurrent PROLOG may well be very important in such circumstances.

There are a couple of drawbacks in using the current Concurrent PRO-LOG system. One is that the language does not have the flexibility of LISP, so that the user cannot manipulate processes in his programs. Therefore he cannot write schedulers himself. This prevented us from writing a more sophisticated simulation system. Right now, all the circuits watch the clock tick by tick, and perform operations on data when the time comes that is written on the data. This might be quite inefficient if the number of ticks that each circuit has to wait is very large. One can avoid this in a truly time-event-driven simulator, in which each circuit tells the scheduler when it wants to perform an operation. The scheduler has an access to such information for all the circuits, and it essentially gives a control to the circuit that wants to perform the earliest. When the control comes back, it gives the control to the next-earliest process. SAKURA was implemented this way. In order to achieve this in Concurrent PROLOG, we need to write a scheduler, which knows how many processes are running, and which processes should be run next. This, I believe, can be done in Concurrent PROLOG, but not without writing a lot of programs.

The second drawback is that the current implementation of Concurrent PROLOG is very slow and space-consuming. Research in creating an optimizing compiler following Warren (1977) is crucial.

The other drawback is that an efficient random-access storage mechanism does not exist. We need such a feature in order to simulate the storage system of the computer systems. We represented a random-access storage by a predicate and used assert and remove predicates to cause side-effects. This, however, causes sequential search, and can potentially be very inefficient.

Appendix: Program Listing

```
memory(InStream, OutStream) :-
    clock(S?) //
    addressHead(InStream, X1, S) //
    hitDataHead(X1?, O1, S) //
    mapHead(X1?, X2, 0, S) //
    writeTrHead(X1?, X2?, X5, S) //
    storageHead(X2?, X5?, X3, S) //
    readTr1Head(X3?, X4, S) //
    readTr2Head(X4?, O2, S) //
    merge2(O1?, O2?, OutStream).

addressHead([],[],[Time|Tail]).
addressHead(Itail,Otail,[Time|AS]) :-
    wait(Time),
    address(Itail,Otail,[Time|AS]).

address([[Command,Va,Idata,Itime]|Itail],Otail,[Time|AStail]) :-
    Time)=Itime|
      stAddrTime(Itime,StartTime),
      finAddrTime(StartTime,Otime),
      call(cacheSearch(Va,Result,Addr)),
      print('***address time='), print(Time), print (' '), print(Result),
      print(' CacheAddrIs='), print(Addr), n1,
      nextAddress([Command,Va,Idata],Result,Addr,Itime,Otime,Itail,
         Otail,AStail).
address(I,O,[Time|S]) :- addressHead(I?,O,S).

nextAddress(Instr,hit,Addr,Itime,Otime,Itail,[[Instr,hit,Addr,Otime,
      [[address,Itime,Otime]]]|Otail],AStail) :-
    print([[address,Itime,Otime]]),n1,
    addressHead(Itail?,Otail,AStail).
nextAddress(Instr,cleanmiss,Addr,Itime,Otime,Itail,[[Instr,cleanmiss,
      Addr,Otime,[[address,Itime,Otime]]]|Otail],AStail) :-
    print([[address,Itime,Otime]]),n1,
    addressHead(Itail?,Otail,AStail).
nextAddress(Instr,dirtymiss,Addr,Itime,Otime,Itail,
      [[Instr,cleanmiss,Addr,Otime,[[address,Itime,Otime]]],
      [Instr,dirtymiss,Addr,Vicltime,
      [[address,Vicltime,VicOtime]]]|Otail],AStail) :-
    Vicltime is Otime+1,
    addressHead(Itail?,Otail,Astail).

hitDataHead([],[],[Time|HS]).
hitDataHead(I,O,[Time|HS]) :-
    wait(Time),
    hitData(I?,O,[Time|HS]).
```

```
hitData([[[fetch,Va,Idata],hit,Addr,Itime,History]|tail],
    [[[fetch,Va,Idata],Odata,OHis]|Otail],[Time|HStail]) :-
  Time⟩=Itime|
    Otime is Itime+,
    cacheVec(Addr, ,Odata, ),
    print('*** hitData time='), print(Time), n1,
    append(History,[[hitData,Itime,Otime]],OHis),
    print(OHis), n1,
    hitDataHead(Itail?,Otail,HStail).

hitData([[[store,Va,Idata],hit,Addr,Itime,History]|Itail],
    [[[store,Va,Idata],[],OHis]|Otail],
    [Time|HStail]) :-
  Time⟩=Itime |
    Otime is Itime+1,
    call(setCacheVec(Addr,Va,Idata,false)),
    print('*** hitData time ='), print(Time), n1,
    append(History,[[hitData,Itime,Otime]],OHis),
    print(OHis), n1,
    hitDataHead(Itail?,Otail,HStail).
hitData([ |Itail],[[misses]|Otail],[Time|HStail]) :-
    hitDataHead(Itail?,Otail,HStail).
hitData(I,O,[Time|S]) :-
    hitDataHead(I?,O,S).

mapHead([],[],MapLastBusy,[Time|HS]).
mapHead(I,O,MapLastBusy,[Time|T]) :-
    wait(Time),
    map(I,O,MapLastBusy,[Time|T]).

map([[Instr,hit,Addr,Itime,History]|Itail],
    [[Instr,hit, , , , ,[hit]]|Otail],MapLastBusy,
    [ |MStail]) :-
    mapHead(Itail?,Otail,MapLastBusy,MStail).
map([[[Command,Va,Idata],Miss,Addr,Itime,History]|Itail],
    [[[Command,Va,Idata],Miss,Ra,Addr,Fault,Otime,OHis]|Otail],
    MapLastBusy,[Time|MStail]) :-
    Time⟩=Itime |
    mapTime(Itime,MapLastBusy,MapItime,Otime).
    call(mapSearch(Va,Fault,Ra)),
    print('*** map time='), print(Time), print(' RA='), print(Ra), n1,
    makeMapHis(History,Miss,MapItime,Otime,OHis),
    mapHead(Itail?,Otail,Otime,MStail).
map(I,O,MapLastBusy,[Time|S]) :- mapHead(I?,O,MapLastBusy,S).

makeMapHis(His,cleanmiss,I.O,OHis) :-
    append(His,[[map,I,O]],OHis).
makeMapHis([[address,AI,AO]],dirtymiss,I,O,[[address,AI,AO],[map,I,O]])
    :- AO is I-1.
```

```prolog
mapTime(Itime,MapLastBusy,Mapltime,Otime) :-
     max(Itime,MapLastBusy,MapSt),
     Mapltime is MapSt+1,
     storageLastBusy(Map3Wait),
     OutMapStTime is MapSt+8,
     OutMap3Wait is Map3Wait+5,
     max(OutMapStTime,OutMap3Wait,Otime).

mapSearch(Va,false,Va).

storageHead([],[],[],[Time|HS]).

storageHead(M,W,O,[Time|T]) :-
   wait(Time), storage(M,W,O,[Time|T]).

storage([[Instr,hit,Ra,Addr,Fault,MapTime,MapHistory]|MapTail],

     [ |WriteTrTail],
     [[Instr,hit,Ra,Addr,Fault,ReadReg,_|[[ignore]]]|Otail],
     [ |SStail]) :-
   storageHead(MapTail?,WriteTrTail?,Otail,SStail).
storage([[Instr,dirtymiss,Ra,Addr,Fault,MapTime,MapHistory]|MapTail],
     [[Instr,WriteReg, ,WriteTrHistory|WriteTrTail],
     [[Instr,dirtymiss,Ra,Addr,Fault,Readreg,Otime,OHis]|Otail],
     [Time|SRtail]) :-
   Itime is MapTime-2, Time)=Itime |
    setMemory(Ra,WriteReg),
    Otime is MapTime+5,
    append(WriteTrHistory,[[storage,Itime,Otime]],OHis),
    print('*** storage write time='), print(Time, nl,
    print(OHis), nl,
    storageHead(MapTail?,WriteTrTail?,Otail,SRtail).
storage([[Instr,cleanmiss,Ra,Addr,Fault,MapTime,MapHistory]|MapTail],
     [ |WriteTrTail],
     [[Instr,cleanmiss,Ra,Addr,Fault,ReadReg,Otime,OHis]|Otail],
     [Time|SRtail]) :-
   Itime is MapTime-2, Time)=Itime |
    getMemory(Ra,ReadReg),
    Otime is MapTime+5,
    append(MapHistory,[[storage,Itime,Otime]],OHis),
    print('*** storage read time='), print(Time), a1,
    print(OHis), nl,
    storageHead(Maptail?,WriteTrTail?,Otail,SRtail).
storage(M,W,O,[Time|S]) :- storageHead(M?,W?,O,S).

getMemory(Addr,Val) :- Val=Addr.

setMemory(Addr,Val).

readTr1Head([],[],[Time|Tail]).
readTr1Head(I,O,[time|T]) :-
   wait(Time), readTr1(I,O,[Time|T]).
```

```
readTr1([[Instr,Result,Ra,Addr,Fault,ReadReg,Itime,History]|Itail],
        [[Instr,Result,Ra,Addr,Fault,ReadReg,Otime,OHistory]|Otail],
        [Time|R1Stail]) :-
    Time>=Itime |
        Otime is Itime+7,
        append(History,[[readtr1,Itime,Otime]],OHistory),
        print('*** readtr1 time='), print(Time), nl,
        print(OHistory), nl,
        readTr1Head(Itail?,Otail,R1Stail).
readTr1(I,O,[Time|S]) :- readTr1Head(I?,O,S).

readTr2Head([],[],[Time|[]]).
readTr2Head(I,O,[Time|T]) :-
    wait(Time), readTr2(I,O,[Time|T]).

readTr2([[[fetch,Va,Idata],Result,Ra,Addr,Fault,ReadReg,Itime,History]
         |Itail],
        [[[fetch,Va,Idata],Result,Ra,Addr,Fault,ReadReg,Otime,OHis]|Otail],
        [time|R2Stail]) :-

    Time>=Itime |
        Otime is Itime+7,
        call(setCacheVec(Addr,Va,ReadReg,false)),
        append(History,[[readtr2,Itime,Otime]],Ohis),
        print('*** readtr2 fetch time='), print(time), nl,
        print(OHis), nl,
        readTr2Head(Itail?,Otail,R2Stail).

readTr2([[store,Va,Idata],Result,Ra,Addr,Fault,ReadReg,Itime,History]
         |Itail],
        [[[store,Va,Idata],Result,Ra,Addr,Fault,ReadReg,Otime,OHis]|Otail],
        [Time|R2Stail]) :-
    Time>=Itime |
        Otime is Itime+7,
        Call(setCacheVec(Addr,Va,Idata,true)),
        append(History,[[readtr2,Itime,Otime]],OHis),
        print('*** readtr2 store time='), print(Time), nl,
        print(OHis), nl,
        readTr2Head(Itail?,Otail,R2Stail).
readTr2(I,O,[Time|S]) :- readTr2Head(I?,O,S).

setCacheVec(Addr,Va,Data,Dirty) :-
    retract(cacheVec(Addr, , , )),
    asserta(cacheVec(Addr,Va,Data,Dirty)).
setCacheVec(Addr,Va,Data,Dirty) :-
    asserta(cacheVec(Addr,Va,Data,Dirty)).

writeTrHead([],[],[],[Time|HS]).
writeTrHead(I,M,O,[Time|T]) :-
    wait(Time), writeTr(IM,MO,[Time|T]).
```

```
writeTr([[Instr,dirtymiss,Addr,Itime,History]|I],
     [[Instr,dirtymiss,Ra,Addr,Fault,MapTime,MapHis]|M],
     [[Instr,WriteReg,Otime,OHis]|O],
     [Time|T]) :-
   Wrltime is Itime+1,Time>=Wrltime |
     cacheVec(Addr,_,WriteReg,_),
     Otime is MapTime+1,
     print('*** writertr time='), print(Time), nl,
     append(MapHis,[[writetr,Wrltime,Otime]],OHis),
     print(OHis), nl,
     writeTrHead(I?,M?,O,T).
writeTr([[_, hit|_]_|I], [_|O], [_|T]) :-
   writeTrHead(I?, M?, O, T).
writeTr([[_, cleanmiss|_]_|I], [_|M], [_|O], [_|T]) :-
   writeTrHead(I?, M?, O, T).
writeTr(A, M, O [Time|S]) :-
   writeTrHead(A?, M?, O, S).

merge2([[misses]|A], [B|C], [B|O]) :-
   merge2(A?, C?, O).
merge2([D|A], [B|C], [D|O]) :-
   merge2(A?, C?, O).
merge2([], [B|C], [B|O]) :-
   merge2([], C?, O).

clock(Cardinals) :-
   clockNext(O, Cardinals).
clockNext(S, [S|Tail]) :-
   U is S+1,
   print('>> Time is '), print(S), nl,
   clockNext(U, Tail?).
clockNext(S, []).

stAddrTime(Itime, StartTime) :-
   addrTime(LastAddrTime),
   LastAddrTime1 is LastAddrTime+1,
   max(Itime, LastAddrTime1, StartTime).

finAddrTime(St, Fin) :-
   Fin is St,
   retract(addrTime(_)),
   asserta(addrTime(Fin)).

init :-
   asserta(cacheSize(O)),
   asserta(storageLastBusy(O)),
   asserta(victimAddr(O)),
   asserta(addrTime(O)).

max(A, B, A) :- A >= B | true.
max(A, B, B) :- B > A.
```

```
cacheSearch(Va, hit, Addr) :-
    cacheVec(Addr, Va, Data, Dirty).
cacheSearch(Va, Result, Addr) :-
    nextVictim(Addr),
    call(victimState(Addr,Dirty)),
    call(cleanOrDirty(Dirty, Result)).

victimState(VictimAddr, Dirty) :-
    cacheVec(VictimAddr, _, _, Dirty).
victimState(_, false).

cleanOrDirty(true, dirtymiss).
cleanOrDirty(false, cleanmiss).

nextVictim(Addr) :-
    retract(victimAddr(X)),
    X1 is X+1,
    cacheSize(CacheSize),
    asserta(victimAddr(Addr)).

dorado(In, Out) :- init, memory(In, Out).

test :-
    dorado([[fetch,15,_,O], [fetch,16_,5], [store,17,_,15]], X),
    write(X).
```

REFERENCES

Clark, D. W. *et al.* (1981). Memory system of a high-performance personal computer. Tech. Rep. CSL-81-11, Xerox Palo Alto Research Center.

Deutsch, L. P. (1983). The Dorado Smalltalk-80 implementation: Hardware architecture's impact on software architecture. *Smalltalk-80: Bits of History, Words of Advice* (ed., Krasner). Reading, Mass.: Addison-Wesley.

Deutsch, L. P. and Bobrow, D. G. (1976). An efficient incremental automatic garbage collector. *CACM* **19**, 522–526.

Deutsch, L. P. and Schiffman, A. M. (1984). Efficient implementation of the Smalltalk-80 system. *Proc. ACM POPL, Salt Lake City, Utah, Jan. 1984.*

Goldberg, A. J. and Robson, D. (1983). *Smalltalk-80: The Language and Its Implementation.* Reading, Mass.: Addison-Wesley.

Lampson, B. W. and Pier, K. A. (1981). A processor for a high-performance personal computer. Tech. Rep. CSL-81-1, Xerox Palo Alto Research Center.

Lampson, B. W. *et al.* (1981a). The Dorado: A high-performance personal computer. Tech. Rep. CSL-81-1, Xerox Palo Alto Research Center.

Lampson, B. W. *et al.* (1981b). Instruction fetch unit for a high-performance personal computer. Tech. Rep. CSL-81-1, Xerox Palo Alto Research Center.

McCall, K. (1983). The Smalltalk-80 benchmarks. *Smalltalk-80: Bits of History, Words of Advice* (ed., Krasner). Reading, Mass.: Addison-Wesley.

Mitchell, J. G. *et al.* (1979). Mesa language manual. Tech. Rep. CSL-79-3, Xerox Palo Alto Research Center.

Shapiro, E. Y. (1983). A subset of concurrent Prolog and its interpreter. ICOT Tech. Rep. TROO3.

Suzuki, N. (1983). Implementing Smalltalk-80 on Sword. Tech. Memo, Univ. Tokyo.

Suzuki, N. and Burstall, R. (1981). Sakura: a VLSI modelling language. *Proc. Conf. on Advanced Research in VLSI*. Dedham, Mass.: Artech House.

Suzuki, N. and Terada, M. (1984). Creating efficient systems for object-oriented languages. *Proc. ACM POPL, Salt Lake City, Utah, Jan. 1984*.

Suzuki, N., Frank, E., Kubota, K. and Ogata, I. (1983). Sword: A bytecode emulating microprocessor. Tech. Memo, Univ. Tokyo.

Suzuki, N., Ogata, I. and Terada, M. (1984). Design of a 32-bit virtual machine for Smalltalk-80. Kigoushori, 28-3, Information Processing Society of Japan.

Thacker, C. *et al*. (1981). Alto: A personal computer. *Computer Structures: Readings and Examples*, 2nd edn (ed. Sieworek, Bell and Newell). New York: McGraw-Hill.

Unger, D. (1984). Generation Scavenger: A nondisruptive high performance storage reclamation algorithm. *Proc. Symp. on Practical Software Development Environments, Pittsburgh, April, 1984*.

Unger, D. *et al*. (1984). Architecture of SOAR: Smalltalk on a RISC. *Proc. 11th Ann. Int. Symp. on Computer Architecture, Ann Arbor, June 1984*.

Warren, D. H. D. (1977). Implementing Prolog—Compiling predicate logic programs. DAI Res. Rep. 39–40, Univ. Edinburgh.

Wirfs-Brock, A. (1983). Design decisions for Smalltalk-80 implementors. *Smalltalk-80: Bits of History, Words of Advice* (ed., Krasner). Reading, Mass.: Addison-Wesley.

Index